MW00777770

ETHEL MERMAN, MOTHER TERESA... AND ME

A Memoir

Photo by Stephen Mosher.

ETHEL MERMAN, MOTHER TERESA... AND ME

My improbable journey from châteaux in France to the slums of Calcutta

A Memoir by
Tony Cointreau

Prospecta Press
PO Box 3131
Westport, CT 06880
www.prospectapress.com

With affection and gratitude to Sharon Nettles,
an outstanding editor and a good friend.

With appreciation to Leah Abrahams of Mixed Media Memoirs, LLC,
for guidance and support in this project.

Cover and interior design by Jason Davis.

  ISBN: 978-1-935212-34-8 hardcover
  ISBN: 978-1-935212-33-1 eBook

Manufactured in the United States of America

Publisher's Cataloging-In-Publication Data
(Prepared by The Donohue Group, Inc.)

Cointreau, Tony.
  Ethel Merman, Mother Teresa ... and Me : my improbable journey from châteaux in
France to the slums of Calcutta: a memoir by Tony Cointreau.

  p. ; cm.

  Includes bibliographical references.
  ISBN: 978-1-935212-34-8 hardcover
  ISBN: 978-1-935212-33-1 eBook

  1. Cointreau, Tony. 2. Singers–Biography. 3. Merman, Ethel–Friends and associates.
4. Teresa, Mother, 1910-1997–Friends and associates. 5. Mother and child.
6. Autobiography. I. Title.

ML420.C656 A3 2014
782.42164/092

For Jim Russo
My Angel Protector
Eternity

TABLE OF CONTENTS

Part II: The Last Mother

Ethel Merman, Mother Teresa... and Me

A Memoir

Part I

The First Mothers

PROLOGUE

Ethel Merman and Mother Teresa had a lot in common. At first glance, that might seem highly unlikely, but in my years with them both, I discovered that though the differences were huge, surprisingly, there were also great similarities.

Often I would be in a restaurant with Ethel Merman, "the Queen of Broadway," who was known for her loud voice and brassy persona onstage, and after dinner I would ask her, "Would you please, very quietly, so no one else can hear, sing your favorite song for me?"

And—always—she would then begin to sing, "Our Father, Who art in heaven, hallowed be Thy name...."

Not many people knew about it, but Ethel also served as a volunteer at Roosevelt Hospital for many years, beginning when her mother was hospitalized after a devastating stroke, and continuing until Ethel herself was too ill to work any more. She was wonderful with sick people. She would sit at their bedsides and hold their hands and comfort them, something you might have expected from Mother Teresa.

One morning as I sat next to Mother Teresa, who was considered a living saint, on her balcony in Calcutta, she was particularly tired after a long meeting with some of her Sisters. I leaned close to hear her weakening voice over the sounds of traffic from the main road below, expecting to hear words of wisdom.

"How much does your hotel cost?" She whispered. When I told her, she said, "I don't mean per week, I mean per day."

"That *is* per day, Mother," I said. "*I* did not take a vow of poverty."

"No," she laughed, "*you* took a vow of *luxury*."

I knew her sense of humor well, and was not surprised at her laughter—something you might have expected from Ethel Merman.

Ethel Merman and Mother Teresa, along with a remarkable woman named Lee Lehman (the wife of Robert Lehman, the chairman of Lehman Brothers), were like mothers to me, and the three of them helped to heal the parts of me that had been damaged as a child. Their humor, their support, and their compassion finally gave me the unconditional love I had been seeking my whole life.

DOTIE AND JACQUES

I was brought up in another era, a time when parents from a certain level of society had little to do with the daily care of their children. People were hired to raise the children while Mother and Father watched from a discreet distance. This is not to say that they didn't care what happened to their offspring—every aspect of their children's lives was carefully monitored—but they didn't feel the need to be involved in the daily chores of raising a child. This is the way it had been done for generations and they saw no reason to change it.

My father, Jacques, was a descendant of Edouard Cointreau, who had started a liqueur business in Angers, France, in 1849. One of his two sons, also named Edouard, took over the company in 1875, and created the orange-based liqueur we know today as Cointreau. Under his leadership the company became a worldwide enterprise. I shall always be grateful for being one of his great-grandchildren.

My mother, Dorothee Richardson, whom everyone called Dotie, came from an old Boston family of Irish descent, the Dowlings; I suspect they had a much more impressive lineage than bank account—more "breeding," as they called it then, than money.

The main difference between the Dowling and the Cointreau families seemed to lie in the fact that one was impoverished nobility while the other was a working class family who created an international business. One worked very hard "keeping up appearances" while the other worked very hard creating a family fortune.

Money had always been scarce in Mother's family. Therefore she decided at an early age to capitalize on her looks and natural dramatic ability, and become an actress. Soon her extraordinary beauty and presence helped her to land her first role in a Broadway play called *Deburau*, at the Belasco Theater. From there she went on to star in silent films under the name of Dorothy Richards.

Since the driving force of Mother's ambition was the financial security she had been missing for most of her early life, she abandoned her acting career to marry Lawrence Wilder, a wealthy shipping magnate who, she claimed, was twenty years older than she. She always laughingly said that she married him because she fell in love with his Hispano Suizo car, "the Rolls Royce of the 1920s."

Mr. and Mrs. Wilder led a glamorous life, traveling on the great ocean liners and entertaining international dignitaries at their homes in Washington, D.C., and New York. Their lavish homes, photographed for the fashion magazines of their day, were filled with the museum pieces with which Mother decorated her homes for the rest of her life.

My beautiful mother was born with a strong sense of style and was always particular about her looks and her clothes. After her marriage she traveled with an army of wardrobe trunks, one of them especially made to carry her shoes. Her private ladies' maid—only one of the large staff that was required to maintain their lifestyle—was always there to look after her. Even when she went for a stroll, the chauffeur followed her slowly with the car, in case she tired.

Mother never really explained why she eventually divorced Larry Wilder. The most she would say was that although she was very fond of him she could no longer live with a man who drank to excess. I've often wondered, however, how much the fact that Mr. Wilder lost a great deal of his money in the stock market crash of 1929 had to do with the breakup of their marriage.

I believe that Mother loved her first husband in her own way, but did not fall in love until she met my father. Many men had fallen in love with Mother, and some of them remained in love with her for the rest of their lives. She once admitted to me that the physical side of a relationship was not important to her; and it suited her that, for these men, she simply represented an untouchable princess. I came to believe that my father was wise enough to understand his wife's chaste affection for them all.

Jacques Cointreau, of course, had lived all of his life in France, dividing his time among an apartment in the exclusive Sixteenth Arondissement in Paris; his family's summer home, Château Brillant, in the Loire Valley, where they spent only one month each summer; their seaside home, La Villa des Cerises, near La Baule in Bretaigne; and Angers, the seat of the Cointreau business, where he went to school.

After his graduation, his two uncles, André and Louis Cointreau, welcomed him into the family business and sent him around the world to promote Cointreau liqueur. It was on one of these travels that he eventually met my mother.

The first time my parents met was at a gala in New York City in 1935, celebrating the maiden voyage of the ocean liner the *Normandie*—the ship that my father forever considered the most beautiful of all time.

Ethel Merman, who was already a star, sang that night when my parents met—many years before she would become like another mother to me. In retrospect, it seems almost prophetic.

Jacques was actually Dotie's sister Ashie's blind date for the party on the *Normandie*. But Ashie was not taken with him the way my mother was. Later that evening, Mother told her, "I'm going to marry that man."

Dotie was not really religious, but once she made up her mind that she was going to marry Jacques, she went to St. Vincent Ferrer church in New York City and made a novena (nine days of prayer) to

St. Anthony. On the ninth and last day of the novena, she was coming down the front steps of the church when she saw Jacques walking by. He had just arrived in New York on another business trip and was as delighted as she was at the chance encounter.

On January 14, 1936, Dotie and Jacques were married in a civil ceremony in Paris, with only the Cointreau family in attendance. Instead of the usual reception, they celebrated with a costume ball at the Hotel Meurice.

A few months later, after the sudden death of Larry Wilder, they quietly re-married, this time in front of my mother's family at St. Vincent Ferrer church in New York City.

My mother and her older sister, Ashie (a name that stuck when Mother as a child could not pronounce her sister's real name, Agnes), had spent nine years in a convent school in France, while their mother studied singing and went on to become a star of the Paris Opera. After she married my father, Mother moved back to Europe for the second time in her life. This time it was to Angers, where her new husband worked in the family liqueur business.

From Jacques' mother Geneviève they rented a large house with a gated entrance and gardens, in the middle of the city of Angers, where they lived with a butler and a staff to care for the two of them. Mother had the antiques from her first marriage shipped over to Angers, and decorated the house, with its high ceilings and oversized rooms, in exactly the same style as her former homes.

The newlyweds were devoted to each other. He adored her and she adored being adored. They were both approaching the age of forty and frankly admitted that children were not a priority in their lives and that they did not particularly care whether they had any or not. Therefore, when my brother Richard was born on January 27, 1939, they placed his full care in the hands of a Swiss nurse, Lucy. My parents had picked her out of a photo of the latest graduating class of a school for baby nurses because she was the only one looking down

4

and smiling at the infant in her arms. Little did they know that this might not have been the best criterion for choosing a baby nurse.

Although my parents were aware that Hitler's army was advancing through Europe when their first child was born, they had no idea that by June of 1940 the idyllic world they were living in would soon come to an end.

THE WAR

It was only as an adult, going through my parents' personal papers and letters after their deaths, that I came to realize what extraordinary events they had lived through before my birth. The people that I had thought of as just my parents, involved in international business and a seemingly frivolous social life, had actually survived two world wars in Europe, and, like many people of their generation, had had experiences as dramatic as any that I had seen in the movies.

My father was well over the age limit to re-enlist when France entered World War II, but in 1940, at the age of thirty-nine, he managed to convince the French army that he would be a welcome addition to their ranks.

He knew he might have to leave the family at any moment to join his battalion, but my parents' main concern was for the safety of my brother, Richard, who was only a year old. As reports came in that the Germans were approaching Angers, my parents decided that the wisest—but by far the most difficult—course of action would be for Mother to take Richard to America. This meant that she would have to drive through France, Spain, and Portugal to Lisbon in time to board the last ship bound for America.

What it was like to escape from Europe in wartime with baby Richard and his nurse, Lucy, was eloquently expressed by my mother herself in letters that she took time to write to her mother and Ashie during her drive across war-torn Europe. Here are excerpts from her letters.

In her first letter, dated June 13, 1940, Mother wrote:

> *Really, darlings, I never could attempt writing you all the doings, emotions and activity of my present life—it's bedlam. Amongst everything have dashed to Prefecture with necessary papers filled out so I can get permit for Lucy and myself to leave country. Today must go to police station for permit of circulation so I can be allowed on the roads to Bordeaux. You can never imagine all the red tape we have to go through—I want everything in order so that when we can leave nothing will delay us.*
>
> *The trip will be hard, very hard, I'm not kidding myself. Traffic in main streets here is like traffic in N.Y. side streets at theater time. Files and files of cars all covered with mattresses, arriving from Paris and suburbs and going Lord knows where. Here in Angers we are already jam packed—so they have to go on and on and sleep under the stars.*
>
> *Barrages of soldiers stopping everyone to examine our papers. It's real war now—but everyone stays calm—the French spirit is admirable—Jacques is always a wonder of optimism and courage.*

On June 16th she wrote:

> *Since my last letter everything has changed in my life. Friday night the 14th at 10 p.m. we heard the bridges on the Loire would shortly be blown up so we had to leave as soon as humanly possible. That night I got about three hours of sleep. Next morning—wild dash to Prefecture to get my necessary papers which we were*

awaiting. At 3:30 p.m. we had to go back to Prefecture with suitcases strapped on top and in car. At 3:45 p.m. we were off.

Over the years, I heard one of my father's first cousins, Pierre, who was a teenager when Mother left Angers, speak in awe about seeing my mother come down the stairs of her home that day. He said it was an impression that would last a lifetime—she was impeccably groomed, not a hair out of place, and wore spotless white gloves. She looked as though she were on her way to a tea party rather than setting out on a perilous journey.

For the first time in years, Mother was forced to travel with just a few suitcases instead of wardrobe trunks, but she wrote, "My fur coats are on my LIST." However, being of a practical nature, Mother also made sure that she had a hundred liters of gasoline in the car since it would be next to impossible to find any on the roads.

Her letter continues:

> *I shan't go into details now of feelings I had leaving Jacques behind me, and my beautiful home with everything I own left just as it was, which I never hope to find again. I can't let myself go. I need every bit of strength and courage I have to carry off our trip. Our little darling is a grave responsibility.*

Mother's first stop would be in Cognac, where André Renaud, an old friend of the family and the owner of Remy Martin Cognac, lived.

> *Leaving Angers was longest as there were only single files of cars allowed to cross bridges in one direction at a time. After that I drove as I had never driven before in my life—between 80 and 110 kilometers an hour. Maybe it doesn't sound much to you but you have no*

idea how the roads were crowded, just files and files of columns of refugees.

At 9:15 exactly we were in Cognac and I had found André Renaud and his family. It was such a relief—no words to describe it even—finding Renaud and not having to sleep somewhere in the car as thousands of others had to.

Mr. Renaud gave her the different currencies from his safe that he knew she would need to successfully complete her journey through Spain and Portugal.

It's lucky Ashie has album of baby and pictures of our interior of home, as I couldn't save anything. At least we will have tangible souvenir—but I don't give a d--- about that. It's funny how little possessions count— only hope Jacques keeps safe.

All the Cointreaus have gone different directions— sauve qui peut! [Every man for himself!] Will keep you informed when I know my plans.

On June 22, Mother wrote from San Sebastian, Spain:

Just one week ago today since I left Jacques and our lovely home. One week which seems like a hundred years— Since then all communications were cut off from that part of country and I have no news of Jacques or anyone.

The Germans occupied Angers on Tuesday [only four days after her departure]. I wish we hadn't left so much good champagne in our cellar for them. I had to leave everything just as it was—didn't have time to take

*with me any of my silver or linens. I guess everything we
had is gone for good.*

*I know Jacques was preparing to move back with
the rest of Quartermasters Corps, but as all that part
of country has been taken, they may all be prisoners
now—it's too awful to even think about.*

*You can't imagine how lonesome it feels being so far
from everyone—cut off from all communications, and
all the time the worry over Jacques.*

Wherever she went through war-torn Europe, the struggle for visas
was intense, as people attempted to escape before the German army
could reach them. Mother was almost crushed and her clothes were
torn by the mobs outside the Spanish Consulate. But through it all
she fought like a tigress and no matter what, made sure she looked her
best at all times—ammunition she knew she might need to charm
officials along the way.

Bridges and borders closed immediately behind her:

*We got to Hendaye and joined the files of cars waiting
their turn to cross frontier, one mile long from bridge.
More military papers to be gotten—special permit to
take car out of country—inspection of baggage. Anyway
by 5:00 p.m. we were on bridge. French gates closed
behind us!*

Altogether it took nine days for Mother, Richard, and Lucy to
make the trip from Angers to Lisbon, where they finally boarded
a packed ship with the relatively few fortunate souls able to book
passage to America. Once they were safely on board my mother
realized that the nausea she had been experiencing had not been due
to the smell of fish in the port city of Lisbon but to the fact that she
was pregnant with me. With everything else she had to contend with

at the time, this was not an event that Mother welcomed. According to Lucy, Mother vented her frustration by breaking a hairbrush over Lucy's head. Naturally, it was Lucy's hairbrush, not Mother's own.

HELLO, LITTLE BABY

After Mother arrived in New York and had made peace with the fact that she was expecting a second child, she placed herself under the care of the top obstetrician in the city. She decided that I would be born at Doctors Hospital, which in those days was set up to feel more like an expensive hotel than a regular hospital. I have been told that on any given evening, you could find a cocktail party on your floor.

As the expected date of my birth drew near, Mother informed the doctor that she didn't want to be leaving for the hospital alone in the middle of the night, and therefore she would be entering Doctors Hospital on February 6, 1941. On the morning of February 7, she would do her hair and makeup, after which she was to be put to sleep while he delivered her child.

On the morning of February 7th, Ashie and a family friend were at the hospital waiting for my mother to come out of the delivery room. As they wheeled a half-conscious Dotie down the hall, Ashie anxiously asked how she felt, and was mortified when Mother replied in front of everyone, "I feel as drunk as you do every night of your life," which was probably not far from the truth.

In her room, after it was all over, Mother was lying in bed fixing her hair and makeup when a nurse showed up in the doorway with a baby—me—in her arms. Mother, whose maternal instincts only went as far as life or death situations, waved to the nurse in the doorway, said, "Hello, little baby," and went back to fixing her hair.

However, I do have two pictures of Mother holding me shortly after we went home from the hospital.

At the time of my birth, the only news Mother had received about my father was that he had been killed in action. Still in mourning, she named me after him, calling me "Jacques," and true to the French tradition, put a name on my birth certificate that was longer than I was—Jacques-Henri Robert Mercier-Cointreau.

ESCAPE

At the same time that my mother was fighting to get out of Europe with Richard and Lucy, my father, who had rejoined his battalion, had been captured by the invading army and sent to a prisoner-of-war camp. The Germans marched his company all day and then stopped for the night in a cathedral, where one of the priests recognized him. The priest woke him in the middle of the night and offered to help him escape, disguised in clerical garb. My father later told us that the stupidest thing he ever did was to refuse, and say, "I cannot abandon my comrades."

Conditions in the German prisoner-of-war camp in France were so inhumane that for most of my father's life he found it impossible to speak about them. Years later, upon his death, I discovered a package filled with drawings he had made after his life as a prisoner-of-war— the only way he could express the horror of his existence during that time. Through winter, summer, spring, and fall, all that the prisoners-of-war had to protect them from the elements was a tent over their heads. There were no walls to keep out the cold, the snow, the rain, or the heat of summer.

Once the German officers began to trust him, they sent him to buy supplies in the nearest town. With each trip he gradually made friends with the shopkeepers. These simple people were the real heroes, who, at peril of their lives, offered to give him shelter and helped him to procure the papers he would need for a successful escape.

The time came when he knew if he didn't escape that very day while he was in town, he might never find another opportunity. Instead of returning to camp as his captors expected, he put his plan into action and fled. The brave people he had befriended hid him on their farms before taking him to a safe place where he could board a train back to his family.

Obviously the trip home to Angers would be dangerous—very dangerous. German officers were on the train and exposure was a constant fear. At every station along the way, his false identification papers would be examined and German officers would scrutinize each passenger. When he first boarded the train, he held his breath while a German officer inspected his papers for an inordinately long time. He then gave my father a long hard look, and without comment handed the papers back to him and moved on to the next passenger. My father told me that this was the worst moment of his escape.

When he finally reached his family, they sent a coded telegram to my mother in New York informing her that not only was my father alive, he had escaped from a prisoner-of-war camp. However, he was not content with having escaped German captivity—he now intended to find a way to rejoin his family in America.

After the initial shock wore off, Mother knew that even if my father were able to get to America, he would need permission to enter the country—an exceedingly difficult task for a French citizen in wartime. Mother told me later that it was all she thought about, twenty-four hours a day, no matter where she was or what she was doing. Even in a movie theater, when a new idea occurred to her of someone who could help them, she would run out to the nearest phone. Mother deluged every influential contact she had in Washington with letters and phone calls to get permission for my father to enter the country. She was determined that the same perseverance that had brought her and her child to the safety of America would also bring her husband home.

Her relentless efforts finally paid off, and she anxiously awaited the coded telegram from Angers, signed "Newman," a curiously Jewish name they had chosen, to let her know when and how he would arrive.

My father, who had only traveled on the great ocean liners of that era, made this voyage to America on a vessel that was not much more than a Spanish fishing boat; the trip took twenty-two days. Upon his arrival in New York, Mother dismissed everyone in the house so they could be alone when she introduced him to his new son.

My father had had no idea that my mother was expecting another child when he was captured by the German army, but on the day I was born, he turned to a comrade in the prisoner-of-war camp and inexplicably announced, "Today I have another son."

After his experiences in the prisoner-of-war camp, for the rest of his life Father had a fear of being in a large space, such as a church or a theater. Mother watched him carefully and never forced him to do anything he was uncomfortable with. I remember as a child seeing him break out into a cold sweat when he accompanied us to church on a religious holiday. Mother saw it too, and insisted that it was all right for him to stand in the back of the church near the exit, where she knew he would be more comfortable.

Many days, especially in the beginning, he could not even leave the house. It would sometimes take him hours to get up the courage to go out into the street. This complicated his life and made it difficult to go back to work.

Since World War II was still on when my father arrived in New York, his family in France suggested that he build a Cointreau factory in America. He soon found a site in Pennington, New Jersey, and built a plant there in 1942, the same year that he became an American citizen.

He spent the next twenty-four years as the president of Cointreau in America, manufacturing and promoting the liqueur in the United States, a country that he had always loved. This is why I had the good fortune to be brought up in New York City, in a country that I too have always loved.

"Mother Only Loves You when You're Perfect"

"Mother only loves you when you're perfect!" was a constant refrain in our house when I was growing up.

Although Richard and I knew our parents loved us, our contact with them was limited. At five o'clock every day, our Swiss nurse, Lucy, bathed us, combed every hair into place, dressed us in clean pajamas and robes, and nervously paraded us into Mother's elegant pink bedroom for a visit. Lucy knew if we had so much as one hair out of place, she would be in danger of losing her job.

Mother would be sitting at her dressing table, making herself even more beautiful for whatever social engagement she and my father had planned for the evening, and would always offer Richard and me each a cheek to kiss gently so as not to disturb her makeup.

From an early age, I engaged in an exhausting pursuit of perfection that was focused on my mother. I worshiped my mother but she had little interest in children's games or jabber. Sometimes, though, she could be childishly playful and so loving that my father would joke about our *"adoration perpétuelle"* or our seemingly endless affection for each other. Those were my happiest moments.

Other times she would be irritable and impatient. I thought if I could act like a perfect grownup, she would never notice that I was locked in a child's body. That way I could be as perfect as I thought she wanted me to be.

Several times a day I geared myself into believing that from that moment on everything about me would be perfect—my looks, my clothes, my conversation—everything—thus ensuring my mother's undying interest and affection. After a short while, though, I would notice that my clothing was slightly wrinkled, or one single hair on my head was not in place, or maybe it was that I opened my mouth and something that sounded childish came out. Something always had to be fixed before I could start again.

One afternoon when I was in the first grade, Lucy was walking me home from school. As we reached the corner of 62nd Street and Madison Avenue, we saw an elegant, impeccably groomed woman coming towards us. It was my mother! I was so proud. She reached down and showered me with hugs and kisses. After she left us, I was floating on air until I noticed the scuffmarks on my little leather jacket—a stark contrast to her perfection—and I hoped she hadn't noticed. I wondered how I could avoid ever wearing the jacket again.

I never felt the need to be perfect for my father the way I did for my mother. Father was a gentle, distant man whose only interaction with his children was to pat us on the head when he came home from the office. Only once, when I was little, do I remember having the audacity to climb onto his lap. We were at the seashore in New Jersey, and the Fourth of July fireworks had frightened me. While trying to run away from the noise, I found Father in the hotel bar, smoking a cigar and drinking brandy with his friends. His arms felt so comforting, but within moments I heard him call for my nurse to take me away.

Despite his disinterest in small children, I thought of him as a god whose word was infallible. When I was three or four, old enough to fear the terrors of World War II, I overheard him say to his guests that the Allies would win and we would soon be safe. I believed him implicitly and never worried about it again.

19

ை ஞ

My older brother, Richard, instead of trying to please our parents and be a perfect little person the way I did, put on a tough veneer and rebelled. This was his main form of expression, the best way he knew to make himself noticed.

Throughout my childhood, Richard was also verbally and physically abusive towards me—a situation that everyone else, including Lucy, chose to ignore. I'll never know the reason for his resentment. Maybe he blamed my birth for having taken away what little attention he had had from our parents for the first two years of his life. I grew up not having any idea that his degree of bullying was not normal behavior for an older sibling.

When I entered the first grade at the Browning School for Boys, I longed for a new mahogany desk that I had seen in a store. I had outgrown the tiny table with baby-sized chairs I had previously used for writing or drawing pictures, and the mahogany desk would be perfect for doing my homework. My parents gave it to me for Christmas—it was my main Christmas present that year—and I cherished it. I loved looking at it, touching it, sitting in front of it, and even the way books and paper and a yellow pencil contrasted with its surface. In less than twenty-four hours, my brother had carved my name across it with a knife. I was heartsick. As usual, our parents said nothing.

And I said nothing more about it; I knew it was futile for me to say anything. By then I had learned that I would simply have to endure whatever hostile acts he invented as retribution for my having been born.

But as I grew older, his abuse became more dangerous to my physical self.

I can never forget the morning he shot me. I got out of bed at six a.m. to go to the bathroom. As I walked away from my bed, which was only a few feet away from Richard's, he pulled out a BB gun that he kept within reach of his bed. While my back was turned, he took aim, without getting up, and shot a BB into my left buttock.

My screams of pain brought a furious Mother running into the room. Rather than comfort me, she berated me for waking her up, and then she dug in to extricate the BB. Although I had no doubt that she loved me, she had little patience for any disruption in her life.

I was eight years old then, and it took me until the age of eighteen to realize that Richard was never going to be my best friend and buddy. It was time for me to declare my independence and no longer accede to his demands that I be his slave. It was then that he made a move that would be a red flag for any psychiatrist.

After coming home from school one afternoon, I decided to take a leisurely bath. While I was soaking in the warm water on that cold winter day, my brother casually walked into my bathroom, unzipped his pants and urinated on me. I was livid, but my parents, who were having a cocktail in the library, barely responded to my fury at this final insult.

Not long after that, my brother informed me, "You're the only person I ever wanted to kill!"

It took years after that, during which time we went our separate ways, for both of us to come to terms with our relationship and become real brothers.

But my need to be perfect to please my mother was something that would affect me for the rest of my life. It is something that you can come to terms with, be aware of, and even think you are free of it, but at some level it never really leaves you, and it will pop up again when you least expect it.

MÉMÉ

One of the things I enjoyed most about living in New York City was that I could be near my maternal grandmother, Martha Richardson, whom I called Mémé. Although Mémé lived in Boston, she would come and stay with us on holidays such as Christmas or Thanksgiving.

Mémé had been born and raised in Boston and had already shown evidence of an extraordinary singing voice at the age of five when she sang the role of "Little Buttercup" in Gilbert and Sullivan's *H.M.S. Pinafore* at the Boston Opera House. Throughout her years in convent school she longed for a career in grand opera, but it was out of the question for a well-brought-up young lady of that era to consider a life on the stage. However, her parents, who themselves loved music, eventually allowed her to study singing at the New England Conservatory of Opera.

In the late 1890s, while continuing her studies at the Conservatory, Martha did what her family expected of her and married Samuel Richardson, a reliable older gentleman of English descent. She bore him two little girls, Dotie and Ashie.

Although Martha appeared in recitals and concerts throughout the Boston area, she wanted to become an opera star, and the only way to accomplish that was to go to Europe and study with the great teachers. Already fluent in French, in 1905 she left her husband in Boston and, accompanied by her mother, went to Paris with her two daughters to continue her musical training. Today, it is almost impossible for us to comprehend the shockwaves such actions created in Boston a century ago.

According to one of the newspaper clippings in her scrapbook, now disintegrating with age, my grandmother, without even a letter of introduction, managed to reach the preeminent teacher of the time, M. Juliani, for an audition.

Juliani had listened to hundreds of hopeful and highly recommended singers from around the world, and accepted few of them as students. "Sing!" he ordered Martha.

As her first notes filled the room, Juliani's eyes opened wide and he half rose from his chair. At the end of her song, he threw his arms around her neck and cried, "Come tomorrow! Don't fail to come tomorrow for your first lesson!"

On December 17, 1910, Martha Richardson made her debut with the Paris Opera as Leonore in Verdi's *Il Trovatore*. The international reviews were unqualified raves. They praised the purity, sweetness and power of her voice and described how, on that evening, the French and American flags hung outside the Opera House in her honor.

During the thunderous ovation, her two little girls, Dotie and Ashie, who were sitting in a box close by the stage, were heard happily crying out, *"Maman—Maman!"*

After four years of international acclaim, it looked as though my grandmother's success would go on forever. Little did she know that World War I would abruptly change her life in ways she never could have imagined.

According to newspaper reports, she had been on the streets of Paris with her two children when a German aeroplane overhead dropped a bomb that exploded on the sidewalk in front of her, killing two women.

The very last clipping in her scrapbook is eerily similar to my mother's story when she too would flee France with my brother, Richard, for the safety of America at the outbreak of World War II.

My grandmother told the reporter:

> I had not intended to leave Paris immediately, but when I learned that the French Government was removing to Bordeaux, I made haste to prepare for departure. In the hurry that followed, I was obliged to leave behind all of my valuable stage costumes. In less than three hours, I packed four trunks, five valises, and other baggage.

The next day she boarded a ship, *La Touraine*, and escaped to America, as her daughter also would, twenty-five years later.

The last clipping in my grandmother's scrapbook ended with,

> *Mme. Martha Richardson, who for four years has sung leading roles in grand opera in France, has fled from the bombs falling on Paris and arrived safely in Boston with her two young daughters. Madame Richardson was scheduled to sing* Aida *at the Grand Opera in Paris on September 8, but, sadly, the Opera House closed its doors on September 3.*

World War I effectively ended my grandmother's career as an opera singer. After she arrived back in Boston, she sold her piano and never sang again. My mother told me that only once, at the end of a large dinner party, was her mother inspired to sing Gounod's "Ave Maria," moving everyone to tears. She never explained the reason for the eternal silence of her magical gift—not even to her children.

When I first met Mémé, she had a regal bearing and still wore her hair swept up and held in place by diamond combs from another era. Wherever she went, one could still feel the magnetism that had mesmerized her audiences many years before.

I loved Mémé and felt she loved me and thought I was perfect just the way I was. She also treated me like a little adult and encouraged my early love of music. The only time I can remember desperately wanting to stay up beyond my bedtime was during her visits—I was happy just being in the same room with her.

One of the greatest memories I have of Mémé was once when I was four or five, and we were alone at my aunt Ashie's house, where I went every day to practice the piano. While I was playing the piano, Mémé looked far into the distance and started to sing—just for me. I immediately stopped my childish playing and sat rapt in the magic of this enormously private moment.

From the very beginning, Mémé touched a sensitive chord in my soul. I was no more than five years old, sitting in my parents' living room in New York, when I saw her discreetly get up and go into my mother's bedroom. I could sense something was wrong and found her sitting quietly on my mother's chaise longue with her hands clasped, looking at the floor. Realizing that she was not well, I sat next to her, and for the first time in my life consciously felt the healing energy of love flow between two human beings.

After a few moments, I heard her ask, "Do you want something, darling?"

I looked up and replied, "I just wanted to see if you were all right."

Mémé took my hand and we sat peacefully together until she felt well enough to rejoin the others. Many years later, after my mother's death, I found a letter among her papers in which Mémé mentioned that moment we had shared on the chaise longue and how touched she had been. She added, "He will always be loved. Yes, he has what it takes!"

On a Sunday morning in November 1947, when I was six years old, Ashie (whom I always called Tata, a childish pronunciation of

"Tante Ashie") brought Richard and me home from church. As soon as we walked in the door, we saw the devastated look on Mother's face. Tata, who was very intuitive, immediately said, "It's Mother, isn't it?" Without saying a word, Mother fell into her sister's arms, weeping. That was the first and last time in my life that I ever saw my mother cry.

The phone call had come while we were in church. Mémé, who had been at home in Boston, had awakened early that morning and told her housekeeper that she was not feeling well. She went into the living room, sat down in an armchair, and waited for the housekeeper to bring her a brandy. By the time the housekeeper returned, Mémé was dead.

After Tata went home to pack for the trip to Boston to bury their mother, Lucy took me into my bedroom and explained, "Mémé is in heaven with the stars."

I said, "I don't want her in heaven with the stars, I want her here with me."

I was confused and frightened but Lucy offered no comfort. So I went alone into a dark hallway that connected her room with mine and started to cry. Later, still fighting back tears, I went to my mother's room, but I was not allowed to go in. I had never seen such a look of sadness on my mother's face before, and I could only stand helplessly in the doorway and watch while she packed. There was no way for me to accept that Mémé would never hold me in her arms and make me feel special and loved and wonderful again. I remained inconsolable and cried myself to sleep that night.

On the other side of the coin was my other grandmother, my father's mother, Geneviève, from whom my older brother, Richard, and I never felt any love. Real love—or the lack of it—transcends all the pretty words and cannot fool children. In the summertime, after the war was over, we would go to France and visit her château outside of Angers. Life at my grandmother's château could be fun because of the animals, beautiful parks, and wonderful places for kids to get into mischief. But as time went on, I saw a darker side of Maman Geneviève that did not coincide with the perfect picture she presented to the world.

Maman Geneviève

Night had already fallen when we pulled into the station, and I clutched the hem of my mother's tailored grey suit with my little hands so that I would not fall down the steps and under the wheels of the train. It annoyed her when I wrinkled the hems of her dresses, but this time she didn't seem to notice.

As my eyes adjusted to the dim light, I saw a cluster of elderly figures dressed in black, as in a funeral cortege, coming towards us. The men all wore black armbands, a symbol of mourning, and the women's faces were hidden behind heavy black veils. I turned my head away, hoping that these ghostly apparitions would disappear. One was even more frightening than all the rest—my father's mother, Geneviève, who coldly appraised me before moving on to my older brother, Richard, who was eight.

I was six years old in 1947 and had enjoyed my first trip from our home in New York City to France on the magnificent British ocean liner, the *Mauretania*. I already adored traveling first class and meeting movie stars such as our shipmate Rita Hayworth. Richard, however, couldn't have cared less about the glamour that surrounded us. He felt it was a waste of time to dress up every evening in the little white jacket, short black pants, and black tie that made up our formal attire. We would first sit with our parents in the bar drinking ginger ale with a dash of grenadine, and then move on to the grand dining room to start our dinner with all the caviar our little hearts desired.

After the *Mauretania* docked at Le Havre, we had a long train ride to Paris. My parents passed the time at a table with cocktails and a leisurely lunch, while I stared out the window at the devastated cities and the charred remains of homes. But there was one house that affected me more than the others. The only thing left standing was the chimney, and I wondered what had happened to the family that had called that house their home.

At first it all seemed unreal, as though I were still in the comfort of the United States, watching a newsreel with my aunt Tata at a movie theater in New York City. But by the time we reached Paris, I was consumed by the devastation and somberness of post-World War II France.

This was my introduction to the Cointreau family, and to Paris—the "City of Light." As far as I was concerned, the light had gone out of this city and the ravages of war terrified me.

All I could do was cling to my impatient mother and silently beg her not to abandon me. For the first time that I can recall, a cloud of deep depression descended on me and I had no possible defense with which to fight it.

The drive down dark streets and past ornate buildings to my grandmother's home in the Sixteenth Arrondissement of Paris did nothing to allay my apprehension. It may have been during that ride that I took a profound dislike to anything old or antique, associating it all with the aura of war. One of the most beautiful cities in the world was rapidly becoming my worst nightmare.

My grandparents owned an entire six-story apartment building, but had kept the largest apartment on the top floor for themselves. When we reached the lobby, it was in total darkness; the light went on for only a few minutes when you pushed a button. If you had luggage or fumbled for your keys, you had to find the button and push it again for a few more moments of light. In the center of the lobby stood a tiny, ornate brass cage that turned out to be the elevator.

Once we entered the apartment, I had no more excuse to hang on to my mother and ventured into a dimly lit foyer. My independence was short lived, however, when I walked straight into a life-sized figure of a Chinese warrior dressed in full battle gear. He was not very tall, but he was large enough to tower over and terrify a small six-year-old boy. After I realized that he was only a statue, I looked around in the semi-darkness and saw that much of the apartment was filled with my step-grandfather's collection of war memorabilia and the heavy, ornately carved Oriental furniture he had acquired during his years as a French general stationed in China as an army doctor during the Boxer Rebellion.

Afraid to lose sight of my parents amid these relics of another war, I followed them to their bedroom. It had white walls, Louis XV furniture, and some lamps that seemed to give off the only light in the apartment. The nicest part of the room was that my mother would be in it, but even as frightened as I was, I was not invited to share it with her.

Instead, my brother and I were taken to a dreary room in the back, overlooking a dark courtyard. It had two single beds, faded flowered wallpaper that was peeling off the walls, and a bare light bulb of dim wattage in the center of the ceiling. I was already depressed, but my heart sank even lower at being trapped in this squalid room.

The next morning, the sunlight streaming into the front of the house slightly improved my mood, but by midday I was aware that in a few hours, when evening came, my parents would go out with their friends, leaving me alone with my fears.

In the afternoon, after lunch, my parents opened the large French windows in their sunny bedroom, which overlooked the Eiffel Tower, and took a nap. I lay down between them and waited, afraid to fall asleep—I was convinced that after they woke up, got dressed for the evening, and left the house, something terrible would happen and I would never see them again. I tried to be Mother's perfect little boy and not show my increasing panic. I didn't scream or cry, but I was

30

sure my parents could see the silent terror in my eyes as I watched my mother prepare to leave me.

As distant and as impatient as she sometimes was, I loved my beautiful mother—with her oval face, large blue almond-shaped eyes, and a natural white streak in her hair, starting at the widow's peak—more than anything in the world. She was my lifeline. If I were to lose everyone else in my world, I could have survived. But if my mother were to go away and never come back, there was no way I could go on living.

As far back as I could remember, when my mother went out for the evening, I would lie awake and wait for her to come home. Still dressed in her evening gown, she would always bend over my bed and envelope me in the scent of her perfume and cigarettes. Sometimes she would sing silly songs she had learned from her mother. Then she would lean down to kiss me goodnight and cover one ear with a blanket. I don't know why she covered my ear with the blanket; I think it was something her mother had done for her. After she left me, I would burrow deep down to the bottom of my bed and lie perfectly still for the rest of the night so that the kidnapper in my nightmares would not see me when he climbed through my bedroom window.

The nights in Paris were agony, but the days were not much better. The only time I dared to relax was in the early morning, when I knew that my mother *had* returned during the night and was safely in bed.

The deep depression and constant terror of losing my mother in Paris continued for two long weeks, until we finally left for Château Brillant, my grandparents' summer home outside the city of Angers in the Loire region of France. The castle is actually named Château de Châteaubriant; but my grandmother had seen the sun shining on it from afar and decided that she would always call it Château Brillant, which is the name that I have always called it.

Even when we traveled by car, Mother made sure that it was in grand style, and an old admirer of hers put his ancient Rolls Royce at my parents' disposal for the summer. The Rolls, a relic from another age, even had little bud vases for roses on each side of the back seats.

It was already dark outside when the Rolls rattled through the massive iron gates and onto the graveled courtyard of my grandmother's château. The servants, who had last seen my mother, my father, and my brother at the outbreak of World War II, were lined up outside the front door. They eagerly greeted my parents and hugged and kissed my brother and me on both cheeks.

Mother attempted to be gracious, but she was tired after the long ride from Paris. At the first opportunity she tore Richard and me away from the friendly crowd and hustled us inside.

I looked around the entrance gallery and saw a massive stone staircase on my right, winding up to the second floor. Facing us was a statue of a Grecian woman; on the left was a huge fireplace.

I was not allowed to linger for long and was taken up to the second floor, where my brother and I were put into a large corner bedroom called the "Throne Room." It was beautifully decorated, with an enormous four-poster bed that had a tapestry canopy and corner drapes. Large windows opened on the front and side of the house. This place was certainly more to my liking than the dismal room I had been assigned to in Paris.

I was asleep in a heartbeat but it seemed as though only a few moments had passed before Richard and I were awakened by the sound of birds singing—the most beautiful sound I had ever heard in my life. We looked at each other, ran to the window, threw open the shutters and looked out in awe at the endless expanse of woods and gardens. Without a moment's hesitation, we put on our bathrobes and hurried downstairs, where we unlocked the front door and ran outside to explore.

Our greatest mistake on this first morning was an attempt to tiptoe across the wide swath of gravel in front of the house. Had we been smarter we might have looked for another, less noisy, route. After a few steps we heard Mother's scolding voice from the second floor:

"What are you doing outside at this hour, and waking everyone up by walking on the gravel?" We immediately froze, but as soon as we thought she had gone back to bed, we stepped onto the grass at the side of the building and circled around the property.

Over the years, as we returned from June to September, this vast property would become as familiar to me as the back of my own hand. But on that first day at Château Brillant, there was so much to discover, and every inch was exciting.

Behind the house we found a formal garden that covered an area larger than a city block. There were statues, manicured trees, and mazes of paths lined with pink roses. In the center sparkled a pond with large goldfish. At the far end of the garden there was an eighteenth century pavilion; inside, its high roof was painted like a blue sky with gold stars and drifts of white clouds. Later Mother told us that this was where our great-grandparents would sit and have tea brought to them in the afternoon. I wondered how the servants had managed to keep the tea hot, since the pavilion was so far from the kitchen.

To the right of the house we discovered a tennis court, and next to it, a huge jungle gym. We were still too close to the house to make any noise, so we decided to explore two trails going into the woods. Both trails led to an open circular temple made of marble, with tall columns supporting the roof. It was at the highest point of the property and had benches to sit on to admire the surrounding countryside. From there we followed a manmade stream that crossed through the woods and emptied into an old-fashioned wading pool surrounded by an intricate waist-high wrought-iron fence.

On our way back to the house we came upon the gardens, which contained every imaginable kind of flower, vegetable, and fruit tree. Three greenhouses, each a city block long, were filled with tomatoes and grapes of all colors. It was almost impossible to tear ourselves away from the sweet grapes, warmed by the sun.

Our last stop was at two enormous stone buildings facing the château. Their interiors had been destroyed during the war, and now they were mainly used to house cars. Even what had once been the chapel had been turned into a garage.

It was getting late so Richard and I crept into the house, carefully relocked the front door, and tiptoed back into bed before Mother could discover that she had been disobeyed.

I was usually a shy little boy but on my first day at Château Brillant I enjoyed meeting the head gardener, Auguste, who had started working at the château at the age of sixteen. He and his wife, Maria, a plump red-faced woman who ruled the kitchen, had lived and worked on the property for almost fifty years.

In New York I was never allowed into the kitchen but Maria instantly welcomed me into her domain. She chatted with me while she supervised a kitchen staff of four, who cooked for as many as thirty people a day on an immense woodburning stove. The intricacies of the old-fashioned ways were all that she knew.

Maria told me that during the war, the gardeners and servants had all been forced to stay on at Château Brillant to care for the Germans, who had taken over the château. My grandparents had moved into what had been my parents' home, three kilometers away in Angers. Once a week the Germans allowed them to come and retrieve food from the garden.

During one of our afternoon chats, while Maria prepared seemingly endless vegetables for the evening meal, she gave me a real insight into the heroism of the farmers who had lived and worked on my grandmother's farms surrounding Château Brillant during the Second World War.

On a beautiful spring day just before the liberation of France, a young American soldier slipped into the area without being caught. The farmers all knew about it and hid him in various places around their farms. The Nazi soldiers suspected his presence in the neighborhood, and gathered up all the families who lived on the farms. Among those courageous folks were, of course, Maria and Auguste. Mothers, fathers, children and grandparents were lined up against the long white wall across the road from the large gates of Château Brillant.

The Germans aimed their guns at the line of people and demanded, "Where is Johnnie?"—the name they used for any American soldier.

No one said a word. I could imagine it must have been difficult for them even to breathe, knowing the ruthlessness and cruelty of the Nazi regime they had lived under since 1940.

These brave and simple people remained silent as the German soldiers cocked their rifles and demanded once again, *"Where is Johnnie?"*

Just as they were prepared to annihilate whole families, an elderly grandmother dropped to her knees, with tears streaming down her tired cheeks, and pleaded with the soldiers.

"Please, we have no idea where the American might be. *Please,* don't kill my babies. Take *me,* if you must, but we know nothing about the American!"

For some inexplicable reason, the commander called a halt to the execution and allowed the farmers and their families to go back to their homes in peace.

And the Nazis never found "Johnnie."

On the other hand, shortly after I heard Maria's heart-wrenching story, I was having tea with my grandmother and a lady friend of hers when the lady began telling us about the hardships that she had endured during the occupation.

"My dear," she told us, "you won't believe the horrors we lived through because of the *sales Boches!* [Dirty Germans!] Can you imagine, I had to eat the skin of the Camembert cheese!"

My grandmother wanted to choke me when I spoke up and said, "It really doesn't sound nearly as terrifying as some of the other war stories I've heard."

I was asked to leave the room.

෨ ෩

When the Americans reached Angers in the summer of 1944, General Patton and his soldiers fought the Germans on our land. Many of the Germans fought from the safety of the château but were soon outnumbered. The next morning when my grandparents entered the gates they were elated to see dozens of American soldiers asleep in the fields next to the house. They approached to greet the men with open arms before they realized that they were all dead. In the château they found General Patton, in what would later be my bedroom, mapping out his next military strategy.

By 1947, the only traces left of the Germans were the bullet holes and, in one of the two living rooms, bloodstains where one of the Germans had been shot in the leg and had bled on the flowered tapestry loveseat. Every summer Maman Geneviève would bring out a bucket of water and soap and try to scrub away the bloodstains, but she refused to ever have the bullet holes in the *boiserie* and mirrors repaired.

At Château Brillant some of the fears I had experienced in Paris began to disappear. Once we arrived in the country, I knew that my mother would not be going out at night without me. My grandmother's château would be a self-contained world where we would only visit other members of the family in the surrounding countryside, together.

Although the surroundings were everything a child could dream of, there were two things that less than thrilled me. In the evenings, after dinner, we would sit out back on the terrace and watch flocks of birds overhead. My nocturnal visits with the family outside ended abruptly when I discovered that these were not birds, they were bats. The other fear I developed at that time was when I went to my room one night, looked in the mirror, and saw a huge spider on my neck. From then on, this slightly neurotic child had to search his room with a fine-toothed comb every evening before he would climb in bed. Each article in the room, including paintings, had to be thoroughly inspected, front, side, and back, to be sure that there were no creepy-crawlies in the vicinity.

One night, a bat got into Château Brillant. Maman Geneviève captured it—I don't know how—and I saw her place it in a glass dome on the mantel over the fireplace in my bedroom. I was both horrified and angry and told her that I would not sleep with that creature in my room, and insisted that she take it away.

In Paris, I had been so concerned with losing my mother that I had given little thought to Maman Geneviève, a strong-willed woman who at an early age had learned to wield her power for her own advantage. She had offered me scant comfort in my moments of fear and panic in Paris, but at Château Brillant, she became a force to be reckoned with.

My grandmother, Geneviève Cointreau, had been born into a small family of newly acquired wealth and privilege. Maman Geneviève and her brothers, Louis and André, were the only heirs of Edouard and Louisa Cointreau, who had built the family liqueur business into a major enterprise.

In the 1890s, Geneviève Cointreau had married Maurice Mercier, a well-known artist who created stained glass windows (some seventy years later, in the cathedral in which her funeral was held, the light on her coffin was filtered through the stained glass windows that he had made). They had two sons, Jean and Jacques (my father).

In 1906, when Jacques was four and his brother Jean was six, their father died, leaving Maman Geneviève alone, with two little boys to bring up.

Jean was determined to be an artist—art was his life—and he had a long and successful career. Watercolors, flowers, children's books, posters, movie posters, Cointreau posters, stained glass windows for a cathedral in France—he did it all, and worked until he died, at the age of ninety-five.

My father wanted to be a surgeon, but when he graduated from school, he was the only direct descendant of Edouard Cointreau of his generation who was old enough to enter the family business, and so he did.

My father's uncles, Louis and André Cointreau, who had acted as surrogate fathers, groomed my father for a career in the Cointreau company, and his uncle Louis took him around the world with him as they promoted the liqueur on an international basis. From the beginning André and Louis insisted that it was important for business reasons that Jacques add his mother's maiden name, Cointreau, to his father's name, Mercier, thus becoming Jacques Mercier-Cointreau.

It was around this time that Maman Geneviève met Dr. Henri Coullaud, a General in the French Army who was a *Commandeur de la Légion d'Honneur*, and had been awarded the *Croix de Guerre*. He was living on not much more than an army salary when he asked for her hand in marriage. Before the wedding, the General insisted that his future bride sign a paper that all but disinherited Jean and Jacques from her fortune, in favor of any children they might have together. They eventually had one son, Denis, so I consider myself fortunate that the document became worthless when the General died several years before Geneviève.

The General turned out to be a great intellectual with a remarkable library that he would retreat to every afternoon. I appreciated his wry sense of humor and the fact that he did not appear to be intimidated by Maman Geneviève. At the dinner table he would often, in front of the family and guests, turn to her and exclaim as a statement of fact, *"Geneviève, tu est une enmerdeuse!"* Loosely translated it meant, "Geneviève, you're a pain in the ass!" He always said it with a laugh, but I suspected that he really meant it.

Maman Geneviève got up at seven o'clock every morning, marcelled her hair with a curling iron, and pinned it up in back. She always wore one of two white summer dresses—alternating them each day. Maman Geneviève's frugal habits were a family trait that my mother always referred to as "*l'economie* Cointreau." At Château Brillant, she cut up newspapers that she doled out to be used as toilet paper (Mother, of course, brought her own from America), saved small pieces of string and paper, and kept little pieces of soap. From sunup till sunset Maman Geneviève ruled Château Brillant, as well as the surrounding farms, which she also owned, with an iron hand.

In those days French servants were often considered no more than slaves, which suited my grandmother perfectly. At 8:30 one morning, I was having breakfast in my mother's bedroom when I heard a commotion down the hall. I saw Mathilde, one of several housemaids, running towards my grandmother. Tears streamed down Mathilde's face as she begged Maman Geneviève to allow her to go to her mother, who was dying in a nearby town.

My grandmother coldly replied, "You may go after lunch has been served and your work finished for the day."

Even though I was only six years old, this struck me as so blatantly cruel that I ranted and raved until she finally relented. But in the end Mathilde was so frightened of Maman Geneviève that she only dared leave later that evening after her work was done.

The next day Maman Geneviève asked me, "Why don't you come with me this morning while I tour the property?" I was a bit wary as I followed her obediently through the gardens and past the chicken coop to the rabbit cages. There I saw about two dozen white rabbits, many of them fluffy babies. Maman Geneviève pointed to a nice plump bunny all alone in a cage set apart from the others, smiled at me, and asked, "How would you like to have this one for your very own?"

I would have preferred one of the cute little babies, but I loved animals more than anything in the world and I was not going to question my sudden good fortune.

That night, when I sat down to dinner with the family, my grandmother turned to me and said, "Jacques-Henri, you have displeased me, so your dinner will not be like everyone else's."

Then Maman Geneviève rang the bell and the butler entered with a large silver platter. On the platter was my bunny rabbit. My dinner had arrived.

Family Battles

That first summer at Château Brillant was the beginning of years of battles between my grandmother and me.

Although I found little to admire in my paternal grandmother, I never feared her. To me, the monster we called Maman Geneviève was a bully who could intimidate others who either wanted to inherit her fortune or were in no position to defend themselves. I was neither.

I believe that what infuriated her most about me was the fact that in spite of being a sensitive child, I never hesitated to stand up and defend those who could not defend themselves. Injustice was something I could not endure silently. Maman Geneviève resented me and wanted nothing more than for me to bow low and acquiesce to her power like everyone else. I may have been sensitive to a fault, but I also had courage—two things that I found can live together in harmony.

Mother was always telling me not to cry. She could not even allow *herself* to cry. I once saw her lie rigid on her bed at Château Brillant, her fists clenched and her face contorted, fighting tears of rage after Maman Geneviève had insulted her. If I hadn't known better I would have thought she was having a seizure.

Earlier that afternoon, Mother had encountered Maman Geneviève in the hallway outside the bedrooms, where they discussed the lobsters they would have for dinner. At one point Maman Geneviève, with her usual charm, turned to my mother, and said, *"Tu radotes,"* which means, "You're talking a load of drivel."

Instead of confronting Maman Geneviève about her rudeness, Mother took to her bed, fighting the tears of rage that threatened to engulf her. I sat helplessly beside my mother, knowing there was little I could do to help her release the emotions she always held in check. So I went to confront Maman Geneviève myself. When I found her on the back stairs of Château Brillant, I stopped her, looked her right in the eye, and with all the venom I could muster at that young age, spat out, emphasizing each word, *"You made my mother cry!"*

She refused to respond to me, and just stood there silently, staring at me. She was not accustomed to being confronted by anyone, especially not by a child. Unbeknownst to me, Maria, the elderly head cook, who had been with the family for decades, had overheard me, and came up the narrow stairs behind me. She looked sadly at my grandmother, and said, "If your mother, Madame Cointreau, could see you now, she would be saddened and ashamed"—a particularly brave thing for a servant to say, especially in those days.

One day when Maman Geneviève and my brother and I were out walking, Richard shot a tiny sparrow in the wing with his .22 rifle. It fell to the ground, and Maman Geneviève reached down and picked it up. With a demonic smile on her face, she held the baby bird near my face and twisted its little neck until it was dead. Then, with the same hideous smirk still on her face, she looked me right in the eye and said, "I'll bet *you* wouldn't do that!"

I looked right back at her and answered, "No, I wouldn't!"

I knew that the little sparrow could not survive on its own with a broken wing, but I was disgusted at her perverted joy in trying to goad an eight-year old child into submission with this act of violence.

Another time, I looked out the window at Château Brillant and saw a very large snake, at least five feet long, slithering down one of the tree-lined alleys toward the house. My grandmother was with me in the living room and immediately called for the head gardener, Auguste, to take care of the matter.

I thought nothing more of it, after he had hit it over the back of the head with a hoe and carried its limp form away.

A few minutes later Maman Geneviève asked me if I would be so kind as to throw a few pieces of paper into the furnace—something that surprised me, since I did not even know there was a furnace at Château Brillant. I knew that it was not for heating that enormous establishment, since no one but Maria and Auguste lived there in the winter. If someone wanted warmth in cold weather, each room had a large fireplace.

I easily found the room with the furnace, which was accessible from a door outside and was no bigger than a closet. Once inside I could hear a loud banging sound. When I opened the little door of the furnace, I saw the head of the large snake rising out of the flames. Its mouth and eyes were wide open and staring at me from only a couple of feet away in an agony I could only imagine. The banging sound was its thick body hitting the metal sides of the furnace as it continued to burn. It was like looking into the pit of Hell. I quickly shut the door, fearing that the agonized creature might find a way to jump out of its fiery prison and attack me. I understood immediately that my grandmother knew only too well the horror that I would find in the furnace that day when she handed me the trash to discard.

Over the years, Maman Geneviève never gave up in her attempts to break my spirit. But she never could.

I was not the only one she fought with, though. Château Brillant was a perpetual battlefield. Maman Geneviève resented her daughters-in-law and fought a losing battle for dominance over her sons' lives, since they had married strong women. To add to the conflict, the daughters-in-law didn't get along with each other, either.

I remember when my father's half-brother, Denis (the General's son), married a young airline stewardess called Marie-Geneviève. The wedding reception took place on a beautiful summer's evening at Château Brillant, and we were all delighted to welcome this pretty blonde lady into the family. By then Denis had become a doctor in Angers, only three kilometers away, so he and his new bride fixed up an apartment at Château Brillant where they could live year round.

The first summer they were in residence at Château Brillant, we arrived for our annual vacation to find that my grandmother and her new daughter-in-law were already at odds with each other. In time, especially after the General's death in 1954, the petty squabbles turned into open warfare that involved us all.

All of the main bedrooms were on a long corridor that ran the length of the château. My grandmother's room was at one end to the right of my room, and Denis and Marie-Geneviève's suite was at the other end, on my left.

Since I had never been able to go to sleep easily, I usually stayed up late reading in bed after everyone else had retired. One night I heard footsteps quietly making their way past my room. Being of a curious nature, I went out into the darkened hallway and heard my uncle Denis's voice coming from my grandmother's room. I listened closely and was stunned to hear him try to convince his mother to leave him the majority of her assets, thereby leaving her other two sons, my father and Uncle Jean, out in the cold.

Denis also spoke about suitcases filled with gold coins that my grandmother had buried on the property before the Germans came. Maman Geneviève was the only person who knew where to find them—and he wanted them all.

As soon as I heard him say "Goodnight," I sneaked back into my darkened room and got into bed. I didn't make a sound as I heard his footsteps pass my door on the way back to his apartment and his wife. Then I turned on my light, wrote down everything I had heard, and hid the information behind a painting above my bed.

The next morning, I went to my parents' room, told them what had happened the night before, and gave them the paper on which I had written down Denis and Maman Geneviève's conversation. I figured what my mother and father did with it then was their business. That night, when I again heard footsteps going down the hall, I turned out my light and went back to listen in the hallway.

This went on for several nights. The scenario was always pretty much the same, and my grandmother, to my relief, remained as stubborn as ever, refusing to do what he asked—even when he threatened, "If you don't do as I say, you will never have a day of peace for the rest of your life."

On the last night of my vigil, I was back in my bed with the lights out when I heard him stop at my door and open it. I didn't dare breathe. Then he quietly closed it and moved on to his suite.

At first, I couldn't understand how he had become suspicious of my sleuthing. Then it became clear—his wife, Marie-Geneviève, must have been at the other end of the hallway, also listening to Denis's conversation with his mother. I couldn't see her in the dark because, unlike me, she had a small hallway to hide behind, and could have easily seen me the night before.

During the day, I always managed to be in the way when Denis tried to be alone with his mother and convince her to show him where the gold had been buried. Although nothing was said, it was evident that he was beginning to lose patience with my constant interference with his plans.

I never understood why, but that summer, I was often sick to my stomach at Château Brillant. One night I thought I was going to die from throwing up. The next morning, however, I seemed to rally, and even managed to keep down a little food.

After lunch, my parents had planned for the three of us to go and visit some friends from New York who were staying at Chenonceau. When I said that I might still be too sick to make the trip, my uncle Denis—the doctor—gave me some medicine and said that in his professional opinion, the very best therapy would be for me to go to Chenonceau with my parents that afternoon.

We had not driven far when I became even sicker than before. In retrospect, I wish my parents had turned the car around and returned home. Instead, I suffered during the entire trip, and lay in bed while they dined with their friends.

It was after eleven o'clock at night when we got home and I was able to crawl into my own bed. It was then that Maman Geneviève told my parents that while we were gone, Denis had finally persuaded her to give him the suitcases filled with gold coins. Now they were all his. I couldn't believe it.

After everyone had gone to bed, my uncle Denis came back to my room, opened the door, stuck his head in, and with a big smile on his face said, "I knew you'd be sick if you went to Chenonceau today."

My grandmother never gave in to Denis on his other demands, but no matter what she did, there was never going to be a happy atmosphere in the house after she gave him the gold.

All hell finally broke loose at luncheon one day when Denis's wife turned on me for not having given her a straight answer to a trivial question she had asked me that morning. The truth was that by then I trusted no one and kept my mouth shut. When she began to berate me, my mother became irate. No one was allowed to attack her children, and no one I had ever met—certainly not the much younger Marie-Geneviève—was a match for my mother. Any pretense of family togetherness ended abruptly when my mother called Marie-Geneviève a *"boniche de l'air,"* which roughly translated means "an airline maid," referring to her one-time job as a stewardess for Air France.

That day Denis and his wife left Château Brillant forever.

One might think that was the end of the debacle, but I'm afraid that was not the way things were played out in my family. Denis went on to sue his mother. My parents told me that he dragged her through the courts, claiming that she should give him a greater portion of her assets than her other sons. They also said that he lost his lawsuit, and

46

was not looked upon favorably by the court for having sued his own mother.

What a shame that a family blessed with so many riches had to waste so much time and energy living a life filled with greed. And as far as the other branches of my family are concerned, this is only the tip of the iceberg. A few years ago, I read in a French magazine that the Cointreau Liqueur family history makes the television shows *Dallas* and *Dynasty* seem tame.

After my first trip to Europe at the age of six, I gradually grew to realize that my father was by far the best of all his relatives. He was a kind and generous man who was fortunate and smart enough to have made his life in the United States, far away from the backstabbing and intrigue that plagued a whole generation of the Cointreau dynasty.

However, Maman Genevieve and family battles would turn out to be the very least of my problems. There was a much darker experience waiting for me back in New York in the fall of 1949, a year I will always think of in terms of "before" and "after."

MY *ANNUS HORRIBILIS*: AUTUMN 1949 – SUMMER 1950

Autumn: Mr. Fuller

For as long as I could remember, two phrases besides "Mother only loves you when you're perfect" were drummed into my head: Tata never tired of saying, "Bluebloods never give in," and Mother—who was not comfortable with my childhood tears—was always reminding me, "Men don't cry." I think Tata said it tongue in cheek, but Mother was serious.

Mother's admonishment was once again wasted on me when I dissolved in tears on my first day in the fourth grade at the Browning School for Boys in New York City. I was only eight, much younger and smaller than the other students in my class, which left me feeling vulnerable—as though I were coping with not just one aggressive older brother, but a whole roomful of them. I dreaded the year ahead.

   Mr. Fuller, my new homeroom teacher, saw my tears and made a special effort to comfort me. He became my friend. Lucy saw him every day when she picked me up at school, and I could see that she had a crush on him, but he was *my* friend. From the beginning of the school year he gave me a special honor. I was proud when he asked me to stay with him in the afternoons after everyone else had gone, and put books and projects back into place.

It wasn't long before he began to give me certain instructions that I knew I had to carry out precisely, and that had to remain our secret.

His desk was at the opposite end of the room from the door, facing sideways. First I had to stand next to his chair, with my back to the door, while he sat so deep into his desk that even I could not see what he was doing; only my back was visible if someone came to the door. I had to get as close to Mr. Fuller as possible while he reached for the opening in my pants. Then my mind went blank and time stood still. The last thing I could remember was looking down at the top of his grey hair from what seemed like a great distance. I never had to do anything—only stand there, perfectly still, while he did whatever he wanted with my body; I was the object.

When Lucy showed up to take me home, I always wondered how it had gotten so late. Hard as I tried, I could never comprehend where the time had gone. And Lucy, who had an extraordinary ability to ignore *anything* when it suited her, never questioned the situation when she came to pick me up after my solitary afternoons with Mr. Fuller.

On a sunny autumn day my school took a group of children to the country. Mr. Fuller said that he had a special surprise for me and I mustn't tell anyone. He took me away from the others and told me to follow him into the woods and up a hill. There was a little stream running down the hill. It was only trickling water and I couldn't understand why he made me walk up the middle of the stream instead of going along the side where it was dry.

By the time we reached the top, my shorts had gotten slightly wet, so he insisted that I take *all* my clothes off to dry. The sunlight filtering through the trees onto my naked body only highlighted my vulnerability. I was confused, not knowing what Mr. Fuller expected of me this time, and embarrassed by my nakedness. He positioned me in a certain way, and told me not to look back. None of his instructions made sense to me, but I obeyed him without question.

49

Then I sensed his presence behind me. Endless time seemed to pass while I waited patiently in the pose he had indicated.

I hardly dared to breathe.

Then without warning he made his move, and I was too young and too innocent to protest or even to understand what he was doing, as he struggled to violate my young body in the worst possible way. I simply went numb.

One of my friends calling from the bottom of the hill finally brought me back to reality and Mr. Fuller into frenzied action. He insisted that I get my clothes back on, and nearly threw me down the hill. My little pal looked at me as I ran down the hill, buttoning my pants, and said, "You shouldn't take off your pants with him. You don't have to do that." I was stunned by the notion that a child could have such boundaries.

By the time we reached the others, the pain had seared through to my consciousness. It nearly took my breath away. I hadn't realized how badly Mr. Fuller had hurt me, and I didn't understand the magnitude of what he had just done to me. The kids and teachers continued to play games while I lay on a tree trunk that had fallen down. I looked around for the only person I thought would understand and make it better, but Mr. Fuller wouldn't come near me. And I never cried.

My mother, who had never met Mr. Fuller, answered the phone the next Saturday when he called to say that he was supposed to take some children to the country for the day. He told her that none of the other kids were able to make it, but he would be happy to take me anyway. Mother instinctively felt uncomfortable with the idea and made an excuse as to why I couldn't go.

That night Mr. Fuller was arrested while sexually molesting another little boy. The story was in all the newspapers and Monday morning when I went to school, a new teacher had taken his place.

I never saw Mr. Fuller again, and even though my mother questioned me, I never gave him away. After all, I thought he was my friend. As far as I was concerned, that was my relationship with Mr. Fuller: he was my friend. It had nothing to do with sex; I didn't understand sex at that age. It was uncomfortable, terrible—but he made it clear to me that it was *my responsibility* to be sure that no one knew what was happening while I was standing next to his desk; it was *my responsibility* that no one found out about our secret. It would be my fault if someone found out.

I did not tell anyone for forty-two years. I had no idea what price I was to pay for my silence.

Winter: The Hospital

A few weeks after Mr. Fuller had been arrested, I woke up feeling sick to my stomach and had to stay in bed all day, waiting for the doctor to come and see me. After a quick examination he told my parents that I would have to go to the hospital right away to have my appendix removed.

I wasn't particularly frightened, since Tata had often described the hospital as a wonderful place where you can pick up the phone at any time to order ice cream. The only reason I was upset was because I was not allowed to get dressed for the trip. The very idea of going out in public without the proper clothes filled me with acute embarrassment. My father, however, ignored my protests, put a blanket around me, and carried me into a taxi. Mother, who was suffering from neuritis in her shoulder and arm, got out of her bed to accompany us to the hospital. I could see Mother's concern for me, mingled with the physical pain she was enduring.

It was dark when we arrived at Doctors Hospital on the Upper East Side of Manhattan and the situation there was not at all what I had been led to expect—certainly not private phones and ice cream. I don't remember any pain, only fear at the increasing number of doctors and nurses examining me and trying to stick needles in my arms. They decided that it was an emergency and scheduled the operation for ten o'clock that evening. By this time I knew that whatever I had been told had been a lie. I wanted no part of the hospital and tried to tell them that I was fine, couldn't they please forget about the operation and let me go home.

Surrounded by strangers who ignored my pleas, I became increasingly tearful until a young Asian nurse bent down next to my bed and put her arms around me. She spoke softly and made me feel that she really cared. I wanted to spend the rest of my life being comforted by her. Thanks to her I let them do the unthinkable—stick a needle in my arm with a minimum of fuss. As was the case with so many of the guardian angels who would appear to me in a moment of crisis and then disappear, I never saw her again.

After the operation, I emerged from a very real dream state in which many people that I had known were coming by to see me. When my thoughts cleared and the post-operative discomfort began, I found myself in a white room with two single beds and a wooden screen with a dim light behind it. I looked over at the other bed and was surprised to see Lucy, sleeping peacefully. I hadn't known that Mother had arranged for her to spend the night in the hospital with me; I'm sure she thought it would be comforting for me to awaken with someone I knew in the room. I started to cry and asked Lucy to come over to me, but she wouldn't. She whispered, "You mustn't speak to me because your nurse might get angry if I interfere with her job."

The nurse heard me wake up, came out from behind the screen and handed me a basin to throw up in while Lucy lay silently a few feet away. Once again I wondered why she refused to protect and comfort me. There were so many things that I couldn't understand.

At dawn Lucy went home to take care of my brother, and another private nurse came on duty to care for me. I didn't cry when she gave me an injection every four hours; on some level of consciousness I must have understood that the drugs took away the pain for a little while.

My aunt Tata came to visit me every day. She was wonderful to be with because she always treated me like a little adult. My first morning in the hospital, she sent me one of the best presents of my life—a whole rose bush. It was covered with dozens of little pink roses and sat on the windowsill where I could look at it all day. My mother told Tata that it was silly to give such an expensive gift to a child. But it made me feel special.

One afternoon a few days later, my father came to see me for the first time, with a gift in his arms. Mother came with him.

I had no idea, as I unwrapped the package, that something was about to go terribly wrong. I had just taken the present out of the box when my mother gave me the news that a family that we knew well would come to visit me in the hospital. The words were barely out of her mouth when my world suddenly went into slow motion. I became frozen with terror and could no longer speak.

I had no explanation for what was happening to me. All I knew was that something within me had suddenly snapped and the thought of any visitors, even those I knew well and had always liked, struck terror in my heart. Nobody knew at the time, least of all me, that as a consequence of Mr. Fuller's abuse, what I was experiencing in the hospital that day was the first of several nervous breakdowns.

Even though I was paralyzed by fear, my parents remained oblivious to the storm silently brewing inside me. Father was angry at my not acknowledging the new brown leather bedroom slippers he had brought me, and Mother was furious that I was too rude to thank my father for his gift. They promptly left their mute and ungrateful child alone with the nurse.

The next day, when our friends showed up, was not a pleasant time for any of us. I was no longer frozen but had reached a state of hysteria which embarrassed my parents and left the visitors wondering what they had done wrong.

When I went home after ten days in the hospital, I took the terror with me. It was no longer possible for me to go anywhere outside of the house without panic setting in. We couldn't receive visitors without my hiding out in the farthest corner of the apartment. If I had to go to a store, I would have to be walked around the block several times before I could finally enter the building.

Mother had difficulty understanding my behavior, which upset me because I could no longer be her perfect little friend, and my father had no idea how to handle the situation. So they left it to Lucy to cope with me as best she could.

Richard had somehow gotten it into his head that I might die from my appendix operation and had temporary feelings of guilt. The day I came home from the hospital, he was nice to me—almost solicitous—for the first time in my life, and it felt good. But about twenty minutes later, when he realized that I was not going to die and that I was the same little brother he had always resented, it was all over. I had always assumed that his abusive behavior was normal, that it was the way all older brothers treated their younger siblings. For the first time in my eight years I clearly saw what might have been. It made me sad.

Spring: First Holy Communion

A few months later, in the springtime, in spite of the emotional breakdown I had had in the hospital, my parents decided it was time for me to make my First Holy Communion. We were not a religious family but they felt it was important for their children to receive the sacraments of the Catholic Church. I was informed that I would have to go through a training period to learn the fundamentals of the church and, more importantly, make sure that my soul was pure enough to receive the sacraments.

I had always been intrigued by spirituality and the idea that someone knew the secrets of the universe, and had wanted to send away for booklets by groups such as the Rosicrucians, who advertised in my comic books, though I never did. This fascination was probably the reason that I peacefully followed my mother on my first visit to the Helpers of the Holy Souls in New York City.

We rang the convent bell and a tall, solemn woman in long black robes silently opened the ornate wooden doors. I held on to Mother's hand as we left the sunshine outside and entered the darkness. The only light was filtered through the religious figures in the stained glass windows. Mother and I sat close together in the long entryway, which was lined with wooden benches. For once, I felt more curiosity than anxiety while we waited to meet the Mother Superior, who would enroll me in my classes.

Within a week I joined a class of about twenty children. We rarely interacted, just quietly studied our lessons and sat for long periods of time in silent contemplation. The nuns turned out to be nameless, faceless, black-robed figures with cold discipline flowing through their veins. A sympathetic word or touch for the children was not a part of the program.

Strangely enough, I was taught nothing about the real meaning of the Catholic faith or God's love. As far as I knew, religion was a dull textbook of rules and the Mass was just a boring forty-five minutes while the priest showed his back to the congregation and mumbled in a foreign language.

The last three days before the ceremony were intense; it was the last chance for us children to mend our ways. We contemplated our faults and went to confession on each of those days, to be sure that we had been properly absolved of our sins. But how could I ever be sure that I was perfect enough to receive Holy Communion?

It was a solemn moment when the Mother Superior called me into her tiny office. She sat with a large crucifix behind her head and asked me about my parents, and if they went to church on Sundays. When I answered truthfully that they did not strictly follow the rules of the Church, the old nun informed me that it was my responsibility to see that they went to Mass every Sunday and confession at least once a month.

I cautiously approached my parents and told them what the nun had said. Mother and Father were not happy. They said that the nuns were being paid to see that I made my First Communion, and the rest was none of their business.

Now my dilemma was multiplied. Not only did I have to worry about my own perfection, but had my parents' souls on my conscience as well. I knew it was a losing battle and that I would only further irritate my parents if I persisted.

As the final day drew near, I was told that a little girl and I had been chosen to go up to the altar during the ceremony to recite a special prayer. Did this mean that I was ready? Or would I have to find out on the day itself, when God would decide whether or not to strike me down as the priest put the body of Christ on my tongue?

When the big day arrived, I was dressed in a dark suit with short pants and a white bow tied around my arm. I was taken to the convent early, and made to sit in a large circle with the other children. I sat facing the large windows, wishing that I could miraculously fly away. Surely I could not be perfect enough for this solemn religious occasion.

Terror once again enveloped me as I fought back the tears. The children across the way looked up from their silent contemplation when my sobbing became audible. No one moved for the longest time. Finally a little girl came over from the other side of the room and put her arms around me in a motherly way.

I was trembling inside as we filed into the chapel. My parents, Tata, and Richard were already seated with the other families.

Shortly before the moment of truth, the anticipation became too much for me. I knelt down and fainted. I regained consciousness to the humiliation of being dragged up the aisle by a large nun, and was unceremoniously laid out on the floor of the vestibule.

Mother was mortified at the scene I had caused, but the nuns were not to be fooled with. As soon as I could sit up, they took me back into the chapel where I received the sacraments with the other children and recited the special prayer at the altar. I could only hope that God had been too busy elsewhere to notice me receiving the communion wafer. I also prayed that since I survived *that*, and recited the prayer perfectly, my parents would ignore the embarrassment I had caused them by fainting in public.

In years to come, I discovered that a friend named Ronnie, who had made his First Communion at the same time, had been told by the Mother Superior that if his mother did not divorce his stepfather and remarry his father, she would burn in hell for all eternity. Ronnie didn't faint in church, but within weeks he had a nervous breakdown.

Soon after my First Communion, my parents began to plan our annual summer trip to France—where, at my Aunt Mimy's beautiful summer home, La Richardière, yet another emotional trauma awaited me.

Summer: The Rabbit

Aunt Mimy had been a childhood playmate of my father. Her family had little money, so the moment she was old enough she married my father's very rich and much older uncle, Louis Cointreau, who died shortly after she gave birth to their son, Pierre. Then she was able to marry for love, and wed the Count D'Epenoux, who had a beautiful château filled with exquisite museum-quality furniture. They lived part of the year in his château, part of the year at Aunt Mimy's summer estate, and part of the year in Paris.

La Richardière, Aunt Mimy's summer estate, not far from Maman Geneviève's château in France, was a massive house well hidden from public view by a long, winding road, and was surrounded by many acres of woods and gardens where my father had enjoyed hunting parties when he was young.

As far as I was concerned Aunt Mimy could do no wrong. She had a voice and personality that was a cross between Ethel Merman and Maria Callas, and a large body that she always insisted was on a diet. In spite of her weight, Mimy had a pretty face with delicate features, and a seductive smile that was not dimmed by the fact that her teeth were slightly discolored from smoking the Spud menthol cigarettes my mother brought her from America.

Her electric personality mesmerized me; at nine years old, I was already fascinated by larger-than-life characters. I was used to catering to adults and enjoyed being near the aura of such a glamorous woman. And Aunt Mimy was my godmother, so she noticed me a bit more than my brother.

My brother Richard and I were only two years apart, but he was always much larger than I. He was built stout—wide and strong—while I was slender, more bones than muscle. In spite of his abuse, I still wanted to follow him around and tried to be his buddy.

One sunny summer day at La Richardière, Richard was acting mysteriously and implying that something interesting was going to happen soon. As usual he made it sound enticing and then pushed me away.

I surreptitiously followed my brother when he went through a door leading to the dark basement of the house and disappeared. The entrance was dimly lit and muffled voices came from afar. I traced the sounds through a labyrinth of concrete and stone dungeons until I found a doorway. I peeked cautiously through the opening, and saw a large bare stone room with several men standing at the far end in a semicircle. Richard was in their midst, looking up at something with an anticipatory smile on his face. A cold feeling of dread came over me as my eyes adjusted to the light and I focused on the thing hanging by its hind legs above my brother's head. It was pure white and squirming—the softness of its fur in sharp contrast to the hardness of the men and the stone walls. At first I didn't understand. I stood frozen outside the doorway, my eyes glued to the ecstatic expression on my brother's face.

The first move was very sudden. And then I understood. One swift club on the back of the bunny's head and then a quick thrust with a sharp knife to gouge out its left eye so it would bleed to death. The creature was still wriggling around and trying to free itself, so the man gave it another whack on the back of the head.

They were so intent upon their mission that no one had seen me in the doorway. They did not know the sickness in my body as I slowly backed away. I couldn't run. I could barely walk back out into the sunshine. All I wanted was to find my mother.

When I saw her she was reclining on a lounge chair in the back of the house, reading a book. Knowing that she would be displeased if I were sick in front of her, I moved cautiously towards her and sat down on the stone floor nearby.

"Mummy, I just saw something awful."

"What am I going to do with you? You're always nervous about something!"

"But it was really awful, Mummy."

I knew that my sensitivity sometimes tried my mother's patience, so I was not surprised that she gave no response and returned to her book. I walked around the corner to be alone with my thoughts. Maybe if I had been a little quicker I could have stopped them. But they were so big. And Richard would have been angry with me too.

Pale and unhappy, I rested against a large tree and tried to figure out how my brother could enjoy watching an animal suffer. After a while, I became aware of someone looking down at me—a tall, blonde German.

German prisoners of war had been allowed to go to work for very low wages in French households at the end of World War II. Aunt Mimy, never one to miss a bargain with the dozens of people she needed to run her estate, had hired some of them to work in the fields and gardens.

At first I was uneasy. I had heard many terrible stories about the Germans. Also, I had only seen this ex-prisoner-of-war working on the land, but had never spoken to him.

The man knelt down and gently asked me my name.

"My name is Jacques-Henri. And I just saw the most awful thing."

"You don't look very well. Why don't you tell me about this awful thing?"

The young German listened intently to as much of the story as I could articulate and agreed that it was a terrible thing to have witnessed. He said that I was a brave young man to have wanted to save the rabbit but there was really nothing that I could have done. This was the fate of all the rabbits that were being raised for food on the estate.

He was kind, not at all the way the Germans had been portrayed. And although he made me feel better by explaining what I had just seen, I never understood why the rabbit had to suffer such a cruel death.

When the bell rang for lunch, I thanked my new friend and ran back into the house. As hard as I looked for him, I never saw him again.

A few days after the incident with the rabbit, knowing how difficult it was for my mother to deal with my emotional problems, I carefully planned a whole scenario. I was so excited about a wonderful moment that I was creating, a secret gift of gratitude that I would give to my mother. No one else ever need know about it. She couldn't help but forgive my imperfection and love me more for it.

That evening I could no longer wait. It had to be tonight when she came in to say goodnight to me in the pretty blue and white flowered room at La Richardière.

Tonight I would put on my pajamas, brush my teeth, wash my face, carefully comb my hair, get into bed, and wait for Mother. If the nanny was around, I would ask her to please leave us alone for a while. Richard would not be in the way, since he was allowed to stay up later. I was so sure that nothing could go wrong. My heart was pounding with anticipation.

How wonderful it felt to be surrounded by the crisp linen sheets and the warmth of the blankets while I waited for her to appear. Oh, my God, she looked so perfect as she walked in that I almost lost my nerve. The nanny was slightly miffed and reluctantly left the room when I announced that I wanted to be alone with my mother for a little while.

I started slowly. "Mummy, I want to thank you for being so good to me since my operation. I've been so nervous all the time but I know I'm getting better and I wanted to thank you for being so patient with me."

She gave an embarrassed little laugh as she quickly got up to go, and said, "Yes, sometimes one feels like saying 'Thank you' for something."

Somehow I was not too surprised that my mother didn't seem to understand the importance of the moment. I didn't really understand it too well myself. Maybe I hadn't said it well enough. I knew that I could never try again. I had done my best and the moment was gone. Strangely, there was a kind of afterglow from simply having said the words.

The Doctor's Report

By the time we left La Richardière, my parents could no longer ignore my escalating emotional problems. I had become even more obsessed with my own cleanliness and perfection, and was increasingly fearful of the outside world. Since my parents knew nothing about what Mr. Fuller had done to me, they were confused by my neurotic behavior, and were finally forced to seek professional help.

That summer, Mother took me to see a doctor at the Children's Hospital in Paris. Several child psychologists put me through a battery of tests, but in those days child molestation was not as openly acknowledged as it is today, and no one asked me the most important question. My "secret," being sexually abused and raped by Mr. Fuller, was not brought to light.

So when the hospital wrote a letter with their findings for my parents to give to a doctor upon our return to New York, their opinion was:

This child is suffering from an obsessive neurosis. He has always been scrupulous, full of doubts and fanatical about being perfect. He has already suffered from several compulsive obsessions (perfection in his grooming, perfection in his schoolwork, etc.). Very fixated on his mother with a striking ambivalence.

He suffers from acute anxiety attacks (fear of going into class, fear of entering a public place) which were triggered by two emotional shocks at several weeks' interval: an appendectomy and a first communion which seemed to awaken all his feelings of guilt.

The Rorschach test shows a basic anxiety with obsessive elements. The TAT by Murray shows an obvious castration complex.

A course of psychoanalysis appears to me to be indispensable and urgent. The parents understand the situation and are committed to having their son undergo the necessary treatment.

Back in New York, my parents' physician, whom I knew well, had a talk with me at our home. It consisted of his patiently urging me to look into his face and say, "Hello." Once he had accomplished that task he announced in a loud voice that I no longer needed any psychiatric help.

The subject was never brought up again.

TATA

One thing that helped me survive the following years was my love of the piano. My parents had allowed me to study piano ever since I was tall enough to sit on a bench and reach the keys. Until I was eleven, we did not have a piano, so every day when we were in New York I went to Tata's house to practice. She was the one person who always listened to and encouraged me in my childhood dreams.

As far back as I could remember, my only desire in the world besides wanting to be perfect enough to deserve my mother's love was to dedicate my life to one of the arts. The one hope I clung to at that young age was that I would someday have a career in show business. It might seem like a bit of a stretch, but I confided to Tata that it would either be that, or become a missionary. She understood.

When Tata had been a young woman in a convent school in Boston, she had fallen in love and eloped with an aristocratic young man from a diplomatic family in Portugal. She lived with her young husband and their baby in his family's castle, far away from Boston and home. Tata said the family treated her with such disdain that she suffered agonies of homesickness and finally went home to visit her mother, leaving her young son in the care of her in-laws. When she returned, they had disappeared with him. Tata, who had phlebitis in her leg, traveled on crutches from one end of Europe to the other in search of them, but could not trace them because of the family's diplomatic immunity. Ultimately she realized that these people were too rich and too powerful for her to win back her son. Therefore she lavished all her maternal love on my brother and me.

I also enjoyed Tata's sense of humor, which had earned her a place at the Algonquin Round Table with Dorothy Parker and other great wits of her youth. However, by the time I was five, Tata had retreated from life and into a world of alcoholism. She tried, often unsuccessfully, to wait until 5:00 p.m., but as soon as she had her first drink of the day, she continued drinking until she passed out.

As much as I loved a sober Tata, the other Tata, the one who changed so drastically after her first drink, frightened me. But during the years that I practiced the piano at her house every day after school, she loved me enough to control herself and never drank while I was alone with her.

I was thrilled when my parents finally took their grand piano out of storage in France and brought it to America. However, I still visited Tata several times a week. The day the piano arrived, I sat down to play—and play, and play, and play. I had not counted on the fact that listening to such a possessed child for hours on end would be too much for my mother's sensitive nerves. Too often when I touched the keyboard I could hear Mother's voice from the chaise longue in her bedroom, telling me to stop playing so she could rest. Eventually I lost heart, closed the lid on the keys, and let the piano simply become a beautiful addition to the living room furniture. My musical aspirations would have to wait.

Panic Attacks

I was twelve years old when my parents planned a trip to Nice, in the south of France, to visit old friends. They decided that this time they would leave Richard and me with Maman Geneviève at Château Brillant, where for once no one was fighting and there was some kind of peace. As for me, everything had seemed fine as long as I was out of Paris and in familiar surroundings—until I decided to go to a department store in Angers with my grandmother and my brother.

Suddenly I couldn't breathe. Frantically I searched for a familiar face in the crowd. Where was my family and why were all of these strangers jostling me around? The front door seemed so far away and everyone wanted to get there first. My heart was racing, my legs were starting to give way, and my head was spinning as the crowd carried me forward. Oh, God, I was scared. Maybe I was having a heart attack or dying or going blind. Fear gave me the strength to fight my way outside into the fresh summer air. My legs were still shaking when I saw Maman Geneviève and Richard standing nearby and I nearly cried with relief as I got into the safety of the car.

Unbeknownst to me, what I had just experienced in that crowded store in Angers was an intense, full-fledged panic attack, different from any I had experienced before, and different from the level of anxiety I had learned to cope with every day. It seemed to come out of nowhere, during a period of relative calm in my life, and caught me by surprise.

From then on, whether in France or the United States, I lived in fear of my next attack. Walking a city block or going back and forth to school became a nightmare. Every time I left the house, I became weak with terror at the horrific things I imagined would happen to me. It was better if I was not alone, but it must have seemed strange to other people when I kept putting my hand to my head in an effort to control the panic, the spinning, and the threat of impending blindness. Many years later, I discovered that there was a name for this—agoraphobia. But at that time, no one knew what to call it, and, again, no one wanted to deal with it.

During this first summer of acute panic attacks, Maman Geneviève suggested that I might feel better if I wrote a letter to Mother, as long as I didn't worry her by mentioning my new problem. Richard just stayed out of my way.

One night as I lay awake with the rising panic, I felt I had no choice but to go in and wake up Maman Geneviève before I died of fright. She allowed me to get into the large bed with her and my step-grandfather, the General, who was still asleep. Knowing her as well as I did, I soon realized that she was only feigning concern in order to keep me quiet. I went back to my own room to wait out the night as best I could.

The only moment of that long night that I found humorous was when the General had awakened, unaware that there was a third person in the bed. The old man, who had a great sense of humor and little patience for Maman Geneviève, sat on the edge of the bed and decided to use the urinal rather than walk down the long hallway of the château to the bathroom. (In those days servants were expected to clean out the chamber pots and urinals stashed inside the bedside tables.) As the General took out the urinal, he offered it to his wife and asked her laughingly, "Do you want to piss, Geneviève?" The old man laughed even harder when she furiously whispered for him to be quiet because the boy was in the room.

Over the years, I relived the story of my step-grandfather and the urinal many times in my mind. I understood from an early age that as long as I could still find something to laugh about, I could survive. It was the times when my sense of humor would disappear that I had to watch out for.

My First "Other Mother"

I never felt that I was perfect enough for Mother, especially after my experience with Mr. Fuller. But over the years I found three "other mothers" outside my family, who were able to nurture me.

The first person to take me under her wing and ultimately become another mother was Lee Lehman, the wife of Robert Lehman, the chairman of Lehman Brothers Banking Investment Corporation. At that time, there were no "Brothers"—Bobbie, as Robert Lehman was called, had inherited his position from his father, along with enough stock to make him the major stockholder. In those days, the company was involved in a considerable portion of the financial business conducted in the United States and around the world. Bobbie had married Lee in 1952, and he treated her daughter Pamela, from a previous marriage, as if she were his own.

When I met the Lehmans, in 1954, on Halloween—a night on which I often meet the most significant people in my life—it would forever change not only my life, but also theirs.

My date for the evening, Marcia, a sweet girl dressed as a daisy, had invited me to a costume party at her friend Pamela Lehman's home. Pam, a pretty, dark-haired, voluptuous thirteen-year-old, was dressed in the colorful hot pink costume of a French can-can dancer. Unfortunately for the daisy, who had a crush on me, Pam and I hit it off from the start.

One of the most memorable evenings of my life began as I walked into the Lehmans' apartment on Park Avenue. In the foyer I saw the

Renoir painting *Girls at the Piano*, a van Gogh *Self-Portrait*, a Matisse, and two life-sized Degas ballerinas. In the massive living room there was more of one of the five greatest private art collections in the world. But I scarcely noticed the art then; I was used to opulent homes and thought that everyone lived this way. What I did notice was the most beautiful woman that I had ever seen in my life, other than my mother, when she walked in and sat down next to me. This was Lee, Pam's mother, whom the press had recently labeled one of the ten most beautiful women in the world, along with Elizabeth Taylor and Ava Gardner. When the Lehmans' art collection was shown at the Louvre in Paris—the only private collection up to that time that had ever been shown there—the press asked Bobbie what his greatest treasure was, and he said, "My wife." I was instantly in awe of this brown-eyed auburn-haired beauty with fine classic features. I may have been only thirteen, but she treated me as though I were an adult.

Years later, I found out that the minute I had walked through the front door, she had turned to Pam, pointed at me, and said, "He's ours." And I was.

Soon Mrs. Lehman asked me to call her "Lee" when only she and Pam and I were together; but I was still to call her "Mrs. Lehman" when Mr. Lehman and other adults were present.

Over the next few years, as Pam and I became inseparable, the Lehmans welcomed me into their home and treated me like a son. Not only did they invite me to travel the world with them on school holidays, but they also asked me to stay with them each summer for a few weeks at their house in Sands Point, overlooking the Long Island Sound, before I headed off to Europe with my parents.

While Mr. Lehman went to work in New York every day, commuting by yacht, Lee and Pam and I amused ourselves by going out to lunch and shopping. I was a great swimmer, and Pam and I often took a dip in their Olympic-sized pool. We were included in the Lehmans' dinner parties every weekend. After dinner, we would all go to the Lehmans' own private movie theater, where we sat in lounge chairs and screened pre-release movies sent over by Twentieth Century Fox, as Mr. Lehman was on the board of directors.

Lee was a very good artist, and she always initiated some sort of art project for the three of us to be working on. She bought a little kiln so we could paint and fire various ceramic objects. She always said that the best way to learn about great art was to copy it, and even when we traveled we would study paintings by copying them. I still have a painting of flowers that I did in Jamaica, a copy of a painting by an artist we admired.

Another thing I loved about Lee was that her generosity knew no bounds. When Pam and I were invited to a party at the Sherry-Netherlands hotel, her mother dressed her in one of her own dresses, a beautiful black and fuschia satin evening gown, and covered her with magnificent jewels. The Lehmans had a little chest that they kept behind a screen painted by Vertes, in the dining room. In the chest, they kept cartons of cigarettes. That night, before going out, I went to the dining room and took out a pack of Newport cigarettes, which I put in the pocket of my dinner jacket.

When I entered Lee's dressing room, where she was putting the final touches on Pam's hair, she took one look at me and said, "You can't ruin the line of your jacket with that pack of cigarettes. I think we can do something about it." She then went into her bedroom and came back with a beautiful slim eighteen-carat gold basketweave cigarette case which she had had made in Venice the year before, and said, "Here, try this." I put the cigarettes in it and put it in my pocket, where it fit like a glove. She looked at me again and smiled and said, "It's yours." Then she went back into her bedroom and brought out a gold Van Cleef and Arpels lighter, also basketweave, which she handed to me. "I'm sorry, but this you have to return. It was a present from Bobbie."

I instinctively knew that Lee received as much joy in giving me the cigarette case as I did in receiving it.

രി ിൈ

Being around the Lehmans was like a salve that protected me from the ugly realities of a world that I had difficulty coping with. At first, whenever I left their house I mulled over every moment that I had spent with them and was sure that I had somehow made a horse's ass out of myself, and none of them would ever want me to come back. These people were beautiful, glamorous, funny, accomplished, and I desperately wanted them to like me. Finally I realized that no matter how awkward I felt I had been, I was perfect enough for *them*, and they *did* want me back.

Sometimes Mr. Lehman was very fatherly with me. Once when I was having trouble at home, he sat me down on Pam's bed and closed the door, and we had a little heart-to-heart talk. He explained to me that my parents were giving me a hard time because they were disappointed in my brother, not me. It was a very kind gesture on his part.

And, years later, on my twenty-first birthday, I was sitting in Lee's dressing room with Lee and Pam, and Mr. Lehman kept coming in every five minutes with yet another present for me. One was a pair of garnet cufflinks that I wear to this day, and another was a crocodile wallet with my initials on it. I don't remember the rest, but there were several others that he kept bringing in to celebrate my birthday. Then they took me to dinner at 21 Club. When Bob Hope came over to the table to say hello to them, Mr. Lehman told him, "It's this young man's twenty-first birthday—could you tell him a joke in honor of his birthday?" Bob Hope declined to tell me a joke, but he did wish me "Happy birthday."

Lee was always there for me, no matter what. If something went wrong in my teenage life I could always go to her. She would listen to my problems and talk to me for hours. But I could not tell even *her* about Mr. Fuller and the anxiety attacks and phobias I had lived with for all those years. As much as I tried to run away from the specter of Mr. Fuller, I realize now that it was never far away.

When I traveled to Haiti with the Lehmans at the age of sixteen, Mr. Lehman was having a massage by the hotel pool and insisted that I have one too. Though I didn't understand why, the thought of a stranger touching my body terrified me. What was even more frightening was that my massage would not be by the pool with everyone else but that I would have to go to a private studio back in the woods. The more I argued against it, the more the Lehmans argued that I must experience this wonderful massage. By the time I was alone with the masseur in the studio, I was rigid with fear. Only the extreme good manners I had been brought up with forced me to stay and endure this private agony. And what excuse could I have given the Lehmans for what they would have considered bizarre behavior?

I do believe Mr. Lehman was an honest man, but I discovered that he was not averse to doing business with monstrous dictators such as Haiti's Papa Doc Duvalier.

During this same trip to Haiti with the Lehmans, we were at a private dinner party in someone's home, when I, in my naiveté, blurted out, "Who is this character?"—referring to Papa Doc. The dictator was so dreaded by his own people that everyone around me turned pale with fear and said, "Don't ever say anything like that!" They knew that all of their lives were at stake if word got out that anyone had said anything about Papa Doc.

Having learned my lesson, my admiration for Lee only increased when she told me about her visit to Duvalier's office with Mr. Lehman. When she and Bobbie walked in, the dictator was sitting back with his feet up on his desk. Not only did he not get up to greet them, he did not even take his feet off the desk. So Lee turned around and walked out. It was an incredibly bold thing to do, but she was offended by his disrespect for a lady. Papa Doc wasn't stupid, though. Lehman Brothers needed Haiti and Haiti needed Lehman Brothers, so Lee got away with snubbing a dictator.

ॐ ॐ

The one questionable part of my friendship with my new "mother" was that by the age of sixteen I was expected to become her playmate and drinking buddy—a role that I was more than willing to take on. Of course, I knew all about doing whatever I had to do, to please the grown-ups in my life. It might not have been looked upon as appropriate behavior but the relationship was a lifesaver for me.

The first time I remember having a drink with Lee was on an airplane coming home from Canada, where the Lehmans owned thousands of acres of land and pretended to camp out in beautiful cabins with wood-burning fireplaces in every room. There was always someone to make sure that the fire was roaring in your bedroom by the time you retired for the night. And when you went fishing, a guide would cast the rod until a fish started to bite; then you would drop the book you were reading, take the rod from his hands and reel in the fish.

I never fell in love with Lee, as did most men she met, but I was, of course, totally captivated by her. She had come from a modest Italian family in upstate New York, and had never lost her unpretentious ways in spite of the pressures and social obligations required of her as Mrs. Robert Lehman.

When Lee married Bobbie, as everyone called him, he was sixty years old—twenty-seven years older than his new wife—and, although the trappings of luxury appealed to her, the world of the rich and famous terrified her.

In order to cope with being Mrs. Robert Lehman, for the first time in her life she started drinking heavily and taking prescription diet drugs and barbiturates, which often put her in an unbalanced state of mind. When she came home in the evening after a day of diet pills and alcohol, dinner would often become a battleground where Lee would pick one fight after another with her husband. In her frustration, he could do no right. Mr. Lehman (as I always called him) always accepted it meekly and almost seemed to enjoy the abuse, which led me to believe that this giant in the business world had a masochistic side to his personality.

Looking back on it, I believe that he was an emotionally immature man. One moment, he could be my best friend and father figure, and the next moment he would look right through me as though I weren't there. This was the pattern in all his relationships, including his marriage to Lee. Though I don't think Lee did it intentionally, on some level she knew that the only way she could keep his interest was by keeping him unbalanced and insecure. This was not in her nature, and it destroyed her. After she had chastised him enough, he would send over to Van Cleef and Arpels for an emerald and diamond necklace, bracelet, and earrings. Within a few years she ended up with one of the greatest jewelry collections in the world.

One thing they had in common was a love of beauty and art. He was a serious collector of museum-quality art, which is now housed in the Lehman Pavilion at the Metropolitan Museum of Art in New York City. After they were married, Lee was instrumental in creating the collection of Impressionist art that filled their apartment. Every Saturday the two of them would make the rounds of all the top dealers. Not only did she have an excellent eye, Lee was a very fine painter herself. She could copy anything. She spent weeks making an extraordinary copy of one of the Modiglianis in their collection. And when they brought home a Van Dongen to decide whether they wanted to buy it or not and couldn't make up their minds, she decided to paint a copy and signed it "Van Lehman." Both of her paintings now hang in my living room.

Lee once confided in me that when she was young, a renowned astrologer in California had told her that someday a very rich and powerful man would ask her to marry him. The astrologer went on to say that if she accepted, the relationship would ultimately destroy her. She then told me that the first time Bobbie Lehman appeared on her doorstep she recognized the man she had always seen in her dreams and knew that, for better or for worse, they were bound to be together.

Within two weeks of my meeting Lee, she made her first attempt to kill herself. I adored Lee, and I was too young to understand why this extraordinary woman was self-destructing. From then on, each time she overdosed on sleeping pills, it tore me apart trying to keep her alive until the ambulance arrived. I remember the first time I held her in my arms and tried to walk her up and down the long hallway while waiting for the doctor. By the time he arrived he told me my efforts were useless—she was already unconscious. I laid her out on the bed, and noticed that her pubic hair could be seen through the transparent fabric of her nightgown. In my thirteen-year-old innocence, I ran into the bathroom and grabbed a little hand-towel and laid it across her to cover her nudity.

When I told the doctor that I was heartened by the fact that her cheeks were filled with color, he explained that it was caused by the poison in her system. After the ambulance took her away all we could do was wait. I can only imagine the agony for Pam.

As for Mr. Lehman, after his wife's first suicide attempt, he bought her another major piece of jewelry to add to her collection. But the next time she overdosed, in her frustration at trying to reach him on an emotional level, she tried to flush a priceless emerald and diamond necklace down the toilet. Obviously she needed something more than jewels to fill the void in her life.

Lee's downfall was the fact that she never knew that she was much more than a beautiful face. Although she was also blessed with great intelligence and humor and such charisma that she could draw anyone to her, she felt an obsessive need to validate herself by seducing every man in her orbit. Not amused were the many wives who watched their husbands (one of them a President of the United States) become captivated by her charms.

And when it comes to Presidents of the United States, my first real lesson in politics was given by the Lehmans.

I arrived one evening for dinner and was greeted by Lee in the foyer. I noticed immediately that the doors to the library were closed—something I had never seen before.

I asked Lee, "Why are the doors shut?"

"Bobbie is having a meeting with..." and she named several important heads of industry that I had met at the Lehmans' apartment over the years.

Naturally I asked what the meeting was about.

"They're deciding on the next President of the United States," she replied.

With true innocence I asked, "How do they determine *that*?"

I was shocked when she answered, "It's whoever they have in their pocket."

After the next election I was not surprised to see, prominently displayed in their apartment, photos of the Lehmans at the White House with President Lyndon Johnson.

I later discovered that President Johnson had immediately become captivated by the beautiful and charismatic Lee—something that did not please Lady Bird in the least. The whole situation became so uncomfortable for Lee that after a while she refused to go with her husband on future visits to Washington.

I often heard remarkable and private information when I was a teenager, spending most of my time with the Lehmans: Bobbie was one of the most influential political and business moguls in the world. One day he came home and told Lee, Pam, and me something I will never forget—he said that the head of the U.S. Air Force had confirmed to him that the government had proof of the existence of UFOs, but would not release the truth to the American public because they feared it might cause widespread panic in the country.

I don't think Lee ever felt more comfortable than when Mr. Lehman was out of town on a business trip and Pam and I would join her in the master bedroom to eat Chinese food and watch television, far away from politics, big business, and high society. Unfortunately, she couldn't spend her life hidden away from the harsh realities of the world she had married into.

Lee might not have been everyone's first choice as a positive role model for an impressionable young man, but I never heard her say an unkind word about anyone—she was completely non-judgmental and taught me to be tolerant of everyone but snobs. Those are lessons that I never forgot.

—✤—
BOARDING SCHOOL

My parents had always assumed that I would go to boarding school by the age of fifteen. As much as I hated the idea of leaving my family and the Lehmans, there never seemed to be much choice about that, although I was allowed to choose which prep school to enroll in. Since Richard had chosen one in Pennsylvania, I figured I might as well go to the same place. At least I would know someone there.

The extensive grounds of the school were carefully landscaped and dotted with a combination of old New England Gothic buildings and modern three-story brick dormitories. It was certainly a departure from the small private school in New York City that I had known all my life, where there had rarely been more than a dozen students in each class, and I had known everyone's name from kindergarten through high school.

My parents drove me up for my first day. It was an awkward situation for everyone, as complete strangers destined to live together for the next year met each other for the first time. Mother and Father helped me unpack before they returned home to New York City, where they could have a cocktail before dinner and congratulate each other for having flawlessly performed their parental duties.

At first I did not question the appropriateness of the school for someone with my emotional background. As the days progressed, however, it was evident that this monstrously large and impersonal environment was not one that I could easily thrive in—and I felt lost. There was certainly nothing nurturing about a place that did not foster individuality or creativity. What on earth did Richard find to love about it? It was a mystery that I did not allow myself to dwell on. Instead, I continued with the relentless round of classes and sports designed to keep the adolescent mind so constantly busy that it has no time for an original thought.

If I had permitted myself to take an honest look at my feelings, I would have seen a new pattern begin to emerge. For the first time in my life I tried to be bad. And I went at it with a vengeance. At first I played small pranks, to annoy the people in charge. No one ever knew or even suspected that the culprit was the quiet boy on the third floor. And I felt such satisfaction when I heard a teacher go down the hall in a rage over a door that had been unhinged so that it crashed down on him—again—when he opened it. The man didn't even realize that it was always the same door. Over time one would think that he would begin to open it cautiously. Oh, God, it felt so good to throw away the fear of not being the perfect little boy.

After a while the pranks became more blatant. I had no fear of recrimination, more a feeling of satisfaction at pushing the envelope as far as I could, while reveling in the power that comes with not caring. My proudest moment came when I sat in a teacher's office and smiled inwardly as the man informed me that he was on to me. He was nearly apoplectic by the time he ended his tirade with, "You're a worse shit than your brother!" I had waited a lifetime to hear someone say that.

Ironically, the only act that I was ever punished for was something Richard had done. In a written report to the dean, the teacher had gotten our first names mixed up. I knew that my brother was up to his neck in trouble, so I politely took the rap in order to save him from being expelled. I felt a certain sense of superiority at the teacher's stupidity, and only mild annoyance at the extra hours I had to spend in a study hall. There was not much else to do anyway. And it gave me a chance to search my brother out and tell him he was off the hook. Richard did not seem at all impressed by my sacrifice, and we each went back to our respective lives. I never again sought out my brother at school.

Within a month I knew that my misbehavior was a cry of desperation at being in an environment in which I could not survive. I felt as abandoned in the school as I had as a small child in Paris, when I thought that I would never see my mother again. Only now I was bigger and able to express myself in a more destructive manner. My mother came up once to visit, and I told her, in a low voice so that the chauffeur could not hear, "Mother, I really *hate* boarding school."

She dismissed the subject with a laugh and said, "But, darling, *nobody* likes school."

I knew it would be useless to bring up the subject again.

On the day that I was to go home for Thanksgiving vacation, I was in the middle of a biology test when I saw our car waiting outside the window. That was the end of the test as far as I was concerned. I handed in my half-finished paper and flew out of the room.

At home, most of the time I tried not to think about returning to school. I enjoyed the security of my own room, and being in the city that I had always loved.

My last night of vacation, I went to a party at a friend's house and realized that if I went back to boarding school I would die. There was no way my spirit could survive. It was all right for my brother, who was too out-of-control in the freedom of the big city. But after a lifetime of searching for approval and six years of submerging the pain of abuse and rape, I needed the space to develop and nurture my own being. There was certainly no nurturing or approval for me at boarding school. There was only a huge emotional void.

On Sunday morning I knew that my time was running out. I went to the medicine cabinet and took out a bottle of tranquilizers that had been there for ages. I took them all. Then I drank the mouthwash, ate the toothpaste, and swallowed anything else that I could get my hands on. After it was all gone, I calmly went in to lunch with the family.

The moment that luncheon was over, it was time to go with Richard to Grand Central station, where the train was waiting to take us back to school. The pills finally started to take effect in the taxi. When it became apparent that something was wrong and I admitted to my brother what I had done, he was furious. He told me that he had plans to stop in some town along the way with his friends for some kind of mischief and he was certainly not going to waste his time taking care of me. The last I saw of Richard was at Grand Central as I was weaving down a staircase to the train.

By the time the train reached its destination, I was almost unconscious, and only dimly aware of an older student from the school who had made it his responsibility to see that I arrived safely. Back at the school, my self-appointed guardian angel held me up as I signed in, and caught me each time I started to collapse. Even through the haze of drugs I wondered why a stranger would go out of his way to take care of me after I had been deserted by my own brother. His final act of mercy was to steer me to the dining hall, where dinner was already in progress. As was the case with so many of my "angels," I never saw him again.

I held on to the backs of seats and staggered to my table. It was evident to everyone that something was wrong, but they all accepted my naive explanation of having gotten high by mixing an aspirin with Coca-Cola. After all, it was the 1950s and still an age of comparative innocence.

It had been difficult enough making it this far but my heart sank when a teacher informed me that it would be my duty to clear the table for all twelve people after the meal. Little did he know that I could hardly stand up.

I sat there until all twelve diners, including the teacher, had left the table. Then I slowly got to my feet, found an oversized tray, and piled everything on it. Dozens of other students on the same tour of duty watched in morbid fascination as I took a few tentative steps in the direction of the kitchen. Within moments the whole tray turned over and everything but me crashed to the floor. I knew I was in no condition to rectify the situation. I calmly staggered around the debris and made my unsteady way out of the dining hall. No one said a word. I learned later that the other kids had covered for me and cleaned up the mess.

Back at the dormitory, no one disputed my story of the aspirin and Coca-Cola. I lay on my bed and immediately lost consciousness.

It felt as though only a few seconds had passed when the morning bell sounded and I was forced to crawl out of bed and get on with the day. It was through sheer will and determination that I functioned for the next three days and struggled, sometimes unsuccessfully, to remain awake in my classes.

On the third day I was still anaesthetized enough to write a three-page letter to my mother during study hall, and tell her what I had done. I had just finished the letter when I was called out of the classroom by the dean, who told me that several teachers were concerned because I had slept through their classes. I had no choice but to report to the infirmary that afternoon for a checkup. I looked innocently at the dean and told him that I had a touch of the flu but was better now. Little did these naive teachers know that if I had not been very lucky I could easily have died in my sleep three days before. It was another secret not to be revealed to the enemy. As for the doctor, he accepted the story about the flu and sent me back to my classes. He didn't even get out his stethoscope.

The day my mother received my letter, she sat at her desk in her wood-paneled library and wrote that she was quite angry at my foolishness and that we would discuss it further during Christmas vacation. Lucy, who still had a room in our house, told me later that in reality my mother had cried upon receiving the letter. The thought of my mother ever crying, especially in front of another human being, seemed foreign. After all, she had taught me to be in control of my emotions at all times.

Mother as Dorothy Richards,
the silent film star.

Mother departing on one of the
great ocean liners in the 1920s.

My parents in costume for their wedding
reception at the Hotel Meurice in Paris.

A more sedate celebration at my
Aunt Ashie's apartment in New York City,
after my parents' church wedding.
(Ashie at left, and best man Tom Burke at right.)

Mother and me.

One of Father's drawings, depicting his
life in a prisoner-of-war camp in July 1940.

My brother, Richard (on the right), our nanny, Lucy,
and me (on the left) in Central Park, New York City.

Rebellious Richard (on the left)
and me, perfect as always.

My maternal
grandmother Mémé in
costume for one of her
operatic roles.

Me, Mother and Richard in
our first passport photo.

Château Brillant.

Bullet hole from World War II in
mirrored sconce at Château Brillant.

Aunt Mimy with my great-grandmother,
Louisa Cointreau, at La Richardière.

My mother's sister, Aunt Tata—the one
who gave me unconditional love.

This is me at the age of thirteen.

Lee Lehman by the pool at
Sands Point, Long Island.

Bobbie Lehman in the
pool at Sands Point.

Lee in front of Renoir's *Girls at the Piano*.

I was Pam Lehman's escort when she came out at the
International Debutante Ball in New York City in 1959.

Ethel Merman onstage as Mama Rose in *Gypsy*.

Ethel Merman and Little Ethel in 1959, the year I met them.

Here I am looking glum, standing next to my
paternal grandmother Maman Geneviève, 1956.
(Father on the left.)

The Copa girls and me in 1965.

Jim and me in New Hope,
Pennsylvania.

Father and Mother at home,
celebrating their last wedding
anniversary.

Lee in the dress she wore at the
opening and dedication of the
Lehman Pavilion at the
Metropolitan Museum of Art,
New York City, 1975.

Ginny Mancini (Mrs. Henry Mancini),
Vincent Minnelli, and me, on my
opening night at Ye Little Club in
Beverly Hills in 1975.

Jim, Ethel Merman, and me,
at a party in New York in 1980.

A beaming Ethel Merman at
one of my performances.

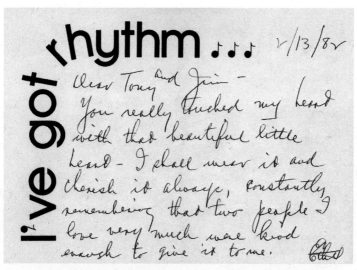

Handwritten thank-you note for a little garnet heart
that Jim and I gave Ethel for Valentine's Day, 1982: "Dear
Tony and Jim, You really touched my heart with that
beautiful little heart—I shall wear it and cherish it
always, constantly remembering that two people I love
very much were kind enough to give it to me. Ethel."

Ethel Merman and her son Bob Levitt in
Catalina, just before her final illness.

"She's Me Pal."

Representing Ethel's family at the unveiling
of the Ethel Merman stamp at Lincoln Center
in New York City, 1994.

Standing outside of Maxim's,
before afternoon rehearsal.

Jim, looking handsome as ever,
before my show at Maxim's.

Performing at a gala at the Hôtel Plaza Athénée in Paris.

Pierre Cardin and me at Maxim's.
He inscribed, "For Tony, in friendship
and the memory of a brilliant evening, Pierre Cardin."

Photo credit Lee Marshall.

My last professional photo in Paris.

Helen Gurley Brown, author and iconic editor-in-chief of *Cosmopolitan* magazine, who insisted that I write this book.

Deep down, however, I *knew* how much Mother loved me and my brother. She never had to change my diapers or breastfeed me for me to know it.

Still, I did not know what to expect when I arrived back home for Christmas vacation. My parents had already started their dinner when I kissed them and took my place at the table. Mother showed her discomfort by not speaking to me and Father acted as though nothing had happened. It was an awkward situation; there was obviously "an elephant in the room" that neither of them wanted to acknowledge.

Later, when there was no danger of the servants overhearing, my mother told me, "I fear you will never develop any character if we allow you to leave a school that you loathe."

Father, however, surprised me. He said, "When I was about your age, I was sent from my home in France to a boarding school in Edinburgh, Scotland. I was so unhappy there that I swore that I would never make a child of mine go through the same torture."

It was a parental standoff.

My mother, however, was not totally inflexible, and wisely suggested that they consult the head of the psychology department at St. Luke's Hospital; he had helped a friend of hers to resolve some problems with her son. This would take the responsibility off my parents' shoulders. It would also be easier for me to deal with an impartial third party.

The doctor recommended that I first have extensive psychological and personality testing at the hospital, before scheduling a private appointment.

When the results were in, the psychiatrist met us in his office. He listened to my parents' story, and then asked them both to step outside so that he could have a private chat with me. I was in awe that anyone would have the power to ask my parents to leave a room.

The doctor turned to me and said, "You don't like boarding school, do you?"

All I had to say was, "No, Doctor, I hate it!"

"All right, I think we can ask your parents to come back in now."

And that's all it took. I never saw the boarding school again.

Years later, among my mother's papers, I found the letter he had written with his findings:

> The series of psychological and personality tests have confirmed my impression that Jacques is a very sensitive boy with many emotional problems, an obsession with his own perfection, and a tendency to withdraw from the world under adversity. The great danger in a boy of this type is the precipitation of a schizophrenic reaction by too much pressure. It is my considered opinion that it is in the best interests of the boy to allow him to withdraw from boarding school and finish the year at Browning, where he can be kept under psychiatric observation and a more careful appraisal of his emotional difficulties made.

Unfortunately, like the last time I was examined as a young boy in Paris, the subject of Mr. Fuller and his abuse was never brought up. My parents did the same thing this time that they had done earlier when another doctor had also recommended immediate treatment—they decided to bury the problem. They never took me to a therapist, and it was never mentioned again.

Being Different

The fact that I was not forced to stay in boarding school made it possible to go back home to my family and the Browning School for Boys. I was also able to once again become a part of the Lehman family, and to search out people and situations that allowed me to grow in my own way.

However, there was another conflict that I could not ignore once I reached my high school years.

As a young boy, I was inept and uncoordinated at athletics. I was also, of course, always perfectly groomed, even on the soccer field—two attributes that do not necessarily endear an adolescent to his friends.

At the age of twelve, when hormones started influencing my classmates' behavior, they suddenly became aware of the "different" ones in the pack, like myself, and like a bunch of wild dogs attacked with the sneers and the slurs that society had taught them. "Fairy," "queer," and "faggot" are just a few that come to mind.

In the 1950s the idea of being anything but a heterosexual was still a cause for intense shame and ridicule. I believe that the fear of being homosexual was so overwhelming that when pubescent children saw what they perceived to be a "sissy" in their midst, they had to go on the offensive, as though homosexuality were a contagious disease. The tragedy for many young boys and girls is not only that stereotypes can be inaccurate, but also that the taunting often leads to a desperate child's suicide.

Of course, in many cases, a sensitive or artistic boy who is not good at athletics grows up to be as heterosexual as most of his friends. Those characteristics are in no way a prerequisite for being gay. In my case, however, I knew that my tormentors were right, and that, hard as I tried, there was no way I could change my real sexuality. I was attracted to men. At that time, my only option was to hope that I could sublimate my desires for a lifetime.

During those early years, I was sometimes able to fool myself for periods of time, since physical contact with a girl could feel good, and my hormones were as active as any other teenager's. But I knew in my heart that that was not what I really wanted. Alone in my bed at night, I felt as though I had been doomed by a vengeful God to a hidden life of shame.

The sad part was that I loved women. They had always played a large role in my life. I loved being close to them. I loved sharing my life with them. The only thing I didn't want was real sexual intimacy.

A problem sometimes arose when one or another of the "macho jocks" made it obvious that they would be more than happy to relieve some of their sexual tension with me. In spite of the temptation I felt, and their obvious and clumsy attempts at seduction, I knew that after they had satisfied their needs they would go on with their lives and out of guilt brand *me* as the aggressor.

Even though I never gave in, one of the more aggressive boys became angry when I felt compelled to end my friendship with him rather than give in. He retaliated in the way I most feared: by lying to his classmates, telling them that we were no longer friends because I had made a sexual advance toward him. There was no way I could win.

As for my parents, they were as clueless about homosexuality as everyone else in their circle of friends. It was the widespread ignorance of the times. After all, it was still a crime for which the authorities put people in jail.

I remember the fear I felt as a teenager the day I overheard my parents planning a dinner party, and my mother suggested inviting an acquaintance of theirs as an extra man. My father said, "No. He's a homosexual and I don't want him in my house." It was not said with any rancor or emotion—it was simply stated as a fact, a fact that did not make me feel any better about myself.

As for Pam, I had more of an emotional attachment to her than a sexual one. Because there was such a strict moral code for boys and girls dating at that time, it was easy for me to make up excuses. "Making out," as we called it then, was fun for a thirteen-year-old, and the first time we made love, at the age of sixteen, during a trip to Jamaica with her parents (Pam and I stayed alone in a two-bedroom guest cottage behind her parents' villa), was a wonderful experience, but not one that I particularly cared to repeat.

Towards the end of our relationship, Pam nicknamed me "Fridgie" (after the word "frigid"). It was sad, because I loved her, and yet could never have fulfilled all her needs.

It never occurred to me at the time that, as often as I may have denied it, sooner or later I would not be able to escape acknowledging my own desires—and when the time came, it caught me unawares and powerless to stop the inevitable.

At the age of seventeen, I was walking up Madison Avenue in New York on a cold winter evening, when I stopped to look in the window of an antique shop. It was getting dark and I knew there was not much time left for me to go home and change before meeting the Lehmans at six o'clock. While studying the objects in the window, I became aware of a handsome older man standing next to me. He was beautifully dressed and asked me if I was interested in art. When I answered, "Yes," he told me that he owned a popular art gallery nearby, and asked if I would like to see his paintings. My heart was pounding in my ears as I followed him down the street. I was not stupid, and knew the moment that I had both dreaded and longed for had finally arrived.

Once inside the gallery, he took me upstairs to a private room where many of the paintings were stored. It was in this setting that I had my first sexual encounter with a man. All I can say is that he was kind and gentle and that it was over very quickly.

The second that it was over, I was overwhelmed by feelings of guilt and shame. I had finally crossed a line and could never go back and erase the experience. I also felt immediate hatred for this man, blamed him totally for what we had just done, ignoring the fact that I had been longing for this opportunity for years.

I literally ran out of the gallery and up Madison Avenue until I reached home. Once inside the apartment, I went into the library to say hello to my parents, and tell them that I only had a few minutes to get ready to go to a dinner party with Pam and her family. My unsuspecting parents had no idea, as I stood there, that all I wanted to do was run into my bathroom and wash away the male smell that seemed glued to my body. I wondered if I would ever be able to get rid of it.

That whole evening, I was filled with a torrent of emotions, the prevalent one being disgust with myself for having given in to desires that I could do nothing to change. At that time, there was no one I could share my dilemma with, no one who could make me feel as though I wasn't the only person in the world faced with this terrible shame.

ARTHUR

The majority of students at the Browning School were children of prominent and often famous parents. I can still walk down Park or Fifth Avenue in New York and remember the sumptuous apartments my school friends called home. At the time I took it for granted that this was the way most people lived.

One of my best friends at Browning was Arthur MacArthur, the son of General Douglas MacArthur. In 1951, during the Korean War, President Harry Truman relieved General MacArthur of his military command. Many Americans considered the General to be one of the greatest heroes in our history, and he arrived in New York amid great controversy and adulation. The Browning School closed early that day so the students could watch the ticker tape parade downtown in his honor. With him were his wife, Jean, and their young son, Arthur.

When Dwight D. Eisenhower rather than General MacArthur gained the Republican nomination for the Presidency of the United States in 1952, the General retired from public life. At the age of seventy-one, he accepted the first civilian job of his life as the Chairman of the Board of the Sperry Rand Corporation. The MacArthur family then settled into their apartment at the Waldorf-Astoria Towers in New York City and Arthur was eventually enrolled in the Browning School for Boys.

The first time we met, Arthur, who was standing behind me at one of the school's water fountains, put out his hand and introduced himself. Although he was two grades ahead of me, I knew I had met a kindred spirit when we sat next to each other in study hall and whispered endlessly about our favorite topic—show business. His father may have been one of the most famous men in the world, but we were two kids who loved swapping stories about movie stars.

Sometimes I would sit on the floor of Arthur's bedroom at the Waldorf Towers while he introduced me to recordings by Lena Horne and Billie Holiday. Later he took me to small art theaters so I could experience for the first time the wit of Mae West and the beauty of Garbo.

Marlene Dietrich was someone we both particularly admired and whom he had met through his parents, General and Mrs. MacArthur. Miss Dietrich had spent much of World War II with the Allied soldiers, entertaining on the front lines, suffering deprivation and even frostbite along with them. She considered those years to be by far the most important time of her life—in the same way that I would later consider my years of service with Mother Teresa, caring for the sick and dying, as the most meaningful years of my life.

I first met Marlene Dietrich when I was fifteen, vacationing in Europe with my family. That summer she was making a movie called *The Monte Carlo Story* in—where else—Monte Carlo. The film introduced Natalie Trundy, a friend of mine from New York, as the ingénue.

In those days everything about Monte Carlo was glamour personified. I met the legendary Marlene on a night when they were filming on the steps of the Casino—a gay teenage boy's ultimate dream.

The next day I was invited to watch them film in the dining room of the exclusive Hotel de Paris.

I was escorted to a director's chair, where I would be able to see close-up. Directly in front of me was a large semicircle of at least fifteen tall lights, positioned around the area where the restaurant scene would be filmed.

Looking to my left, I saw a massive silver ice bucket holding a bottle of Dom Perignon. On the other side of the Champagne sat Miss Dietrich, in an identical director's chair! I had never felt more sophisticated than I did that moment. Dom Perignon and a smiling Marlene Dietrich next to me on a movie set in the Hotel de Paris in Monte Carlo—it was almost more than I could take in.

What I was not thinking about at that moment was the fact that in the past few months I had grown taller by several inches, and my feet were now a size 11—something I had not yet come to terms with. I still pictured myself as the cute and cuddly smallest boy in the class.

At some point, with the lights already lit and everyone ready for a take, I made one of the most embarrassing decisions of my life. For reasons I cannot remember now, I got up out of my chair—completely forgetting that my feet were almost twice the size they had been a few months earlier—and immediately tripped over the base of one of the lights. The entire circle of lights went crashing to the floor like a row of dominos.

And there I stood, mortified. I was sure that the director and crew were ready to send me back to France and the guillotine.

Ah, but that's when the remarkable Miss Dietrich, understanding my teenage agony and distress at the mayhem I had just caused, came over to me and put her arm around my shoulders. With just the look on her face, she dared anyone to make the dreadful situation any worse for me. No one said a word; they simply got busy picking up the lights. Marlene was my champion that day, and I will never forget her generosity and kindness towards a vulnerable and thoroughly humiliated young man.

One evening Arthur and I decided to sneak down to Washington D.C. to see her nightclub act at the Shoreham Hotel. Back then it felt like a daring thing for us to do. We planned to fly down on the shuttle (which in those days cost practically nothing), see the show, and come right back. After the show we waited a while before Arthur called Marlene in her suite. She was most gracious and told him that she was already in bed but would send down her latest recording, which was of Pete Seeger's "Where Have All The Flowers Gone," sung in English and German. She said it was the only copy she had, and we could return it to her in New York.

Before we dropped the record off at her apartment building (which turned out to be a block away from where I lived) we wrote a poem to go with it. We saw Miss Dietrich many times after that, but we never found out what she thought about our "poetry."

Arthur graduated from high school before I did. The next time I saw him, when I was nineteen, I was leaving a movie theater one evening and heard someone call my name. I turned around and there was my old friend Arthur. He said, "Why don't we go have a drink?"

I asked, "Where should we go?"

He replied, "I only know downtown bars." So we went to a downtown bar. For once, I felt completely relaxed about being myself. There was no need for any kind of social pretense; we just shared the things that seemed important to us at the time. At that moment, I knew that this chance encounter would be a turning point in my life: I could go wherever I wished and say exactly what was on my mind with no fear of recrimination.

One of the reasons Arthur was the perfect friend for me to connect with was that having famous last names made us both vulnerable to scandal and gossip. My name was bad enough, but I could only imagine the pressure of being the son of an army hero and icon throughout the world. I don't know how Arthur had managed to cope with being publicized as the epitome of the all-American boy while his father had attempted to run for the presidency of the United States in the early 1950s.

While we were having a drink that first evening we reconnected, I recalled that he also knew one of my best friends from high school. I asked him, "Whatever happened to Mike?"

He answered, "Didn't you know? Mike killed himself nine months ago."

I was stunned, because he was my first contemporary to die. Years later, I still pass by the building where Mike lived and look up at the window of his bedroom on the corner of the second floor, where he died from an overdose of sleeping pills, and wonder why.

After that evening at the bar, Arthur and I saw quite a bit of each other. Mostly we went to small piano bars in Greenwich Village, where we drank cheap champagne and talked all night.

We laughed over everything and anything—even silly things like the way his mother had referred to the actor Basil Rathbone as "Rasil Bathbone." He forever remained Rasil Bathbone to us.

Arthur and I enjoyed relaxing and having a good time just being ourselves, with no social pressure or adults to please. It was an important friendship for both of us.

When General MacArthur died in 1964, Arthur and his mother began inviting me to spend more time with them. They would often take me to dinner at Sardi's before going to see a Broadway show. And any time a star we cared about was appearing in cabaret at the Waldorf Astoria Hotel's Empire Room, the MacArthurs would ask me to join them.

Mrs. MacArthur, a Southern lady, was a petite steel butterfly whom I respected and whose company I enjoyed. However, I'm sure that a large part of the reason she and Arthur invited me was because I was a buffer for their sometimes complex relationship.

Mrs. MacArthur, with her gentle Southern drawl, always referred to her late husband as "The General," and his bust always sat at the head of the table when I would dine at the Waldorf Towers with Arthur and his mother. It was evident that after General MacArthur's death, Mrs. MacArthur's life and her home continued to revolve around maintaining his enormous legend and legacy—something that throughout Arthur's life had always been his parents' main focus.

I have no doubt that The General was a formidable person to have had as a father. Arthur was a sensitive and artistic only child who never showed much interest in the family tradition of going to West Point and becoming a part of the military life. In spite of the fact that he had movie-star good looks, a brilliant mind, and a talent for writing—I always felt that he could easily have fulfilled my mother's idea of perfection—there was no way for him to compete with the great American hero known as General Douglas MacArthur.

By the early seventies I was traveling a great deal, and Arthur and I started losing touch with one another. When I occasionally ran into Mrs. MacArthur on the streets of New York, she would beg me to call Arthur. She always said, "He needs a friend." So Arthur and I would end up talking for a couple of hours on the phone and then go back to our separate lives.

Our next-to-last conversation during that period was a frantic phone call I received from Arthur asking if he could come and see me right away. Ah Cheu, the Asian woman who had been his *amah* or baby nurse and had stayed on to run the house for the MacArthurs, had died and Arthur said that he was running around Chinatown looking for her grave. Obviously he was in some sort of crisis. I waited for hours for him to show up at my home, but he never did. And he never called.

The next phone call came a couple of years later when Arthur, again in a frantic tone of voice, said, "I can't tell you where I am but I'm trying to put the pieces of my life together and you're the only person who can help me make some sense of it."

I tried to calm him down and assured him I would help him in any way I could. Then I heard noises in the background and the phone went dead. Many years passed before I heard his voice again.

Mrs. MacArthur and I stayed in touch over the years. She even gave me a personal letter of reference when I bought a New York apartment in 1980. Every time we spoke, I always asked her about

Arthur, who seemed to have vanished into thin air. Her answer was invariably a vague, "He's traveling. But I'll tell him to call you when he gets back." Her answers never kept me from writing Arthur notes on special occasions. I could only hope that they reached him.

In 1999 I read in the papers that Mrs. MacArthur had reached her 100th birthday, so I sent her a medal that had been blessed and kissed by Mother Teresa. Several months later I received my first phone call from Arthur in more than 25 years. He thanked me for the medal and told me that he had lived a reclusive life. Now every day he went to the Waldorf Towers to care for his mother, who was in poor health.

I was sad to hear him say, "I'm not the same person that I was before. I have no life."

Arthur seemed interested in the spiritual side of my life with Mother Teresa, and before hanging up he told me he could not be reached by phone but asked if he could call me again. I made him promise that he would.

I still miss my old friend. I hope he knows how much his friendship enriched my life.

—✦—

THE GOSSIP COLUMNS

My high school years at the Browning School for Boys were unusual in that I knew practically nothing about proms and other activities that most students take for granted. Instead, I was thrust into a sophisticated social whirl that had nothing to do with the life of a schoolboy.

For example, as a teenager I attended a party in Paris that I will never forget. Yvonne Coty, who had started the Coty perfume business with her ex-husband, was a dear friend of my parents. I had known her all my life, and she always made me feel that she adored me. She gave me my first pair of cowboy boots, when I was around five, and I proudly marched up and down the hallway in them. She also gave me my first pair of gold cuff links for my First Communion; I still have them. Each time she saw me she always said, *"Ce garçon, il a du coeur!"*—"That boy, he has heart!"

Madame Coty, who had remarried and was now Madame Cotnareanu, was one of the richest women in the world, a renowned hostess who was frequently asked by the French government to entertain foreign dignitaries in her homes. My parents and I had visited with her in several of her homes, but my favorite was her mansion in Paris, in the Bois de Boulogne, where the super elite such as the Duke and Duchess of Windsor had opulent homes and were her neighbors. This mansion had a three-story-high entry hall with a glass ceiling made by Lalique, and glass railings on the massive staircase, also made by Lalique. Each room was filled with antique furniture of the finest museum quality.

At this particular party, which I attended with my parents, dinner was a sit-down affair for no fewer than forty guests at the longest dining room table I had ever seen in my life, with what seemed like a butler behind each chair.

After dessert had been served, the curtains at one end of the massive dining room parted and the Ballet Company of Paris danced on a stage outside. I would cherish forever the memory of the party that summer night at Yvonne Coty Cotnareanu's home in the Bois de Boulogne.

The social scene that kept me so busy was not just in Paris, but also in Manhattan. One morning when I was seventeen, riding the Madison Avenue bus to school, I recognized the lady sitting next to me, reading a newspaper, as an important figure in the social and fashion world. Although we had met on several occasions, neither of us said a word. At the time, I was extremely shy, had a huge crush on her, and was sure that no one of her importance would ever remember me. She carefully folded the newspaper to a certain society column and dropped it in my lap as she got off the bus. I picked it up and read that I—"the liqueur heir"—had been at a private party at the exclusive Harwyn Club, and that I was now "the newest glamour boy of the season and a Mecca for all the ladies."

I could hardly believe that they were talking about *me*, although it was true that famous women reacted favorably to me—I treated them with respect, as fellow human beings, with naturalness and innocence, and I enjoyed their company. I was brought up that way, and that was who I was.

This was the 1950s, and New York City was filled with nightclubs well populated by society and the new "café society." It was the era of El Morocco, the Stork Club, and the Harwyn Club, which were at the top of the heap. They all had live orchestras to dance to, and both men and women were expected to dress for the occasion.

There were many daily newspapers in New York City then and they all had gossip columnists whose information came mainly from the publicity departments of the major nightspots. Photographers roamed the clubs, taking pictures of celebrities and socialites for the next day's papers.

The party at the Harwyn Club, mentioned in the clipping, was the beginning of a slew of publicity that ultimately I found difficult to cope with.

Although I was still going steady with Pam Lehman, the columnists insisted on linking me with other young women from prominent families and started inventing stories about me that did *not* please my parents. One of their least favorite was that every morning the butler would come into my room with a hundred dollar bill on a silver tray, as my allowance for the day. And this was many years ago when a hundred dollars was almost worth a hundred dollars!

My mother was also not happy with the place that Lee Lehman, the first of my "other mothers," had in my life, and became quite jealous. On the other hand, having her son going steady with Pamela, the stepdaughter of Robert Lehman, the great investment banker, was a feather in her cap, so I did not suffer many consequences at home.

I had no idea then that shortly after I graduated from high school, Mother would have to deal with my meeting the second of my "other mothers," a woman that I—along with theater-goers around the world—had long admired.

My Second "Other Mother"

When I graduated from high school in the summer of 1959, I had already decided that instead of going to Yale, as Bobbie Lehman wanted me to do, I would pursue my passion for show business. His wife, Lee, who had become my first "other mother," supported my decision, despite his insistence that "all actors are bums."

My own mother was so convinced that she would someday die in poverty, no matter how rich her husbands had been, that I think she was relieved not to have to spend the money on tuition. Besides which, I was not a wild child, but a son my parents fully trusted.

Immediately after graduation, I joined a summer acting class for teenagers at the Neighborhood Playhouse in New York City. A girl sitting next to me on the first day of class said, "My name's Patty. What's yours?"

"Jacques," I said, since I hadn't yet decided that I wanted to be called Tony.

She made a face, but sitting on the other side of her, a pretty, dark-haired girl with sparkling brown eyes and a pixie haircut leaned over, smiled at me and said, "I think Jacques is a beautiful name. My name is Ethel." From that moment on we were the best of friends. Ethel, who was seventeen, told me that she was spending the summer in New York with her mother before going to college in Colorado in the fall.

Within a few days Ethel asked me if I wanted to see "Mom's play."
"Oh, sure, what's she doing?"
"*Gypsy*! Mom's Ethel Merman!"
I thought to myself, "I can do that."

The smash hit musical *Gypsy* had just opened on Broadway, and *everyone* in New York wanted to see "Mom's play."

Ethel Merman, who had never had a singing lesson in her life, had been a star ever since the first time she stepped on a Broadway stage, on October 14, 1930, in George Gershwin's *Girl Crazy*. She stopped the show and made theater history at the end of the first act when she sang "I Got Rhythm" and held a note for sixteen bars. During intermission, George Gershwin ran up the five flights of stairs to her dressing room to advise her, "Never go near a singing teacher!"

I had been a fan of hers ever since I saw her on the "Ford Fiftieth Anniversary" television show in 1953, and instantly fell in love with that huge, belting voice, the sparkling eyes, and indomitable personality. It had long been a dream of mine to meet her.

When I went to pick up Little Ethel to take her to dinner before seeing *Gypsy*, her younger brother, Bobby, answered the door. He led me into the living room, and went to tell his sister that I had arrived.

Ethel Merman, her husband Bob Six, who was then president of Continental Airlines, and her two children Little Ethel and Bobby (both from a previous marriage to Bob Levitt) lived in a beautiful apartment with a large living room, a library, a small kitchen and three bedrooms at the Park Lane Hotel on 48th Street and Park Ave. They had moved there from Colorado, where the family had lived since 1953, when the star had given up Broadway to marry Mr. Six.

While I stood in the living room, feeling like an awkward kid, Bob Six walked by me on his way to the study. Not only did he not acknowledge my presence—which made me feel even more uncomfortable—but he also looked at me as though I were nothing more than a cockroach that had invaded his private space. Within a few moments, to my immense relief, a lady in beige silk Chinese pajamas, which were very fashionable at the time, and her hair in rollers, strutted into the living room. With a big welcoming smile, she put out her hand and said, "Hi, I'm Ethel's mother!" Ethel Merman had arrived in my life.

Miss Merman then took me into the study to meet the "charming" Mr. Six, but hard as she tried, he remained taciturn and disagreeable. His attitude, however, did not put a damper on the way Miss Merman and I related to each other. We spoke of mutual friends like the Lehmans, who, ironically, had introduced Ethel to Bob Six at a party to celebrate the first anniversary of the Broadway production of *Call Me Madam.* We also discussed the painter whose colorful work adorned many of the walls in their apartment and whom I had met the year before in Jamaica while traveling with the Lehmans. Our conversation flowed easily. We felt as though we had known each other forever. But then, I had also felt the same way the first time Little Ethel and I had met at acting school a couple of weeks before.

After dinner, Little Ethel and I went to the Broadway Theater, where her mother had left tickets for two house seats at the box office. I was so naive that I thought house seats were free, and barely had enough money left in my pocket to pay for them.

When I think back upon it, I can see why Ethel Merman considered her role as Mama Rose in *Gypsy* to be the pinnacle of her career. I was mesmerized watching her create this monster of a mother, repelling you and making you love her at the same time. I stood and cheered with the rest of the audience as she belted out the last few bars of "Rose's Turn," which she always referred to as her "soliloquy:"

"Everything's coming up roses
This time, for me,
For me, *for me*, FOR ME, *FOR MEEEEEEEE!*"

Years later, the well known actor-dancer Harvey Evans, who had been in many Broadway shows, said, "A lot of great actresses have played Mama Rose, but Ethel Merman *was.*" On June 19, 1992, Clive Barnes would write in the *New York Post,* "Merman was a belter with a gimmick, and the gimmick was called genius." I couldn't have agreed with him more.

After the show, we went backstage. Miss Merman had invited Little Ethel and me to join her for a late supper at Sardi's. While we waited for her to change out of her costume, Little Ethel took me into the wings and, with her great sensitivity, stood back so I could experience for the first time what it was like to stand alone on a massive Broadway stage. As I looked out into the vast, already dark 1752-seat theater, with only a "ghost light" for illumination, the whole six-foot-two of me felt very small and inadequate—which was strange, in a way, since, later on, the stage would be the only place I would feel at home.

By the time Little Ethel and I arrived at her mother's surprisingly small pink-and-white dressing room, I had to go to the men's room so badly that I shyly asked if there was a bathroom nearby I could use. Miss Merman pointed to a spot hidden behind some costumes where, to my horror, I found a little cubbyhole with barely more than a curtain for privacy. I knew that the other people in the room would be able to hear me as clearly as I could hear them. And I would rather have died than have Ethel Merman hear me urinating.

It was agony flushing the unused toilet and then waiting to get to Sardi's before finding any relief.

Sardi's restaurant was synonymous with show business. Most opening night parties were held there while everyone waited for the reviews to appear in the newspapers. All the great stars congregated at Sardi's after appearing in or seeing a Broadway show, and the red walls were covered with their caricatures. Miss Merman told me that up to that evening, only one caricature had ever been stolen—hers.

At Sardi's that evening, the conversation was mainly with theater people stopping by to say "Hello" to Ethel Merman. There was a constant parade of performers paying their respects to the woman most often referred to as "the first lady of Broadway." Miss Merman was gracious to them all and got a kick out of introducing them to me. Jule Styne, who wrote the music for *Gypsy*, was there with his current flame, Sandra Church, a petite, dark-haired beauty who was playing the role of Gypsy Rose Lee. Others I remember meeting that evening were Dolores Hart, the star who gave Elvis Presley his first screen kiss, and the marvelous actress Eva Marie Saint, whom Ethel introduced as Eva Saint Marie. Nobody, least of all I, corrected her. Many sat down for a while and traded industry gossip with Miss Merman.

At Miss Merman's urging, I tried something I had never eaten before—steak tartare. Originally, the thought of raw steak would have turned my stomach, but not the way they did it at Sardi's. I should have known Miss Merman wouldn't steer me in the wrong direction. However, when I think of it, another of her favorite dishes was one I promise you I would never touch, and that is creamed tripe. Yuck.

When the great producer Billy Rose sat down with us, Little Ethel and I took a break while her mother and Mr. Rose traded inside stories in a low voice so the other tables wouldn't hear. But Little Ethel and I had our own gossiping to do. We had spotted what seemed to our young eyes like an old, overdressed woman with way too much makeup floating around the room talking to everyone. We thought she was trying very hard to be noticed, and felt sorry for her desperation. We both agreed that she reminded us of the eccentric and slightly mad Norma Desmond in *Sunset Boulevard*. Later we asked Miss Merman and Mr. Rose who the lady was. They told us that her name was Mae Murray and that she had been one of the great stars of the silent screen—just like Norma Desmond.

At the end of the evening, Mr. Rose offered to take us home in his chauffeur-driven Rolls Royce. First he dropped off my friend Little Ethel and her mother at the Park Lane Hotel on 48th Street and then proceeded up Park Avenue to 79th Street where I was still living with my parents. On the way, Mr. Rose talked to me as though I were a peer and not just a kid. He told me he had known the real Mama

Rose, and Ethel's character in the musical didn't even come near the terrifying truth of what she was actually like. He added that, in his opinion, the real Mama Rose had been psychotic.

It had been an enchanted evening. First I had a fun dinner with Little Ethel, whose company I had enjoyed ever since our first meeting. The feeling was mutual. She may have had a crush on me but she knew that I had been in a relationship with Pamela Lehman for the last five years. Then I got to see one of the great performances of Broadway history. Finally, I went to Sardi's with one of my best friends and her mother, the greatest star on Broadway, ate steak tartare, met everyone in show business heaven, and went home in a chauffeur-driven Rolls Royce with the legendary producer Billy Rose. Could an eighteen-year-old aspiring actor and lover of the musical theater ask for anything more?

The following Monday morning Little Ethel came up to me at acting class and said prophetically, "You know, if Mom can't have you for *me*, I think she wants you for herself!"

That Ethel Merman would want me to be her friend wasn't really a surprise, though, since I had instinctively felt a strong connection between us the moment we met. It was a connection that would encourage me to break the shackles of my need for perfection—a connection that would continue until her death twenty-five years later.

That summer Pam Lehman was out of town, staying with her parents in Sands Point, Long Island, where I would join them on weekends. Pam was not at all pleased when she read in the gossip columns that I was "dating" Ethel Merman's daughter during the week. The truth of the matter was that Little Ethel and I were just good friends, but I had a hard time convincing Pam of that. Every time Little Ethel and I went to a nightclub, we would ask the orchestra to play "Ain't Misbehavin'," because we weren't. It became "our song." She even gave me a picture of herself on which she had written, "We ain't misbehavin', but it's a blast. Love, Ethel".

One night I was having dinner at 21 Club with the Lehmans, when we spotted Ethel Merman, Bob Six, and Little Ethel at another table. None of them said a word to us. Little Ethel later told me that the reason was that Bob Six had forbidden them to acknowledge my presence because I was with Robert Lehman, a very influential business contact for Continental Airlines, and Mr. Six was afraid that Pam's jealousy of my friendship with Little Ethel might jeopardize his business dealings with Lehman Brothers. However, Miss Merman, who had a strong streak of the naughty little girl in her, wasn't able to resist winking at me when she thought no one was looking.

As I got to know Little Ethel better I found out that Mr. Six was no more charming to his wife and stepchildren than he was to me. At that time, the marriage was already on the rocks and he was having affairs with other women.

From everything Little Ethel and her mother told me in later years, I learned that it had been a house under siege. He had even threatened to kill Little Ethel's pet poodle Midnight. It all looked lovely from the outside but behind closed doors everyone walked on eggshells around "Mr. Robert," as he told the children to call him.

In 1958, a year before I met Little Ethel and Bobby, their real father, Bob Levitt, lay down on the living room couch at his home in Long Island after spending the weekend with his son and daughter, and killed himself with an overdose of sleeping pills. Both children were devastated. Years later, Ethel Merman told me that Bobby was only twelve years old when he heard the news. She heard him crying in his bedroom, but before she could go in and comfort him, Bob Six stopped her and threatened to leave if she went into her son's room. By this time they had all been so bullied by the man that she was afraid to defy him and be with her son when he needed her most. She told me that it was something she would regret until the day she died.

Ethel Merman's decision to go back to Broadway should have been a clue to the world that Colorado and Mr. Six were not working out.

The pain of having endured Bob Six's abuse and the collapse of another marriage was very evident to me the night I went backstage with Little Ethel at the end of a Friday night performance of *Gypsy*. Knowing that Miss Merman was going through a difficult time with her divorce, Little Ethel and I decided to go to the theater at the end of her mother's show and ask her if she wanted to join us for supper afterwards.

We arrived at the Broadway Theater in time for the curtain calls. Miss Merman did not know we were there and was waiting in the wings to take her final bows. She was looking down at the floor, marking time while the rest of the cast went on stage. To my eighteen-year-old eyes, she looked like the saddest woman I had ever seen.

But as soon as Miss Merman's time came to step out on that stage, I saw the most remarkable transformation. The moment the lights hit her, she somehow made them seem a little brighter than they had been for everyone else. It was as though someone had turned on a switch and released a power that could overwhelm and thrill you with its laser-like beam. The entire theater was electrified by a force of nature called Merman, the same force that had thrilled Broadway audiences since 1930. That evening, not only was I privy to the private moment of a very public human being in pain, but I was also inspired by a glimpse of true theater magic in action.

Since I had been brought up never to call adults by their first name, I called Ethel Merman "Mrs. Six." So when she divorced Bob Six in 1960, I called her on the phone and asked, "What do I call you now? Do I call you Miss Merman or Mrs. Six?"

"Call me Ethel," she said.

As much as I loved both Little Ethel and her mother, over the next few years I could see that they did not have an easy time dealing with each other. I often felt like a referee, trying to patch things up between them.

It was a puzzling situation because Ethel Merman had always said that she had such a loving and trusting relationship with her own parents. She used to say that her relationship with her parents, "Mom and Pop Zimmermann," had never changed since she was a little girl. "They always came first with me and I with them."

Whenever anyone tells me that they had an idyllic childhood I immediately become suspicious. I believe that no one has a perfect childhood because we are all products of human beings with their own imperfections. Therefore, Ethel Merman's adulation of her parents never rang quite true in my ears. Yes, they may have doted on their only child, but I always had the impression that Ethel spent her life trying to please her parents—an impossible task in the long run.

Little Ethel was very proud of her mother, and looked very much like a younger version of her. They even walked the same way—both had that famous Merman strut. Little Ethel also inherited her mother's sense of humor and was a gentle soul who loved animals of all kinds and wanted to mother them all, from butterflies to elephants.

Considering the relationship Ethel claimed to have had with her own parents, I never understood why she sometimes appeared to be afraid that her children might hurt her, although it was obvious that she and the children adored each other. When Little Ethel told me, "Sometimes Mom scares me," I couldn't put my finger on it, but I understood what she meant. I could see that Ethel was a formidable personality who sometimes tried to control her children with the same strict code she had learned from her own parents, with considerable friction as a result.

Bobby and Little Ethel had a more complicated relationship with their mother than I did. Bobby referred to me as "the other son—the one who could go anywhere with Mom." Until the day she died, Ethel referred to me as her "other son," and I'm sure my role was easier than being her real son. I was the one with the charmed life. Not being Ethel's real son meant that I could do no wrong. How could I? I had already been taught by my mother how to be "perfect." And Ethel trusted me. This was always a big reason for my close relationships with my three "other mothers," Lee Lehman, Ethel Merman, and, later on, Mother Teresa. Until the day they died, they knew that they could trust me in every way.

After summer acting classes at the Playhouse were over, Little Ethel went on to college in Colorado. We stayed in touch, if not directly, then through her mother. As for me, I felt that I needed to learn more about my chosen profession before I could step on a stage and make a career of it.

The Runaway Heiress

In the midst of my socializing and studying acting with the great Lee Strasberg at The Actors Studio, a friend of mine asked me to join him and his girlfriend at his mother's Fifth Avenue apartment. At the age of nineteen, I had just broken up with Pam Lehman—Pam had finally realized that I was never going to be good husband material—and my friend wanted me to meet Gamble Benedict, who many people thought looked very much like Pam.

An eighteen-year-old heiress to the Remington typewriter fortune, Gamble, on the night of her coming-out party, had run away to Europe with someone the newspapers said was a Roumanian chauffeur twenty years her senior. Her disappearance had made headlines around the world, and knocked the impending Vietnam War off the front pages for six days.

Seventeen years earlier her mother had committed suicide, which had created its own headlines and scandal. Ever since then Gamble had been raised by her grandmother, who controlled her interests in the family fortune.

When Gamble disappeared, her grandmother hired detectives to track her down in Europe and bring her back to the United States, where she was made a ward of the court. This was when our mutual friends decided that we should meet.

A few days after I met Gamble, she invited me to her large townhouse off Fifth Avenue at 5 East 75th Street to meet her grandmother, "Grammie," who rarely left her room and never seemed to leave her bed. According to Gamble, Grammie loved her gin, and bed was the safest place for her to be. When I met her I was shocked to find that this wealthy matriarch resembled nothing more than an old crone; from what I could see, she lived in her nightgown and was seldom properly groomed.

Grammie lived on the fifth floor, while Gamble lived on the floor above her in what had once been the servants' quarters. The first four floors of the house had been kept in total darkness for years, and Grammie had forbidden anyone to go through them. But one day Gamble and I quietly snuck up the stairs, which wound around the elevator, afraid to turn on any of the lights in case someone should notice and inform Grammie. What I saw were large rooms furnished with beautiful antiques. However, years of disuse had rendered the house colorless and reminiscent of Miss Haversham's home in *Great Expectations*. There were no butlers or maids to care for this huge house, only a young couple who lived in the basement and were used to the eccentric ways of a spoiled old woman.

Grammie apparently decided that I was a well-brought-up young man who might be a positive influence on Gamble, and the court agreed. Although I was not the most emotionally stable person that she could have met, I was honest and unwilling to make any rash moves. Thus we were freely allowed to go to all the chic nightspots, and in time, I was trusted enough that we were even permitted to stay out later than Gamble's court-imposed ten o'clock curfew.

We spent almost every evening at El Morocco, the Stork Club, or the Harwyn Club, where the newspapers had a field day with the two of us; photographers tried to take our pictures, and anything we wanted was on the house. At the Harwyn Club, our favorite, if Gamble's Roumanian ex-lover showed up, the *maitre d'* would bar him from entering while we were there.

Within a short period of time we were inseparable. The court ordered Gamble to take a secretarial course, and we would meet after our respective classes were over. Often, before going out in the evening, we stopped for a drink at Tata's apartment on Fifth Avenue. Tata would greet us at the door, newspaper in hand, and entertain us with whatever the gossip columns had to say about us that day.

Up until this time, I had been known as Jacques or Jacques-Henri, the name I was given at birth. My father, whose name was also Jacques, felt that there might be some confusion and people would think that he was the one dating young women—a silly premise at best, but enough to give me grief at home. The day he came home in a temper because someone had jokingly asked him how my mother felt about his going out with young girls, I changed my name from Jacques-Henri to the name I had chosen when I was confirmed by the Catholic Church at the age of fourteen—Anthony, or Tony.

Getting the newspaper columns to change my name was another problem, until I talked to a lady who at that time wrote the then-famous "Cholly Knickerbocker" column. Her name was Liz Smith, and as we all know, she later went on to become famous as a gossip columnist and author under her own name. At first Liz told me, "It's impossible for us to change your name, since you're one of the hottest names we are writing about right now." Instead, she cleverly compromised by writing about me as "Jacques 'Tony' Cointreau." In time they were able to drop the Jacques and everyone was satisfied.

My name became the least of my problems when Gamble suggested that we run away to Alabama, where the laws would allow us to be married immediately. She was still a ward of the court, and I felt that she should have a little more patience and wait until we would be free to be married properly. Not only was her future in jeopardy, but if I defied New York state's court system by eloping with her, I might be arrested if I tried to re-enter the state.

One morning I woke up with a high fever and a severe case of the flu. Gamble called me from secretarial school at noon to say that *they*—the friends of her Roumanian lover—had come to take her back to him. From what she said, I surmised that they thought I had become a threat, and they were not going to let Gamble and her fortune slip out of their hands without a fight. She begged me to come and get her.

Being too ill to get out of bed, I tried to persuade her to come to me. As the hours passed without any word, I was filled with an ominous feeling that I had underestimated her situation with the Roumanians. When Grammie started calling wanting to know where Gamble had disappeared to, I had no answer for her.

The next day the headlines of every newspaper screamed, *"Gamble Gone Again!"*

And so the nightmare began. I was worried, I was frightened, and I could do nothing from my sickbed. Plus, I was harassed from every side by the press.

A couple of nights later, the news came out that Gamble had finally married her slick Roumanian in another state. I struggled out of bed and was very visibly on the town with Little Ethel, who was visiting her mother. Because we appeared at the Harwyn Club, smiling for the photographers, the reporters assumed that I had been playing a game all along and had helped Gamble escape. No one knew that I was as surprised as everyone else—and heartbroken. Gamble's wedding picture on the cover of *LIFE* magazine did nothing to alleviate my feeling of guilt at having been too ill to rescue her when she begged me to.

Not long after their marriage, Gamble and her Roumanian husband moved to Montclair, New Jersey. That was when I began receiving phone calls from her. Though our talks were never inappropriate, Gamble's husband walked in on one of our conversations and was not pleased.

Soon I received a phone call from an older man and his wife—two Roumanian "friends" of his, who said they knew I was a friend of Gamble's, and asked if we could meet for a drink in their apartment, which was only a few blocks away from my parents' home, where I was still living.

When I told my brother that I had agreed to the meeting, he became enraged at my apparent stupidity—one of the few times I felt he was genuinely worried for my safety. He showed me a newspaper article about a Roumanian gang who had thrown a man out of a window. He then made me promise that if I was foolish enough to go have a drink with these people, that I would at least call him from there.

Although I had lived with many fears all my life, I was never afraid of people. In fact, I was quite bold in that respect, perhaps sometimes too bold for my own good.

When I arrived at the Roumanians' home, I discovered, to my chagrin, that they lived on the twenty-sixth floor. The first words out of the older gentleman's mouth—to me, at nineteen, everyone was older—were, in a thick Roumanian accent, "Mr. Cointrrrrreau, won't you please step out on the terrrrrrace?"

I may have been foolish, but I was not stupid. I stuck my head outside and replied a bit shakily, "No, no thank you."

I must have ultimately seemed rather innocent and not much of a threat, so after a quick drink and some small talk, in which I wished the newlyweds well, I easily made my way out of the apartment.

I had not called my brother, and by then he was beside himself with worry. You should have seen him when I arrived home! His relief at seeing me come home all in one piece was quite obvious.

As I had suspected would happen to anyone who took Gamble, a ward of the court, out of state, Gamble's husband was immediately arrested when he ventured into New York City.

It seemed to me that the marriage was off to a rocky start. After several separations and reconciliations, Gamble and her Roumanian divorced for good. After I read in the papers that Grammie was found dead on the toilet, I never saw or heard from Gamble Benedict again.

ANOTHER NERVOUS BREAKDOWN

I had genuinely cared for Gamble and felt betrayed; what made it even more difficult was that the entire affair had been played out very publicly in the press. Although I tried to come to terms with the end of my relationship with Gamble and put it behind me, the constant pressure I had been under triggered another emotional breakdown.

Before long I found myself panicking as soon as evening came. By six o'clock I was definitely on edge. By nine o'clock I was fighting panic, and by eleven I was sure that I was going to have a heart attack, or die, or go blind. In the daytime I had to take a taxi to go even one block away from home.

I had lived since the age of eight with panic and fear, but my parents had never followed up on any of the recommendations to get psychological help for me. Now, at nineteen, I tried to convince myself that my imagined heart attacks and terrors were a perfectly normal way of life. How could I know that my need for perfection, coupled with the suppressed memories of Mr. Fuller and my early sexual abuse, were still seething under the surface and coloring almost every facet of my life?

I never said a word to anyone about my latest difficulties until one night around eleven o'clock when I was sure that I was going to die. I knew I should at least tell my mother, but I didn't know what to say. I kept going down the long hallway towards her room but couldn't bring myself to knock on the door leading to her bedroom. Finally I couldn't stand it any longer and burst into her room to tell her that I was dying but I didn't know why. She put me on her bed and called the family doctor. Then she lay beside me and held my hand while we waited for him. I nearly crushed her hand, I was clutching it so hard.

When the doctor arrived, he recognized a panic attack for what it was and calmly sat in a chair and wrote out a prescription for tranquilizers. Each evening I was to take a pill at six o'clock, another at nine o'clock and the last one at eleven o'clock.

The medication was a great help, but the most important thing he did was to convince me that none of the things I feared would actually happen. Even if I felt that I was having a heart attack, I would still be able to run down the seven flights of stairs from our apartment if there was a fire. Nothing bad was going to happen to me. It was all in my head—even my agoraphobia.

During this period of nighttime panic, Mother allowed me to sleep on the chaise longue in her bedroom, and for the first time I saw her kneel by the side of her bed every night and say her prayers. As I improved, I moved back to my own room, knowing that my father had also left the door to his room open for me. Their concern and understanding was a great comfort to me.

That summer my parents suggested that I get away from the press by going to France with them. Obviously we had blocked out my lifelong aversion to Paris and the dangers of returning to Maman Geneviève's home ground.

My father's brother, Jean, picked us up at the Paris airport early in the morning. On the plane I had been looking forward to getting away, but as soon as we approached the edge of the city, all my childhood insecurities and fears came flooding back. I suddenly became as paralyzed and mute as I had been in my hospital bed as a child. It was impossible for me to utter a word.

I was overwhelmed by a deep depression that took me by surprise. I could not rationally understand why the city should affect me this way now that I was older. Within twenty-four hours of arriving in Maman Geneviève's depressing apartment—which was still filled with her late husband's artifacts of an ancient war—I became physically ill and could no longer eat. After a few days my Aunt Mimy came to the rescue and took me to the warm comfort of her country home, La Richardière, to recuperate until it was time for me to join my parents at my grandmother's château.

Back in New York, the gossip columns were filled with erroneous speculation about my sudden disappearance. I learned later that a friend whom I had trusted was making up stories and selling them to the newspapers.

True to form, Maman Geneviève outdid herself that summer as far as her cruelty was concerned. Unbeknownst to me, my father had made the mistake of telling her that I was taking medication for some emotional problems. One evening before dinner when she was struck by a particularly evil mood, she accosted me in the front entrance of Château Brillant with a twisted look on her face. She said, "I know all about you. Your father told me all about it. You're crazy. You should be in an institution."

I was so shocked and filled with rage at her attack that I ran up to my room in tears and kicked a wooden hanger all around the room, wishing it were Maman Geneviève.

That evening I sat at the dinner table with silent tears rolling down my face while my grandmother chatted with the rest of the family as though nothing had happened. The next day, when some friends of mine stopped by, my grandmother attempted to charm them. When I asked her to please leave us alone, I saw a tear appear in her eye. I knew it was just a performance for my friends, so I looked at her and said, "Last night you watched me cry, now it's your turn." My friends were embarrassed as we walked away, but I knew that it was one of the first times in my life that I would refuse to be the good little boy and allow someone to abuse me for their own perverted reasons.

When I was leaving Paris to go back to the United States, Maman Geneviève turned to say goodbye to me, saw the look of contempt on my face, and froze for a moment. When she asked, "Without rancor?", I turned and left without a word.

It was eleven years before I returned.

Back in New York, I designed my own therapy. I had to get better or die. And it wasn't easy. I gave myself pep talks as I took my medications and made myself walk an extra block alone every day. Eventually the panic attacks became less severe, and nothing that I couldn't cope with. The day I was able to stop my medications altogether, I knew I could still come out of a bad situation and survive.

As I gained strength, I felt that the time had come to put my training on the line and try out for a real job in show business.

SUMMER STOCK

Despite what the newspapers wrote about my lifestyle, I needed to earn some money. My parents were happy to keep a roof over my head but gave me only a small allowance for carfare and other essentials. My father always said that the moment I left the comfort of his home I had to be able to provide for myself; after that, there would be no unnecessary handouts. Like every young person, I looked forward to a day of financial independence.

In late spring 1962 I spotted an ad in the trade papers for a summer stock company in New Hampshire that would be doing eight musical comedies in eight weeks. They were holding open auditions in New York City—which meant that anyone could go.

I showed up at the rehearsal hall, signed in, and waited my turn. The song I had brought with me was a spirited "up tune" called "Great Day." When my name was called, I gave my music to the pianist, stood in front of a group of people sitting at a long table, and gave it all I had. I was enthusiastic, if nothing else. After the first eight bars I heard a disembodied voice say, "Thank you!", so I took back my music, left the room and went home, happy just to have survived the experience.

I had been home for only a few minutes when a frantic stage manager called me up to ask why I had left. I had heard only the "Thank you" and not "Would you please wait outside for a few minutes" while the powers that be discussed my fate. Evidently the job was mine!

The night before I left for summer stock, I was walking down Park

Avenue when it dawned on me that I was about to embark on a new life. This would be a new beginning for me, with new friends and a new way of life; now I would have to learn to live with other young people and survive on a salary of $25 a week. Oddly enough, because I would be doing something I really loved, I had no fear of going into this new situation alone.

The theater was in Rochester, New Hampshire, a charming little New England town straight out of a Norman Rockwell painting. The company took over a small, three-story pristine hotel a few blocks from the theater. It housed us all for $7 a week each. Most of the kids shared a room with simple pine furnishings and a connecting bath, but I asked for a single, even though it meant that I shared a bathroom at the end of a hallway. At least my room was the only one that had a private sink in it.

Never having been in a small hotel like this before, I went downstairs on the first day to notify the desk clerk that the maid hadn't made up my room. He informed me that for $1 a night, the maid only serviced the room once a week, when she changed the towels and the sheets!

Eight shows in eight weeks is hard work. We did full-blown productions of Broadway shows such as *South Pacific*, *Carousel*, and *Kiss Me, Kate*, with beautiful costumes and sets. Some weeks I'd be the star of the show, and some weeks I'd have a small role. We were enthusiastic and more than eager to rehearse one show during the day, perform another one at night, and play in between. I loved every minute of it. And as for my agoraphobia, there was always someone in the cast or crew to walk to and from the theater with.

I was particularly proud of the way I played the naive Russian composer Peter Borof in *Silk Stockings*. But when my parents came to see the show, they were not impressed. Summer stock in a small town in New Hampshire was a long way from the sophisticated theater world of London, New York, and Paris that they were familiar with.

It was more what they didn't say than what they actually said that let me know how they felt. I was confused and disappointed but I did my best not to show it.

After they left, the rest of the cast crowded around and asked how my parents had enjoyed the evening. I had to tell them the truth, that it had been less than a success in my parents' eyes. My new friends, all of whom originally came from modest backgrounds in small towns, put their arms around me and told me not to worry, that I had given a great performance. Even a girl who had eyed me suspiciously on our first day of rehearsal and told me that she had seen me when she was the hatcheck girl at the Harwyn Club, had nothing but kind words for me that night. I had never experienced that kind of camaraderie and support in the social whirl that I had come from.

I didn't care if it was Broadway or summer stock, I felt so fulfilled in my new environment that I actually thought if I were to die that summer I would die happy.

ETHEL, JUDY,
MR. SINATRA—AND JIM

For the next three years, I performed in more musical comedies than I could keep track of. I didn't care if they were good, bad or indifferent, as long as I was working. One of these was an Off-Broadway production called *Utopia*. Norman Nadel of the *New York World-Telegram and Sun* simply wrote, "*Utopia* isn't!" I can't say that I disagreed with him. But a job was still a job and meant experience.

In the late 1960s there was still a real and viable world of cabaret in America. After I had done a three-month stint as the production singer at the Copacabana in New York, my agent introduced me to Phil Moore, a well known and respected conductor and orchestrator. Through Phil, my personal and professional lives were about to meld.

We began to put together my nightclub act. A few days before Halloween in 1966, I went to Phil's house to pick up some music. From outside the front door I was introduced to a man standing at the end of a dark hallway. When he said, "Hello," although I couldn't see him at all, I instinctively knew from just hearing his voice that this was the person that I would spend the rest of my life with. I was told that he would be at Phil Moore's Halloween party four days later, and I couldn't wait to actually meet him.

For several years I had been living a discreet gay life, all the while publicly playing the role of the ladies' man about town. I am not sure how many people I was fooling besides myself. And in my heart I knew that I had always wanted a serious, stable relationship.

When I arrived at Phil Moore's Halloween party, I was not disappointed. The voice I had heard down the hallway belonged to Jim Russo, who arrived with a beautiful young actress named Ronda Copland on his arm.

I thought he was quite handsome and beautifully dressed, although I learned later that he never had any confidence in his looks. He also had a kind look in his large brown eyes, and a sense of humor that immediately seduced me. By the end of the evening, we felt as though we had known each other forever. Not only was this the start of a lifelong relationship with Jim, but Ronda became like a sister to me. Once again, as with the Lehmans, Halloween had brought significant relationships into my life.

Jim had been brought up in an Italian family in a small town in New Jersey. After high school, he had attended Georgetown University and was now doing promotion for Capital Records. As I got to know him better, I discovered that his background had been no more idyllic than mine. He had three much older siblings—Bill, Donald, and Louise—and had been born ten years after the youngest, Louise. Throughout his childhood his mother had treated him like a little doll that she liked to dress up, and she never let him go outside and play because he might get dirty. He had no friends and was only allowed to ride his tricycle alone in the basement. Jim never knew what it was like to be told that he was loved, that he was worthwhile, or how it felt to be tucked into bed at night.

Although there were empty bedrooms in the house, Jim's mother made him sleep in the same bed with his sister, Louise, who was ten years older, until he was thirteen and Louise left home to get married. Their mother had ruled their lives so completely that it never occurred to either of them to question this bizarre sleeping arrangement.

Jim adored Louise, and she did her best to give him motherly love, but she was herself too much a victim to be much help to him.

When Jim was six, his oldest brother, Bill, who had served in Europe during World War II, brought home a war bride, a Belgian woman named Paula. Even though she didn't speak English, Paula was an exceptionally loving and understanding woman who gave Jim much of the encouragement and support that he didn't find at home. In a way, she became *his* "other mother."

He grew up as the baby of the family and knew early on that his mother wanted to keep him at her side for the rest of her life—something he was not about to let happen. He always knew that it was only a matter of time until he could move away. When he was in high school, he used to sneak on the bus and ride to New York City—despite his mother's warnings that New York City was a terrible place filled with danger—and he would say to himself, "Someday I'm going to live here."

The day Jim left home to go to Georgetown University, his mother predicted, "You'll be back within two weeks." Once he arrived at school he found that for the first time in his life he felt totally free. Instead of being homesick like many of the other students, he was more than ready to enjoy his new life and new friends. On his first college break at Thanksgiving, he visited a classmate in Chicago instead of going home, and never looked back.

Even though Jim came from a very different world than I did, it was very much the same in certain respects, and we understood each other immediately.

While my relationship with Jim was growing, Phil Moore and I continued to work on my nightclub act. We took material from both my French and American heritage, and put together an act using the best of both worlds.

When we felt that the act was ready, my agent came to the studio to see what we had created. He liked it so much that he booked me to open in the Club Gigi at the renowned Fontainebleau Hotel in Miami. It was a big jump for a cabaret novice and we knew it.

A few nights before I left for Miami, I picked up Ethel Merman at the Berkshire Hotel on 52nd Street, where she was living, and took her down the street to the elegant French restaurant La Grenouille for dinner.

Ethel told me that Judy Garland was also staying at the Berkshire. At that time, no hotel would accept Judy because she was notorious for running out on her bills, but a large company Judy was working for had guaranteed her stay at the Berkshire for a certain number of days. "I really have to call her or she'll be hurt," Ethel said.

At 9:30 p.m. when we returned to the hotel, Ethel called her old friend Judy and was not surprised when the switchboard operator said, "Oh, yes, Miss Garland just got up."

When Ethel got Judy on the phone, she told Judy that she was with me, and that I was a big fan. She knew Judy would like that. Judy immediately told her, "Oh, come on up, I'd love to see you both."

We didn't know that Judy was nearing the end of her life, but we couldn't help but notice that she looked emaciated. The first thing Ethel said was, *"You're skinny!"*

To which Judy replied, *"I'm svelte!"*

"YOU'RE SKINNY!"

"I'M SVELTE!"

They went through this routine several times before falling into each other's arms and hugging. The last time Ethel had seen her, she had been on Judy Garland's television show. Judy jokingly complained to me that Ethel had been difficult to work with, and Ethel laughed that her agent had put it in her contract that she didn't have to do the show if Judy didn't show up for rehearsals. She was being professional, not difficult. Judy laughed too. She was a good egg and always able to laugh at herself and her many foibles.

The first thing that struck me when we walked into her suite was that Judy was wearing White Shoulders, the same perfume that Little Ethel always wore. Judy was dressed in what had once been a beautiful hostess gown of red brocade with sable collar and cuffs; I think it was the same one she'd worn on the Christmas television show she had done with her three children. I was saddened to see that the gown was soiled and had seen better days.

The hotel staff had told Ethel that the maids had not been allowed in Judy's suite to make up the rooms. Apparently this was true: when I excused myself and went to the bathroom, I passed by the unmade bed and found myself knee-deep in dirty towels.

I sat back in the living room, as Judy's younger companion Tom Green kept the vodka and tonics flowing, waiting to hear what these two show business legends would have to say to each other. But after Ethel turned to Judy and told her that I was opening at the Fontainebleau in a few days, the conversation focused on me and *my* career.

Judy treated me as a peer, and was generous with advice straight from her own life. She kept repeating, "Don't let them do to you what they did to me. Don't let them tell you that you're nobody. Don't let them tell you that you're nothing, that you are not a star and that you have no talent. Don't let them use you and just throw you away. You are somebody. You are important. You must always remember that, Tony." It seemed to me that Judy was really talking about herself, but that it was easier for her to do it in terms of *my* life. Ethel just sat there beaming at me like a proud mother.

When the front desk phoned at 11:30 p.m. to say that Miss Garland's limousine was waiting downstairs, Ethel decided it was time to make our excuses and leave. She didn't want to stay any longer in case Judy's drug and alcohol intake would cause the evening to take a bizarre turn. Judy seemed disappointed that we were leaving her alone so early in the evening. Her plaintive voice was almost haunting, following us down the hallway as we walked to the elevator: "Goodnight, Ethel. Goodnight, Tony. Goodnight, Ethel. Goodnight,

Tony"—over and over as if she were trying to draw us back into her world. Every fiber of my being wanted to turn back, but I knew Ethel was far wiser than I, and the right moment had come to make our departure. I now know that there was no way we could have filled the desperate void in Judy Garland's life.

None of us knew then, that happy evening when I was about to begin my solo nightclub career, that Judy would be dead within two years. She was the victim, the one who had been used and discarded, despite the fact that millions of people still loved her. That evening she seemed so normal, sitting with Ethel, Tom, and me in the living room of her suite at the Berkshire Hotel. But then I had to remind myself that she had just gotten up for the day at 9:30 p.m. and was only beginning her daily round of pills and liquor.

For all her seeming paranoia, that magical night Judy totally seduced me with her capacity for laughter—at herself, and at the world and all its silliness. Laughter had always been what attracted me the most to the extraordinary women in my life. I was raised, nurtured, and fed by their unfailing sense of humor. All of the women I was closest to laughed at every facet of life from the slapstick to the tragic.

I was delighted that Judy's flashes of self-deprecating humor seemed to be her armor against some of the tragedies of her own life. My personal mantra has always been that no matter how bad things get, there is no longer any hope the day you can't find something to laugh about. Judy, Lee, Ethel, my aunt Tata, even Mother Teresa later on in my life, all had that gift and made sure they shared it with me. In the end, laughter and love are the only things that never die.

When I arrived at the Fontainebleau Hotel the day before my opening, I had a bad case of the flu and a fever of 102. Unbeknownst to me, Frank Sinatra was also opening there, in the big showroom called La Ronde. Dizzy from the fever, I walked into the giant lobby and saw a life-size cutout of Frank Sinatra on my left and a life-size cutout of myself on my right. I thought I was hallucinating.

The hotel doctor came to see me that evening. Unlikely as it might seem, between a shot of penicillin, a shot of vitamins, and the resiliency of youth, I was in good shape for the orchestra rehearsal the next day.

As show time at the Fontainebleau drew near, I was terrified of what would happen when I stepped out on that stage in front of a sophisticated Miami audience—not to mention the critics whose newspapers had already done feature stories on me. However, from the moment I walked out on the floor the audience could not have made me feel more welcome, and the reviews the next day were equally enthusiastic.

On my way down in the elevator on my second night I felt little of the previous night's apprehension. When I noticed a long line snaking out of the entrance of the Club Gigi, waiting to get in to see my show, I thought, "Wow, word certainly spreads fast!"

My bubble quickly burst when the *maitre d'* ran up to me and announced, "The King is here and he wants to meet you!" It took me a moment to understand that Frank Sinatra had come to see my show and that all these people had come to watch Mr. Sinatra watch me perform.

Once again my stomach started doing somersaults. The *maitre d'* grabbed my arm and dragged me across the room to meet "the King," who was standing at the bar with his guests.

I don't care what anyone else says about Frank Sinatra—to me, he was a very generous man. He paid close attention during my show and applauded each song enthusiastically. He particularly liked a rhythm-and-blues number I sang in French and English called *"Le Coeur Qui Bat,"* or "The Heart That Beats;" at the end of the song, I held a note at the top of my lungs for thirty-two bars while the orchestra played full blast. I think Mr. Sinatra may have been intrigued by my breath control. He even invited another large party a few nights later to see the show again. Both times he went out of his way to make me feel comfortable and to show his appreciation for my work. He was a very gracious gentleman to a young kid starting out in show business.

One of his guests was a tough-looking character called Jilly who looked like he had stepped out of an old George Raft gangster film. He was well known for a restaurant named after him in New York, where Mr. Sinatra and his buddies liked to hang out. After the show, Jilly came up to me and said in his raspy voice, "Hey Kid, when you get back to New York, anything you want—it's yours— De name's Jilly!"

I stammered, "Thank you, Mr. Jilly," and fairly ran from the room. There were times when I didn't feel *that* sophisticated.

An unexpected bonus for me was when Jim showed up to lend support on my opening night. He had been working for Capitol Records and knew the show business scene well. That week we decided that if we were going to be together, he would give up his job in promotion to manage my career.

Jim ended up knowing me better than I knew myself, and his objective eye was exactly what I needed. Over the years, I sometimes found myself getting a little impatient as he adjusted my collar or my hair before I walked out on stage or made a public appearance, and I often referred to him as "Mama Rose," the ultimate stage mother in *Gypsy*. But he was always right.

A Tragic Mistake

After our summer at the Neighborhood Playhouse, Little Ethel had gone to college in Colorado, as she had planned. And although she was no longer in New York, she and I remained in close contact.

When news from Little Ethel became sparse, I started to worry. The first news flash I received was a real shocker. During her first year of college, she had eloped with a tall, athletic student called Bill Geary. A few months later, the reason became obvious. There was a child on the way. When the baby, Barbara Jean, arrived, Ethel Merman played the part of the ecstatic grandmother to the hilt, with pictures for everyone to see.

But I could sense trouble brewing when Little Ethel told me in February 1961, "I'm a baby with a baby."

Other than that, I knew nothing about how she really felt until 1962, when I got a call from her mother inviting me to a cocktail party she was giving for her daughter, who was coming to New York for a visit—without Bill. I was shy about the meeting and didn't know the protocol of seeing a married woman my own age. What I really wanted was to see my friend Little Ethel alone. When she told me at the party that it would be all right for me to take a married lady out to dinner, we made plans.

It didn't take long for her to tell me that she was unhappy in her marriage and that she was planning a divorce. Her mother's only problem with our seeing each other was that if the press got wind of our dates at the hot spots in New York it might cause people to gossip about Ethel Merman's married daughter cheating on her husband with The Liqueur Heir. However, Little Ethel and I didn't worry about the possible scandal and went everywhere.

It was during this time that I fully saw the tension that arose between mother and daughter.

Ethel was still acting like the strict Victorian mother her parents had brought her up to be, and as Little Ethel told me, "Mom makes me feel like a whore." Strangely, there seemed to be a double standard for Little Ethel and Bobby. The boy could get away with murder whereas his sister had always been punished for the slightest infringement of the rules. The girl never had a chance.

Oftentimes Ethel would be on the phone with me, complaining about what a difficult time she was having with her daughter. Later on, I would hear the other side of the story from Little Ethel. Because I was able to hear both sides of each issue, it was relatively easy for me to bring them back together again. I never understood the dramas that were going on about nothing, but was pleased to be a peacemaker. It was evident that they adored each other, but it was not easy to be Ethel Merman's child. In a way Little Ethel was brought up with the same problem I had been faced with—the need to be perfect in order to please.

Both of Ethel's children inherited their mother's sense of humor, as well as a talent for theater and writing. But Ethel sometimes feared that if her daughter went into the theater and was not good enough, it might reflect on *her*. Little Ethel must have felt a great responsibility to be as good as her mother—an impossible task for any child of a legend.

As for Bobby, he was a loveable rascal. He was also very much like his mother—and that's why *they* often locked horns through the years. It's also why he could more easily stand up to her demands. He grew up to be an unusually caring human being who, even in the worst of times, had his mother's full love and admiration. Sometimes it was a grudging admiration, but she always saw the unique brilliance, and I might add genius, in his gift for writing. He's also a very nice guy with a great sense of humor.

I don't believe Ethel ever really understood the pressures her sensitive daughter was under or how Bobby was trying to make his own way in the world. Many times, Ethel called me and cried because she couldn't understand what was happening between her and her children. She loved them both so much, but was unable to bend her own old-fashioned Zimmermann code of ethics. Her code was such that she never said a four-letter word in front of me until I reached the age of twenty-one. I thought it was rather quaint.

During Little Ethel's trip to New York in 1962, after she had decided to leave her husband, she found out that her plans for a new life would have to wait—she was pregnant again. I was dismayed, since she had told me how lost she already felt. And now she felt that her only choice was to go back to Colorado and her husband; staying with her mother was less appealing than going back to Colorado and possibly finishing college. I worried that she was going from one trap to another, but I was still living with my parents and had no resources to help her with.

She must have felt more overwhelmed than ever when her second child, Michael, was born soon afterward, in November 1962. She was now a "baby with *two* babies"—something she was not emotionally ready to cope with.

When Little Ethel and her husband and children moved to Los Angeles, she became increasingly confused about what she wanted to do with her life—whether to be an actress, go back to college, or be a full-time mother. Over the years her emotional problems became too much for the marriage to survive, and in February 1967, when she and Bill Geary divorced, he obtained custody of the children.

Ethel, knowing how confused her daughter was, paid for a multitude of doctors and psychiatrists to help Little Ethel put her life together again. Little Ethel and I spent hours on the phone talking about how it felt to be emotionally fragile. Lord knows, I had had my own ups and downs in that department.

I tried to help and was pleased when she started acting in small roles on television shows. She also told me that she had had her nose refined, and was acting under the name of Nicole Geary so that no one would say she was using her mother's success to get ahead in the business. All I could do was encourage her and let her know I always cared about her.

In August of 1967, Little Ethel returned to Colorado, planning to finish her college education, and asked Bill if the children—Barbara Jean, six, and Michael, four—could visit her for a couple of weeks before school started. The morning after they arrived, Barbara Jean knocked on a neighbor's door and cried, "I can't wake my momma up."

When Bill Geary called Ethel Merman on August 23 to tell her that her daughter had died, it was the worst day of her life. She said it was only her faith and her belief that someday she would be reunited with her daughter that helped her to survive.

I was still living at home when it happened. My mother read the headline in the morning papers: "MERMAN'S DAUGHTER DEAD". Knowing how close we were, Mother came to my room to tell me what had happened. I was in the shower when she knocked on the door. This seemed to annoy her impatient nature, so she shouted through the door, *"MERMAN'S DAUGHTER IS DEAD!"* And that's how I got the news.

The first time we spoke on the phone after her loss, Ethel sobbed uncontrollably. All I could do was tell her that I loved her and how much I hated to see her in this kind of pain. I was stunned and immensely saddened, but my upbringing still did not allow me to release any emotion of my own. I had learned Mother's lessons of self-control well.

Ethel immediately flew out to Colorado, with Bobby at her side.

She couldn't bear to view her daughter's body, but asked for a lock of her hair. Little Ethel was cremated and her mother bought a room that was really a small chapel with an altar for the urn to rest on at the Evergreen Shrine of Rest. At the time she hoped that eventually the whole family would be reunited there in Colorado. A couple of months later when the beautiful little chapel was ready for the memorial service, I was working in a show and unfortunately couldn't go with Ethel when she asked me.

For a long time she kept a picture of Little Ethel and a lock of her hair on a table in her bedroom. On the table was a candle she kept lit twenty-four hours a day. She said, "If President Kennedy can have an eternal flame, so can my Ethel." She eventually stopped lighting the candle because she feared it might create a fire hazard. But the picture and the lock of hair were never far from her bed.

Little Ethel's death wasn't made easier for Ethel to bear when the press labeled it a suicide. But I was with her the day she received the coroner's report, which stated that it had been an accidental death. Ethel always said that she wanted the world to know that it had simply been a tragic mistake.

I knew that a psychiatrist had been prescribing tranquilizers and sleeping pills for Little Ethel and that another doctor had been giving her more pills to lose weight. She sometimes added alcohol to the mix to balance out the highs and lows, which had been induced by the drugs.

According to the coroner's report, she had a minimal amount of these prescription drugs in her system when she died, but she had topped them off with vodka. The vodka had interacted with these powerful drugs and created a lethal combination.

In those days we were not as sophisticated about amphetamines and barbiturates as we are today. I knew young girls of sixteen whose doctors prescribed amphetamines for them to lose their baby fat. Barbiturates like Nembutal and Seconal were easily given to anyone

I knew who wanted sleeping pills. The tranquilizer called Miltown was so popular that I knew women who had gold charms of the pill attached to their bracelets.

Little Ethel was not stupid, and had told me how frightened she was of the possible deadly effects of these medications. But she didn't know the danger of mixing them with alcohol.

Ethel often said after her daughter's death that she would never again have anything stronger than an aspirin in her own house. Unfortunately, it was too late for her beloved daughter.

On the day Ethel received the coroner's report—a couple of months after Little Ethel's death—I took her out to dinner. Her spirits were very low. I hated leaving her alone in this condition, so I took her to see the great French singer-composer, Gilbert Becaud, who was performing his nightclub act in the elegant white and gold Empire Room at the Waldorf-Astoria hotel. She had never heard of him, but I knew that she appreciated great talent and would enjoy his show.

When we arrived at the Waldorf, she was still uncharacteristically quiet, so I requested the discreet table towards the back of the room where I usually sat with Mrs. Douglas MacArthur and her son, Arthur. By the end of the show, I knew I had done the right thing in bringing her, as I watched Ethel begin to come back to life, visibly inspired by this legendary French composer singing his own songs of life and love.

Although Mr. Becaud was aware of her presence, he instinctively knew not to intrude on her grief by introducing her to the audience in too public a way. Instead, after his last song, "What Now, My Love?", which he did in French and then in English, he took a single rose from the piano, walked over to us, and, without a word, placed it on the table in front of Ethel.

MY BEAUTIFUL FRIEND

Throughout the tragedy of losing Little Ethel, one of my best friends, and watching her mother's suffering, I never suspected that more heartbreak would soon come into my life with my first "other mother," Lee Lehman.

One summer day in 1968, in Lee's 49th year, I received a phone call that she had taken another overdose. That day she had listened in on a phone conversation of Mr. Lehman's, and discovered that he was having an affair with a much younger woman. When Lee confronted him, he said, "I will give up Françoise if you will give up Robaire."

Lee was oblivious to the fact that Robaire was a gigolo; he made her feel that she was still young and beautiful. And she was still young and beautiful, but she needed a man's validation. Her answer to her husband was to go to the medicine cabinet once again.

This time my beautiful friend's heart temporarily stopped beating on the way to the hospital and she went into a coma. When she came out of the coma a week later, she had sustained considerable damage to the motor portion of her brain. Her movements became like those of a drunken person, and her speech almost unintelligible.

It was almost impossible for me to accept that she might never be the same, that someone who had been an idol to me and had seemed invincible would be so diminished for the rest of her life.

I didn't know what to expect the first time I saw her. I knew that she could no longer take care of herself as before, and had to have her hairdresser and makeup man come to her home every day. The first time I went to her apartment, I watched her walk slowly down the long hallway towards me. She looked as beautiful as ever. But after I kissed her, she made a remark that I could not understand. I was mortified for her.

That day, Pam and Lee and I went to Lee's mother's house, where I spent the afternoon sitting on the couch next to Lee and keeping up a steady stream of one-sided conversation. When I told her that I had missed her, the only intelligible words she could say were, "Thank you."

I gradually accepted that Lee would never walk normally or speak clearly again. In time Jim and I learned to "interpret" what she was trying to say, and in spite of her handicaps, she retained all of the charismatic attributes she had had before, including her sense of humor, and was as fascinating as ever.

About the same time as Lee's overdose, Mr. Lehman suffered a stroke. Like many who control their universe with power and money, he was terrified of death—the one thing he couldn't control.

It was ironic that in the last months of his life, after seventeen years of marriage, neither he nor Lee could speak intelligibly to each other. A hospital room had been set up for him in their apartment with nurses around the clock, and for most of that time Lee couldn't bear to enter the room. She told me, "All we can do is look at each other."

Mr. Lehman believed that if he lay perfectly still and didn't move a muscle he would preserve his strength and live forever. Unfortunately, that was the wrong thing to do, and he died a year later, in August 1969, in their apartment on Park Avenue.

Lee and Pam called me immediately after Mr. Lehman's death and asked me to come over to the apartment. I walked into Lee's bedroom, where she was lying on her bed, and said, "I'm sorry."

She looked up at me and said, "I am, too."

I was doing a show that night, and she asked if she and Pam could come with Jim and me to see it. It may have seemed like an odd request at a time like that, but I realized that it was either come with us, or sit alone in her apartment, where her husband had just died.

Maybe Lee and Bobbie Lehman's relationship was defined by an exchange that occurred as they were leaving Saks Fifth Avenue in the early days of their marriage. When Mr. Lehman asked her, "Would you have married me if I weren't rich?", she replied, "Would you have married me if I weren't beautiful?"

"They Found My Navel"

In 1966, Tata, who had never been heavy to begin with, began to lose an inordinate amount of weight and went into the hospital for tests. Doctors were unable to come up with a diagnosis and the day before she was to be discharged they decided to do one more test, which involved putting a catheter into a major artery in her groin.

The test was never finished—while inserting the catheter, they blocked the artery and cut off the circulation in her right leg. The doctors waited three days to operate, and by then it was too late to restore the circulation. Gangrene had set in. Tata was sent home to wait out the next six months in agony until the doctors could see how far up her leg the damage would go. She later sued the hospital and won, although she had already died before the case was settled.

Jim and I visited Tata every evening at home and served her her favorite beverage, three parts sweet vermouth and one part whiskey. The last thing we gave her before leaving was codeine for the pain.

Tata was a courageous woman who always greeted us with a smile, no matter how much she suffered. But the evening we entered her front door and heard her moaning in agony from the bedroom, I knew it was time to call the surgeon. He came the next day and scheduled Tata's leg to be amputated below the knee.

Mother and I left the hospital during the surgery, and came back to the sound of Tata screaming in her room. The nurse told us that there was a problem and they had had to remove the bandage. Now two doctors were working on what remained of Tata's leg. She sounded—and I felt—as if they were torturing her to death.

The doctors did not want to give her any painkillers because they were afraid that someone with so little body weight might not tolerate additional drugs after the recent anesthesia. They left the floor without ordering painkillers.

So far I had been able to sublimate any show of emotion in my private life: as always, pain and loss were not to be acknowledged. However, my brain was still functioning. I remembered that the surgeon who had performed the operation had obviously been impressed by my mother's charms, and I insisted that Mother get on the phone and sweet talk him into *immediate* action for painkillers. Within minutes, a nurse appeared to give Tata an injection.

Not only was Tata in terrible pain but she was also concerned that the doctors had taken off more of her leg than she had thought they would. My mother simply went home and left me to deal with the situation.

Tata kept asking, "Have they taken too much off my leg?" She insisted that I look under the sheets and examine the now-bandaged but still bloody stump. I looked, and comforted her as best I could—"No, they've taken off just the right amount, just what they said they would do"—but after a few moments I had to excuse myself and go into the bathroom and sit with my head between my knees in order not to lose consciousness.

Even *that* was not to be acknowledged; I could tell no one, not even Jim. I was still only allowing myself to present the perfect, brave little soldier to the world.

When Tata was ready to leave the hospital, I was wheeling her out of her room when a doctor stopped us and told her that she couldn't leave yet—a spot had been discovered on her lung. Tata insisted that we keep going. With a smile and a wave, she turned to the doctor and said, "I hope it's fatal!"

And it was. For the next four years Tata managed to get herself from the wheelchair to her living room couch, where she spent the day reading and waiting for her five o'clock cocktails. When I was able to, I would do the honors. If not, Jim was more than happy to fill in for me. He always said, "Tata was one of the most fascinating women I ever met. When you were with her, she made you feel as though you were the only person in the world that mattered." Her charm and powers of seduction were totally focused on the person she was with. Although she no longer left her apartment, she knew everything that was going on in the world. And she could always make you laugh.

On the Fourth of July weekend of 1970 Tata called me—it was a Sunday—and said, "Darling, I can no longer get off the couch."

I understood immediately that with no self-pity or complaining, she had deliberately waited until she knew it would be too late to prolong her life. The malignant "spot" on her lung had metastasized to other organs in her body.

My parents were in Europe, so I called my mother's doctor, who was on a golf course in Long Island, and asked him how I should proceed. He told me that he would make arrangements for Tata to be admitted to Lenox Hill Hospital and for me to get an ambulance for whatever time they gave me. He added, "I'll be in tomorrow to see her."

Jim went with me and we waited with Tata for the ambulance to arrive. Her private room was to be ready at eight o'clock in the evening. Just before the attendants lifted her onto the gurney she told us, "Darlings, you won't believe it, but I've lost so much weight that I can't find my navel."

It seemed as though every doctor on the Eastern seaboard checked Tata out while Jim and I waited in the hallway outside her room. After two hours, a young intern told us that they were through and we could go in.

Tata lay on her bed looking like a mask of death, with her hands clasped over her chest.

We went over to her and quietly called, "Tata?", whereupon she opened one eye, saw the obvious concern on our faces, gave us an exhausted but wicked grin and announced in the most dramatic tone she could muster, *"They found my navel!"*

Tata lived another three months. I stayed in town in order to be with her every day.

I had worked hard over the years to prevent my emotions from taking over and this was no different. At this point I went into deep denial and, even though she was obviously failing, I could not acknowledge her imminent death. One evening, as I sat on her bed chatting away as though nothing was wrong, Tata turned towards me and said, "Goodbye, Darling."

I still didn't get it. Later, I realized that all my life she had refused to say "Goodbye" to me; she always insisted on *"Au revoir,"* which means "Till we meet again."

The next morning, my mother, who had returned from Europe, received a call from the hospital. Mother came to the door of my room and called loudly, "My sister is *in extremis.*"

"I'm in the shower—go with Father to the hospital and I'll join you there."

Mother and Father went on to the hospital, where Tata was already dead; she had died with only an intern at her side. Someone called for a priest to give her the last rites.

After the last rites, my parents left the hospital—they left me there to take care of filling out all the papers, and taking Tata's wedding ring off her finger. I put the ring in an ashtray in order not to lose it. It felt surreal for me to be waiting for the man from the morgue to come and get my beloved Tata.

සා ෆා

Mother and Father and I put Tata to rest next to her mother, Martha, in Boston.

At Tata's funeral, my mother was as stoic as she had taught me to be. My armor nearly cracked, though, when I first saw Tata's casket and the reality of her death struck me. And Mother's nearly cracked when she walked away from Tata's tomb. I followed her and took her arm. Mother stopped in her tracks, turned to me with tears glistening in her eyes, and defiantly stated, "I never loved her. It's just so hard to say goodbye!"

At first it seemed like a strange remark, coming from a woman whose life had been so closely bound to her sister's. Finally I understood that my mother simply could not bear the thought that I had almost seen her give in to her emotions.

My mother inherited Tata's apartment on Fifth Avenue. I myself cleaned out all of her personal belongings, carefully turning over to my mother anything of value, such as jewelry. Although Mother had never formally acknowledged my relationship with Jim, she grew very fond of him, and, because the maintenance on Tata's apartment was much lower than any rental we could find in the city, she allowed us to move in. It was our home base for four years. I think Tata would have been pleased.

The only thing of Tata's that I kept was a beautiful leather-bound prayer book that she had received for her First Holy Communion as a young girl. In it she had Scotch-taped her calling card, on which she had written, "I would love to have my beloved Jacques-Henri own this prayer book."

With her great sense of humor, Tata had always said that she wanted inscribed on her tombstone, "Here lies Ashie, straightened out at last."

THE UNIMAGINABLE

At the time of Tata's death in October 1970, my mother had been receiving treatment for breast cancer for a year. Two months after Tata's death, just before Christmas, my father informed me that, according to her doctor, Mother now had no more than six months to live.

Mother, in the last year of her life, knowing that she was going to die, continually told me that I was selfish and inconsiderate. I did not want to fight with her before she died, so the only thing I ever said back to her was, "If I were so terrible, would I have taken such good care of Tata?"

She had to admit that that was true, but continued to berate me. It was easier for me to accept the abuse than to confront her behavior. I thought she was angry that she was going to die and I was going to live on; but I no longer think that's true. Mother couldn't bear to show emotion, just as when, at Tata's funeral, she had said, "I never loved her. It's just so hard to say goodbye." She was doing the same thing with me, pushing me away, because she couldn't bear to say goodbye.

I, having always believed that I could not survive if my mother died, went into an even deeper denial than during Tata's illness: it was not possible for my mother to die, and simply could not happen. If I permitted my real emotions to surface, I feared they might tear me apart until there was nothing left of me but pain.

I accepted a nightclub engagement at a resort in British Columbia for six weeks, beginning January 21, 1971. The night before I left, I went to see my mother at home. She was in bed, wearing a pink negligee, looking more beautiful than I had ever seen her. I lay next to her on the bed while we talked about my work. She and my father and Tata had always fully supported my goals and dreams, and Mother was always happy and proud when I had a good job on the horizon.

I held her hand and became enveloped in the smile that I knew so well. Oh my God, I didn't want to acknowledge that this might be the last time I would ever see her. It couldn't be happening. She would never leave me like this. My world went into slow motion. I survived by focusing on making each precious moment together count. There was only our laughter that mattered anymore. We had never loved each other more than we did that evening. We both knew the truth but had to play out the scenario the only way we knew how—the only way that we could bear it.

My engagement in British Columbia was a great success. But on some level I was still denying the severity of Mother's condition. I had not even given my parents my phone number in British Columbia, and I could not bear to call them for the first two weeks.

The day I finally called home was on my birthday, February 7th. Mother berated me for not being more present, when my father had so much on his hands taking care of her. But it was difficult for her to speak, since the cancer was affecting her throat, and I said, "It's so difficult for you to speak, why don't you put Father on the phone?" I didn't know it then, but those would be the last words we ever spoke.

On February 20th, my father called to tell me that my mother was in Lenox Hill Hospital and would not live through the night. I couldn't believe that "six months to live" had turned into two months. Fifteen minutes before my ten o'clock show, my father called again to say that it was over, my mother was dead.

Still being my mother's perfect child, I went on with the show, and returned to New York the next day. My father, my brother Richard, our old nurse Lucy, and I took Mother's body to Boston and buried her beside Tata and my grandmother Mémé. The only way that I could publicly deal with the loss of my mother was to take so many tranquilizers that I almost nodded off in the cemetery.

That day, Lucy wanted to lean on my arm for support—but it was eighteen years later when she finally thought to tell me the one thing that might have comforted *me*: two weeks before Mother's death, she told Lucy that she had made her peace with God and was ready to go.

I had lost both Mother and Tata within four months. But the day after we buried my mother I was back in Canada, where Jim and Lee were waiting for me. I only missed one performance.

Many years would pass before I could allow myself to grieve. I continued to perform in theater, nightclubs and television—on stage was still the only place that I could allow myself to publicly express emotion.

"And Who Are *You?*"

Mother had always believed that she would someday be a widow like most of her women friends. But she not only died fifteen years before her husband, she died even before her mother-in-law did.

Maman Geneviève had the same strained relationship with my mother that she had with her two other daughters-in-law, strong women who knew how to defend themselves. There was no love lost between Mother and Maman Geneviève, and Mother had made no secret of the fact that she would not go into deep mourning on the day that her mother-in-law died. Besides not liking the woman, Mother had a lifelong and irrational fear of dying in poverty and knew that when Maman Geneviève died she and my father would be even more financially secure.

My father, who had little love left for his mother, could not believe that his beloved wife had died first. There would be few tears shed when Maman Geneviève died.

It had been a family tradition to spend summers at Château Brillant, but after 1960, for the next eleven years I did not even wish to be in the same country as Maman Geneviève.

The day that I finally went back to France, it was to visit my father at his summer home after my mother had passed away. He spent winters in New York City and summers in his home overlooking the Loire River, not far from my Aunt Mimy's estate, La Richardière.

I found Aunt Mimy, who had always been so robust, to be in failing health. Now she was so large that her hips had started to disintegrate and she could no longer walk. The pain was sometimes excruciating. The only way she could dull the physical pain—and her fear of death—was by drinking copious amounts of whiskey before meals, and full glasses of Cointreau afterwards.

I hated facing the loss of one more icon of my youth and felt helpless when she pleaded with me to convince her of an afterlife. I knew that *I* believed in a higher power and that there is a greater purpose for our being here than just taking up space. But how do you explain that faith to someone else?

This was something that my father also brought up with me. At first he hadn't let anyone see the deep sorrow he felt at Mother's passing. He was an independent man who made no demands on Richard and me. His attitude was, "Don't tell me how to live my life, and I won't tell you how to live yours."

But as we grew closer, he told me that after Mother's death he had called a priest from St. Vincent Ferrer (the church where he and mother had been married) to come to his house and visit him because he was so angry at God for having taken his wife away from him "after thirty-five too-short years." Nothing much was resolved, though, and in the end he professed to believe in nothing.

This issue haunted him for the rest of his life. Although I never tried to convince him of my own beliefs, I always answered, "Someday, Pop, you're in for a big surprise!"

One day in the summer of 1972, I announced, "Pop, I want to see my grandmother."

He replied, "No, you don't."

"Yes, I do."

"*I* don't want to see her."

Finally he gave in and took me to her home in Angers. As we entered her massive bedroom, I saw a shriveled ninety-two-year-old woman lying in bed singing children's songs to herself. She looked up and sweetly asked, "And who are *you*?"

"I'm your grandson, Jacques-Henri."

Then she turned to my father in the doorway and asked him who *he* was. She seemed delighted to meet her son and grandson and started to entertain us with her songs. A few moments later she turned to us and asked again, "And who are *you*?"

We went through this several times before I quietly said to my father, "We can go now." Maman Geneviève was still singing to herself as we walked down the long hallway to the stairs.

Thank God for the inner voice that had prompted me to insist upon visiting my grandmother one more time. As we left her room, all the hatred in my heart totally disappeared. Whatever pain she had caused me and whatever demons had possessed her were her cross to bear and could no longer have any impact on my life. I could only feel compassion at the tragedy of her existence.

I am not particularly proud to admit that when I was a teenager I had so much resentment towards my grandmother that, as I was walking behind her at the top of the main staircase at Château Brillant, the thought crossed my mind: "How easy it would be to gently push her down the stairs!" I will always be grateful for whatever good sense held me back from acting on that fleeting impulse.

Not long after our final meeting, Maman Geneviève was standing at the top of the two steps leading to her dressing room, watching her ladies' maid, Marie-Eugenie, walk by. She lifted her cane to hit her faithful servant, lost her balance, fell down the steps, broke her hip, and soon passed away. This time there was no reason for me to mourn, but how ironic that it should turn out to be a fall down stairs that ended her life after all.

Hooray for Hollywood

One of my first important jobs in show business was as the singer with the Guy Lombardo orchestra for a year. During that time, I did two concert tours across the United States, Canada, and the Caribbean; played the Tropicana Hotel in Las Vegas twice (the second time with my name up in lights under Guy's); recorded two albums for Capital Records; played Carnegie Hall in New York City; and performed in the legendary Lombardo New Year's Eve television show, broadcast around the world.

By 1975, although I still loved show business, I became aware of a need for something more, but I wasn't sure what it was. At the time, all I could think of was that a move to Los Angeles might be the answer.

I had been to Los Angeles once, when I was working for Guy Lombardo and had to re-record one song on a new album. Guy had asked me if on my day off I would fly from Chicago, where we were in the middle of a concert tour, to the Capital Records studios, do the work, and return that same day.

It only took an hour to do the recording, so I had some free time before my flight back to Chicago. A friendly cab driver offered to fill the time with a $10 tour of Beverly Hills, where I fell in love with the palm trees, sunshine, warm weather, and unostentatious houses that in those days made up the city. Every street looked like a scene out of an Andy Hardy movie, and I always dreamed of going back.

So when Jim agreed that moving to Los Angeles might open up

new opportunities for my career, I was eager to go. We packed up our belongings and our little Yorkshire terrier, Charlie, in a new Plymouth Gold Duster, and set out on our trip from New York to Los Angeles, California.

We knew nothing about the city. But when we arrived early in the evening, we decided to stop at the Cavalier Hotel on Wilshire Boulevard in Westwood because it looked like our idea of California. All that mattered to us was that it had a courtyard, a swimming pool and lots of palm trees.

After checking in we called the only person we knew in Los Angeles, Ronda Copland, who had been with Jim at the Halloween party in New York the night I met him. Ronda was now pursuing a successful career in theater, movies, and television. We had no idea where she lived but when we told her where we were staying, she said, "I live just around the corner!" and invited us over for dinner.

It seemed like an auspicious beginning, the first of many happy and hopeful evenings we would spend with her as we started our new life in California.

Before long, Jim and I found a small furnished apartment that we loved in Brentwood. As my father had told me, once I left home, I had to earn my living like everyone else; and, although I had always had work, I never knew if the next job would be my last—a common problem for most people in show business. So we knew we had to be careful with our money.

As soon as we settled in, we called Lee Lehman, who had already traveled extensively with us since her husband's death several years before. She had gone everywhere with us and sat through hundreds of my shows—the test of a true friend—and when we were in New York, we saw each other almost every night; we either had dinner together at her home, or went to the theater. Lee said she would enjoy getting out of New York and spending a couple of weeks with us out on the coast.

Lee was in a diminished state as a result of her 1968 suicide attempt, and damage to the motor portion of her brain still made it difficult for her to speak intelligibly or to walk without holding on to my arm. But I had always adored her, and wherever we went, I watched out for her and protected her. Once when we were in Jamaica in the Caribbean, the housekeeper asked her if I were her son, and added, "He's so lovin' to you, Mum."

Lee told us that we gave her life again; without us she would be spending most nights alone in her apartment. As far as Jim and I were concerned, it was never a hardship or an obligation, but something we did out of love. We enjoyed her company, and our time together was always filled with laughter.

The night before we called Lee from Los Angeles, she had attended the opening of the Lehman Pavilion at the Metropolitan Museum of Art, which her husband Robert had helped to plan before his death in 1969. The Pavilion was designed to recreate rooms from the townhouse on 54th Street in New York City where he had grown up, and to showcase the Renaissance treasures that had been in those very rooms.

Mr. Lehman had intended for Lee to have lifetime possession of the Impressionist works they had collected for their apartment, and after her death the major portion of this collection was to go to the Metropolitan Museum. But she found it so unpleasant to live with the 24-hour-a-day armed guards required by the Museum that she soon relinquished the collection to the Met.

Lee arrived in Los Angeles in June of 1975, took one look at our small apartment, and asked if she couldn't take us both to the Beverly Hilton Hotel. Then she got into our modest Plymouth Gold Duster and insisted that we go right to a car dealer, where we traded it in on a beautiful grey Mercedes.

After two weeks, Lee decided to stay longer, and we looked for a house for her to rent, a house that all three of us and our little

Yorkie, Charlie, could live in. We found a house owned by the writer Sidney Sheldon on Rodeo Drive that we all liked. From the outside, it looked like an idealized grandmother's house where you'd go for Thanksgiving. But inside, it was pure Hollywood glamour. Upstairs, there were three bedrooms and three bathrooms, one for each of us. The enclosed back porch held a complete working antique soda fountain and a grand piano. Downstairs, the house was decorated all in white. I found this especially appealing, because in those days I was in what I called my "white period" and wore only white; white gave me a feeling of purity and helped to satisfy my ongoing obsessive need for perfection and cleanliness. There was a pool, a guesthouse, and quarters where a succession of eccentric housekeepers would live.

The first was a French housekeeper called Claire, who arrived surrounded by an enormous pile of Gucci luggage. She turned out to be a lousy maid but had a certain *joie de vivre* that amused the three of us.

At this point in my life, although I was not totally free from fear, I was so caught up in doing the work that I loved that I was able to push aside my childhood emotional traumas and focus on the tasks at hand.

One drawback about living in the Los Angeles area was the necessity of driving. I had a driver's license, but was frightened of being at the wheel of a car. However, when you have no choice, you do what you have to do, so I drove, although I went miles out of my way to avoid the freeways. The only place I felt comfortable driving was in Beverly Hills, with all the little old ladies who drove under the speed limit.

One day when I drove to an audition, I parked my car on a side street in front of a nursing home. I looked in a window and saw an elderly woman in a wheelchair. In the other windows I saw more elderly people, sitting alone. They all looked so lonely. My first impulse was to go to the front door and ask if they needed someone to sing to the patients or just talk to them. But I was not sure of the reception I would get, and I walked away. For years I remained haunted by the thought of what might have been—what I might have brought to those lonely people's lives, and what they might have brought to mine—had I followed my instincts and opened that door.

Soon after we had settled into our new home, a well-connected friend from New York invited us to a dinner party in Beverly Hills. In Hollywood, the name Cointreau instantly created a buzz that caused people to open their homes to me, and started a chain of social events that had less to do with my career than with my name. Once again I was unexpectedly drawn into a high-profile social scene, with my name in the gossip columns. At first I thought this could only be beneficial to my career.

I had never thought much about how others perceived my family name. I had noticed that over the years many people would come up to me with a story about how Cointreau liqueur had impacted their lives. Sometimes it was their first drink or it had marked a special occasion they could never forget. It seemed to hold a glamour and a fascination in many people's past.

When one of the top agents offered to handle me, he told me that my life was what he aspired to—my social life, that is, which he had read about in the newspapers. All he wanted was to be in that social milieu. But I was aiming for something entirely different: I wanted to work. On stage was the one place I knew if I was good or bad, and no one could tell me otherwise. I was sure of who I was and the kind of performance I had given.

However, I could not complain about the life the agent had been reading about in the newspapers—it was very exciting. Although the Golden Age of Hollywood had passed, I was invited everywhere and felt fortunate to be in the company of many legendary stars.

At a party at Tony Bennett's house I found myself

uncharacteristically speechless when I was immediately introduced to two men standing *together* in front of the fireplace—Fred Astaire and Gene Kelly. It was a magical evening, made even more so when Cary Grant came over and asked if I would like another drink.

After dinner, I was sitting on the couch speaking to one of the nicest gentlemen I have ever met in my life, Danny Thomas. At one point in our conversation, he stopped me and said, "I think my wife wants you to sing." There was a small band in the corner of the living room, so with very little prodding, I got up and sang *"La Vie En Rose."*

Another unforgettable evening was at the producer Ross Hunter's house. I was talking to the columnist Dorothy Manners when she looked over my shoulder and said, "Here comes Mae, in her virginal whites."

Mae West was then in her eighties, but she was done up the way we all remembered her for so many years—the long blonde hair and the clinging white gown—hanging on the arm of her muscleman, and swinging her hips when she walked, the way we had seen her do in so many films.

When Ross introduced me to her, I was speechless for the second time in my life. But in her best Mae West manner, she immediately put me at ease when she looked me up and down, smiled, and said, "Hiya, honey."

At the end of the evening, all the other famous faces became just a blur in comparison to the inimitable Mae West, who completely seduced me with her intelligence, her charm, and her persona. It was an almost surreal experience for me, conversing with the famous "Diamond Lil" of Broadway and movie history, the one whose work Arthur MacArthur had introduced me to so many years before in little art theaters in New York City.

Gloria Swanson was another living legend who entered my life when our friends Ellen and Ian Graham invited Jim and me to dine with her.

Miss Swanson had been one of the great stars of the silent screen, and in 1950 she became a legend forever when she gave an unforgettable performance as the faded movie star Norma Desmond in the classic film *Sunset Boulevard*. Ellen was the only photographer that Gloria Swanson would allow to photograph her in the last fifteen years of her life. Ellen and Ian stipulated that when I made reservations, it should be at a restaurant that specialized in seafood, and I should request a discreet table in the back.

The evening literally started off with a bang when Miss Swanson approached our car at the Beverly Wilshire Hotel, where she was staying, and the engine blew up. Jim stayed to take care of the car while the rest of us took other transportation to the restaurant. Even though I knew about Miss Swanson's passion for health food and nutrition, I was a bit taken aback, as we got into the car, at the very first words she ever spoke to me: "You know, Africans eliminate four and a half pounds a day." My only thought, which I was too polite to say, was, "No shit!"

The "discreet table" I had requested turned out to be a huge round banquette in the center of the room, with a spotlight on it. Miss Swanson was so uncomfortable that with within a few minutes we got up and made our exit.

Ellen and Ian then invited us to go to their home, where they had organic tacos in their freezer. When Jim tracked us down by phone, Miss Swanson, who had barely met him, insisted on taking the call and very graciously told him where to find us, and that she was looking forward to seeing him.

The most impressive part of meeting Miss Swanson was how unlike Norma Desmond in *Sunset Boulevard* she was. She was just a good old gal, wonderful, intelligent, friendly, and thoroughly at ease with us.

Knowing that she had a reputation for tremendous charisma onscreen, I asked her exactly what her definition of charisma was. She thought seriously for a moment, and then answered, "It's an energy."

Later, in New York City, she was the only star I ever walked with down Madison Avenue whose mere presence literally stopped traffic—even in her late seventies.

It was during this Hollywood period in the 1970s that my two other mothers, Ethel and Lee, got to know each other well. Ethel loved coming out to the West Coast to promote her latest project on the TV talk shows, primarily Johnny Carson or Merv Griffin. Whenever she came out, we would have a dinner party for her, or go out to dinner after her work was done.

When Ethel was recording her disco album (fourteen of her biggest hits done with a disco beat), she stopped by every night to play us the latest background track the musicians had laid out for her. She was like an excited schoolgirl as she sang along with the music. She admitted she had nearly driven the person next to her on the plane crazy when she plugged in the earphones to her Walkman and rehearsed all the way from New York to L.A. But she had a ball. Every new endeavor was the most exciting thing that ever happened to her and she gave it her all.

When in L.A., Ethel always stayed at the Beverly Hills Hotel, and always in the same room, 102 if I'm not mistaken. Every evening, no matter how late, she would go to the front desk and check all of her charges for the day. That was Ethel—a star, a legend, and still a secretary from Astoria!

Amid the slew of parties, I met Marshall Edson, who owned a Beverly Hills cabaret called Ye Little Club, where Joan Rivers used to try out her new material. He gave me an audition and immediately hired me for what turned out to be the first of several engagements.

Before my first show, I needed a pianist and someone to organize a band—so whom did I call? No less than the great Henry Mancini himself, of course! He was most gracious, and recommended some excellent musicians.

My opening night at Ye Little Club was filled with press and Hollywood celebrities. Before the show, Lee Lehman gave a dinner party at the restaurant next door, but I was too nervous to attend. However, I needn't have worried—once I walked on stage, the audience treated me like an old friend.

It was during this first engagement at Ye Little Club that I collected two of the most treasured compliments of my career.

One was from the movie director Vincente Minnelli, whom I met for the first time on opening night. He had just returned from Venice, where he had directed what turned out to be his final picture, *A Matter Of Time*, starring his daughter Liza. After my show he told me how much he admired my work. Then he said, "Tomorrow I'd like you to come over to the house so I can give you notes like I do Liza!" *That* was an accolade I'll never forget.

The next day Jim and I drove down Sunset Boulevard to his house, which was situated on a huge corner lot. The house itself reminded me of Norma Desmond's mansion in the movie *Sunset Boulevard*—it was evident that no improvements had been made for many years. Where the legends of Hollywood had once been entertained, the carpets were threadbare and the furniture had a look of neglected grandeur.

Mr. Minnelli, impeccably dressed as always, greeted us at the door and took us through the house to the back porch, where we sat and discussed my show. His "notes" about lighting and staging were brilliant—pure Minnelli—but some of his ideas were much too ambitious for the confines of a tiny Beverly Hills nightclub where the lighting consisted of a single spotlight that was either on or off. Even though I could not implement all of his suggestions at the moment, we took notes for later use in a larger venue.

Mr. Minnelli was one of the most generous gentlemen I have ever met—this was the sort of gesture that you don't often find in Hollywood. And we remained friends for the rest of his life.

The second compliment I treasured came from my "other mother,"

Ethel Merman, who had first seen me singing while I was dodging showgirls on the Copacabana stage in New York City. After my show at Ye Little Club, she kissed me and bellowed, "That was great, Tony. *Now ya know what you're doin'!*"

LAVENDER TULIPS

With all the places my career was taking me, it didn't matter if I worked out of Los Angeles or New York. Late in 1979, I was invited to go back to the East Coast to sing at a benefit for Planned Parenthood that Paul Newman and Joanne Woodward were sponsoring in Connecticut. I jumped at the opportunity, and once Jim and I were in New York, it felt like home again. We decided to stay.

Being in New York also brought me back to the city where my "other mothers," Lee and Ethel, now lived. They were both getting older, and being nearby made it possible for us to make the most of the time we had left to be together.

After Little Ethel's death, my friendship with her mother deepened. Over the years, Ethel and I were on the phone several times a day and nothing was too trivial for us to share.

One of the things I loved most about Ethel was her infectious enthusiasm. Every little thing that happened to her was the most exciting thing in the world. However large or small, it didn't matter. When she and Jim and I were invariably seated at the best table in a restaurant, she would turn to us in awe and say, "Wow! Look at us!"

Her little-girl quality was also evident when we would walk home from a restaurant, and she would stop in front of department stores and create elaborate scenarios for the mannequins in the windows. The three of us would roar with laughter while we elaborated on the silly stories she invented. The roles she played on stage may have been loud and brassy but in her heart she always remained little Ethel Agnes Zimmermann from Astoria, Queens.

Sundays, we would often spend the day at flea markets in the New York City area. The one we went to most often was a gigantic one that filled Roosevelt Raceway. First we would have a tuna sandwich and a cup of tea in the coffee shop, while fans looked on in disbelief, and then we would work our way through the crowds milling around the hundreds of stalls, looking for bargains.

Ethel would buy inexpensive pieces of antique jewelry. She would take them home, wash them thoroughly with a toothbrush, and then wear her new "jewels" proudly the next time we went out.

One time she bought stacks of little notepads with other people's names printed on them, apparently abandoned at the printer's. When we asked her why she wanted pads with other people's names on them, Ethel, in her practical way, said that they were cheap and would be useful for taking notes when she was on the phone. I couldn't argue with her reasoning.

Whether at the flea markets or in a restaurant, Ethel always had the illusion that she could be anonymous whenever she wanted to, just by putting on her big round rose-colored sunglasses. On another excursion to the flea markets, she began to bargain for a piece of costume jewelry that she liked, then decided that she wanted to think about it and would come back the following week. Ethel reassured us, "They won't raise the price on it, because *nobody* knows who I am with these glasses on."

When we returned to the stall the following week, the saleswoman took one look at her and said, "Oh, hi, Ethel, you're back!" Ethel was obviously not as anonymous as she thought she was.

After *Gypsy* closed, Ethel no longer wanted to commit to the long runs and restrictions that were always required of her as the star of a hit Broadway show. She wanted to be free to enjoy life. She often told me, "Broadway's been good to me, but I've been good to Broadway. It's time to live for Ethel."

I don't think she ever regretted her decision, but once when we were in a cab passing through the Theater District to attend a matinee, Ethel told me, "I don't understand why, but every time I go to Broadway I get an awful feeling in the pit of my stomach."

She couldn't explain it, but I wondered—was it the memories of her glory days on Broadway when she was a young wife and mother, before the father of her children had killed himself, before her daughter had died, or she had divorced four husbands?

I remember when I went to see Ethel recreate her role of Annie Oakley in a six-month revival of *Annie Get Your Gun* at Lincoln Center in New York. Afterwards, Ethel offered me a ride home. On the way across town, she told me that she prayed every day for a man to love her. That's all she wanted. She said, "I pray so hard that it has to happen." Sadly, it never did.

On April 7, 1983, Ethel was scheduled to fly from New York to Los Angeles to sing "There's No Business Like Show Business" at the Academy Awards ceremonies. A few minutes before she was scheduled to leave, she called me from the Surrey Hotel where she lived, to say that the car was waiting downstairs and that she would call me from Beverly Hills.

During our brief conversation I noticed that she badly mispronounced a word—something that she had often done in the last year. Before, when she had mispronounced a word or a phrase she would laugh and say, "Oh, I'm all right," and say it again properly. This time when she said, "Oh, I'm all right," she again said it the wrong way. It may not have seemed like much but it bothered me all the same. There seemed to be a pattern emerging. It made me uneasy.

When she hung up the phone after our conversation, she went to the large mirror—the one on which her son had had etched:

The light of God surrounds me.
The love of God enfolds me.
The power of God protects me.
The presence of God watches over me.
Wherever I am, God is.

When she reached the mirror to freshen her lipstick before going downstairs, the lipstick fell from her hand. Within moments she was having a seizure. She painfully crawled to the hotel phone to ask for help but found that she could only make garbled sounds. The operator immediately understood something was wrong and alerted the manager to go up to Miss Merman's apartment. Slowly Ethel dragged herself through the living room to the foyer where she managed to unlock the steel bolt on her front door.

The next morning I received a phone call at seven from Ethel's financial advisor and friend, Irving Katz, to tell me that she had apparently had a "mild" stroke and was in the hospital. I was very concerned, but felt she would have a good chance of overcoming a mild stroke. A few minutes later I received a call from a nurse at the hospital saying that Ethel had insisted that she call me so I wouldn't worry when I didn't hear from her that day. Thank God, Irving had prepared me for the call. At the time, I thought that the nurse was only calling me as a convenience for Ethel; I had no idea that Ethel could hardly utter an intelligible word.

Her son, Bob, immediately flew to New York and stayed by her side while she went through an operation on her brain. Everyone was very secretive about her condition and told the press that it was only temporary. This only worried me more.

The first time I visited her at the hospital, I sat in the waiting room with Bob, talking with the elderly family doctor who had treated Mom and Pop Zimmermann. The doctor was very blunt in assessing the situation and did not feel the need to cover up the truth of Ethel's condition in front of me. It was then that I learned for the first time that she had a malignant and inoperable brain tumor, and that in his opinion any treatment would only cause unnecessary suffering and a painful prolonging of her life.

After he left, Bob turned to me and said, "Well, at least now you know the truth."

When Ethel was a little girl, her father would play the piano for her when she entertained the troops during World War I. She was no more than six years old when she sang "She's Me Pal" to her mother, sitting in the first row.

Many times, driving home from flea markets, Ethel would burst into song, and "She's Me Pal" was always one of my favorites. When she was in the hospital and having difficulty communicating, Jim and I had a small needlepoint pillow made for her with the words, "She's Me Pal." The morning we gave it to her, she started to cry, put the pillow up to her cheek, and sang the whole song—perfectly. It was probably the last performance Ethel Merman ever gave.

Ethel was not told the truth about her condition, and went home after a few weeks with only Prednisone to lessen the size of the tumor on her brain. She temporarily regained the ability to communicate, but it was only a matter of time before the tumor continued to grow.

At first, in spite of her seventy-five years, she cried and said, "I'm so young." And she *was* young—young in spirit, and, until the cancer started growing in her brain, filled with energy and health. As time went on, I had to lean very close in order to hear her whisper, "I'll never wear my pretty dresses again." By then she knew it was all over and I understood how much she had loved getting "all gussied up," as she would call it. Finally there was only one word left that she could articulate, "Terrible... Terrible... Terrible!"

In the last eight months she lost her power of speech, the use of her arms, the use of her legs. This was my friend, with whom I had spoken sometimes five times a day on the phone. Nothing was too small or too insignificant for us to share. Our communication had always been so important to her. Every day she lost a little more, until she could only lie in her bed, mute and unmoving. It was agony for us all.

The first time I realized that Ethel could no longer communicate at all was the day she could only greet Jim and me with a rising crescendo of garbled cries. When the nurse told her to calm herself, I took her hand and told her, "Ethel, go ahead—moan, cry, scream—whatever you want. This is just terrible what's happening to you."

On Ethel's last birthday, a month before she died, her son, Bob, asked me if I was coming over. I had already thought about it and told him I couldn't imagine trying to wish her a happy birthday under these conditions. His reply was only one word, "Chicken!" I knew then that he was right and that I just didn't know how to face dealing with a usually joyful occasion under such tragic circumstances. In spite of my fears, I went anyway.

As I walked the few blocks to her home, I spotted some lavender tulips in a store window. This was always her favorite color, so I went in and bought them, all the while dreading what I would find when I walked into her room.

To my surprise, I found her lying in bed with a peaceful smile on her face. On impulse, I took the flowers and placed them all around her, decorating the bed in which she lay, immobile. She smiled and laughed like a young girl as I sat next to her and talked. It was, of course, a one-sided conversation, but seeing that beautiful smile made it easier for *me* to accept her terrible agony too.

On February 15, 1984, Bob called me at 7:00 a.m. to tell me that his mother had died earlier that morning. It had taken ten months.

Ethel had on many occasions told Jim and me that she was looking forward to someday being reunited with "Mom and Pop and my Ethel." That day had come sooner than we all thought.

I went to the hotel where she had lived to say my final goodbyes. I knew my life would never be the same without Ethel. When I entered the apartment, I fought back the tears. My family's mantras that "Bluebloods don't cry," and that emotions were to be controlled at all costs, were now nearly impossible for me to live up to. I walked into the bedroom where she lay and kissed my second "other mother's" surprisingly cold and lifeless cheek for the last time.

A few nights later, Bob took the urn with his mother's ashes and rode downtown in a long black limousine. He drove past all the great Broadway theaters where his mother had thrilled audiences for decades and saw the marquees dim their lights at curtain time for one minute in her honor.

That night, the producer Alexander Cohen told the television newscaster Dennis Cunningham, "*You* can be replaced, and *I* can be replaced. But Ethel Merman can never be replaced."

A year before Ethel had become ill, Jim and I went to her apartment one evening to pick her up and take her out to dinner. While we were sitting in her living room having a drink, she told us she had talked to her lawyer that day about rewriting her will. She turned to me and said, "What'll I do with the gang in the closet? You want 'em?"

I knew that the "gang" referred to the cremated remains of her mother and father, Mom and Pop Zimmermann, and her daughter, Little Ethel, that she had brought home to New York from Colorado, and the ashes of her former husband, the father of her children, Robert Levitt. In her later years she had derived great solace from having their ashes near her, in her closet. At Christmastime she would sing carols to them, and on their birthdays she would sing "Happy Birthday."

She asked the question so casually that for a moment I didn't know if she was kidding, or serious. I didn't know whether I should say, "Yes, of course I'll take them," or what my common sense would dictate, which was that her family might want them. So I told her, "What about your son, Bob, and your two grandchildren? Maybe they would like to have them."

It was instantly apparent that I had said the wrong thing—that she had given it a lot of thought and took my answer as a rejection. I knew her so well that I could see in her face that she was hurt. She tried to look casual and said, "Then I'll give them to Bill," who had been Little Ethel's husband and was the father of her two grandchildren. There was no way I could take back the words I had spoken in ignorance.

Within a couple of years of Ethel's death, I got a call from Bill, who said that he was moving out of town, and asked if I would please take the ashes, which by now included Ethel herself. I always believed that Ethel manipulated events from above, and got her way after all.

While Jim and I were helping Bob make up the list of people to be invited to Ethel's memorial service, Bob asked us, "Is there anything of Mom's that you would like? Anything!"

Jim and I both knew exactly what would mean the most to us: on the table in her foyer was a small Christmas tree that Ethel had treasured and lit every evening of her life. We felt that it represented her spirit more than anything else. We've now had it in our home for almost thirty years, and we also light it every night just as she did.

"Le Tout Paris"

As painful as it had been to watch Ethel's suffering and death, in a strange way her death freed me to leave New York and begin a new phase of my life, far away.

In 1984, I was appearing in a nightclub in New York called Freddy's with "The Incomparable Hildegarde," who was then in her middle seventies. After a lifetime in show business, she could still delight an audience. Together and separately we sang new songs and old favorites in French and English; she even accompanied me at the piano while I sang *"La Vie En Rose."*

On opening night, a reporter for the French newspaper *Le Figaro* saw the show and insisted that Pierre Cardin, who lived in Paris, should hear me sing. What I did not know at the time was that Mr. Cardin was not only one of the great couturiers of the world, but was also a powerful figure in show business in France.

Mr. Cardin arrived in New York a week later and invited me to his apartment to sing for him. When I finished the last note of the song "Memory" from *Cats*, he immediately offered to launch my career in Europe with a gala at the world-renowned Maxim's in Paris, which he owned. He told me that only a handful of people, such as Maria Callas, had ever sung there. It was an offer I couldn't refuse—although, obviously, it meant that I had to return to Paris.

When Jim and I arrived in Paris, the old fears and insecurities of my childhood came rushing back, and depression threatened to overwhelm me. But between Cardin's legendary accomplishments and my family name, the newspapers were already filled with prominent stories about my evening at Maxim's. It was clear that I had to stay.

The afternoon of the gala I went to Maxim's for rehearsal and found myself surrounded by an art nouveau setting and magnificent *boiserie* meticulously preserved from another era. The engineers from Mr. Cardin's theater, L'Espace Cardin, were still setting up the sound system for the evening, so I went upstairs to visit the historic bar I remembered sitting in with my parents many years before.

The bartender, an elderly gentleman, greeted me with stories of my great-uncle André Cointreau, who had been one of their illustrious patrons. Uncle André had been famous for his many mistresses, one of whom had been a well-known French actress of her day.

The bartender's stories reminded me of when Uncle André was in his seventies and attended a luncheon given by my grandmother at Château Brillant. That day he met Juliette, a plump, very pretty, middle-aged "poor relation" of Maman Genevieve's second husband, the General. Juliette, who often stayed with us at Château Brillant, was not disappointed to find herself the object of André's interest, and within a short time she became his last mistress.

When his long-suffering wife, Aunt Flo, found out about Juliette, she tearfully told my mother that she had had enough—she was finally ready to divorce the old rogue. My mother, who was a practical woman, advised her that after a lifetime of putting up with his cheating, it would be foolish at her age not to retain her position as "the wife." Aunt Flo took my mother's advice and remained Mrs. Cointreau for the rest of her life.

What no one else in the family knew was that after that luncheon at Château Brillant, my mother, who had noticed the attraction between Juliette and Uncle André, had suggested to Juliette (who was married to an impoverished intellectual) that an affair with Uncle André would be a good opportunity to improve her financial situation. Despite Juliette's husband and Uncle André's wife, the affair turned out to be a love match. To my mother's horror, whenever she saw Uncle André, he took great delight in recounting his renewed sexual prowess with his new mistress.

Although Juliette was no longer welcomed by my grandmother at Château Brillant and was ostracized by most of the family, I always had a soft spot in my heart for her. I was touched to hear that after Uncle André died in her arms, she kept her promise to him and accompanied his body to the gates of his family home, where she kissed him one last time, got out of the ambulance, and retired to Biarritz on the money and jewels he had given her.

I left the bartender and memories of Uncle André and went to check out the sound system. That evening, when I walked up to the stage at Maxim's, I discovered that Mr. Cardin had also planned to make this a unique event in the world of fashion by inviting many of the great international designers to sit at one table—Marc Bohan, Paco Rabanne, Jean Louis Scherrer, Courrèges, and Claude Montana, to name just a few.

The other guests included what they call *"Le Tout Paris,"* all of the top social world of the city. Show business was represented in part by Jean-Michel Rouzière, the great French stage producer who had introduced *La Cages Aux Folles* in one of his historic Parisian theaters. Since I was not really French, I did not know who he was and thought him slightly mad when he insisted he wanted to build a show around me.

As a matter of fact, I did not know who most of the elite were, except for one American, Pat Kennedy Lawford, the late John F. Kennedy's sister, who years later became a good friend of mine. (Pat remained a friend even after a fragile Louis XVI chair she was sitting in collapsed under her during a dinner party at my home. Her head missed the wall by inches, and, as I helped her up from the floor, she brushed herself off and put everyone's fears to rest by laughing, "You don't put an antique in an antique!")

For the show, we put together a variety of songs in French and English that we thought the audience would appreciate. Mr. Cardin's only request was that I sing "Memory" from *Cats*, as I had done for him in New York.

A few days before the gala at Maxim's, the reporter from *Le Figaro* (the one who had introduced me to Pierre Cardin) gave me a cassette of spiritual songs. I fell in love with one called "Freely, Freely" and decided it would be a perfect finale for this glamorous event.

At the end of the show, I thanked Mr. Cardin and then said, "But let us not forget the One who is truly responsible for this beautiful evening." I sang "Freely, Freely" in its entirety, and then came down from the stage and did it again very softly while I walked through the audience, touching them as I passed.

I don't think many spiritual songs had ever been sung at Maxim's, and the newspapers thought it a daring thing to do. They also said it worked because of my sincerity. I never doubted that it would.

I could not have been called a religious person, but my interest in spiritual songs was not new. It had begun when I was a child and my mother took me to see a movie called *A Member of the Wedding*. I sat spellbound as Ethel Waters sang "His Eye Is On The Sparrow" *a capella*, with one arm around a very young Julie Harris (who many years later I had the pleasure of introducing to her idol, Mother Teresa) and the other around an even younger Brandon de Wilde.

For most of the movie, I never knew that Julie Harris's tomboy character was really a girl. I may have been too young to understand the movie, but not the song. It was my first taste of inspirational songs; and although as a child I would hide in the closet to avoid being taken to Mass on Sundays, I fell in love with the music.

So when a producer of gospel music shows came up to me after my performance at Maxim's and asked if I would like to star in his new show and tour Europe with his company, I jumped at the opportunity. The idea was so appealing that I quickly expanded my repertoire of gospel songs and joined them—thinking that this would be the answer to my dreams. I traveled through France and Switzerland with them, and at first it was a joy.

When we arrived back in Paris for our first gospel concert at L'Espace Cardin theater, most of the Cointreau family—many of whom I had not seen since I was a teenager—showed up. They had never seen me on stage before, but that night they saw one of the most inspired performances of my career. Towards the end of the show I launched into "The Battle Hymn of the Republic." I sang the first verse *a capella*, with only a steady drum beat behind me. Then the orchestra began to play, and I started hearing lone voices singing in different parts of the theater—some of them in harmony. With each chorus, more people joined in, and by the end of the song, the whole audience was singing with me. It was totally spontaneous and one of the most moving experiences of my life.

Although the audiences were consistently wonderful and I loved the music, it soon dawned on me that some of the people I was involved with were the most bigoted, racist, jealous human beings I had ever worked with. When we did our second concert in Paris, months later, I peered through a window that overlooked the inside of the theater and noticed that all the black people had been seated in the third balcony. This so enraged me that I flew downstairs, screamed at the producer and informed him that we had had a civil war in my country over such discrimination. I went through with the show but knew it would be my last.

I was greeting friends and family backstage after this show when a young man came running up to me crying out, "You have to record, you have to record!" His name was Marc François, and he was the man responsible for getting me away from gospel shows and back into "show business." As much as I longed to go back home to America, this was another offer I couldn't refuse.

Within a year Marc was the president of his own company and, even though we never aimed for the most commercial projects, our work was always critically respected. And instead of going home to America, I spent the better part of the next ten years doing concerts and working in recording studios in Paris.

Working for Marc was always professionally challenging and I loved it. But my old demons had not retreated, and being in Paris depressed me as much as it had in my childhood. Each time I went back, the first three days in Paris were always the hardest for me, but the depression never went away completely. It was simply masked by throwing myself into my work.

When I entered the recording studio or a theater, it was like being a mole hidden deep in the ground. I lived in an artificial world with no windows. But the moment I emerged I had to steel myself to face the streets where I had felt so lost and frightened as a child.

Our apartment was in a part of Paris called the Ile St. Louis, with cobblestone streets and quaint shops that resembled a small town. Many people would consider this their dream place to live, but for me it only made life bearable.

In our apartment Jim created a cocoon with colors that lifted my spirits. The drapes were permanently closed so I did not have to face the streets outside. The bedroom, where I spent most of my time, was done in yellow with a colorful material of birds and flowers. It was the best we could do to bring sunshine into my private world, and I stayed in my artificially lit seclusion as much as possible.

I left my apartment for the eightieth birthday celebration at the Folies Bergère for its owner, Helene Martini. The orchestra seats had been removed and tables brought in so that guests could have dinner. All the stars in Paris attended, but I was the only person asked to perform that night. In the middle of the dance floor, facing the dais where Madame Martini was seated, I sang Peter Allen's song, "Once Before I Go"—maybe not very fitting to sing for an eighty-year-old lady, but it was very well received.

As the evening ended, I was surrounded by so many pe
complimenting me on my performance and wishing me well, that
was feeling a warm glow of success at all the praise from this show-
business savvy crowd.

A beautiful woman that I recognized immediately as Dalida, a great
singing star, took me aside. France felt that it owned her, but she had
performed throughout Europe for many years, and had actually been
born to an Italian family living in Egypt. She first told me how much
she had enjoyed my performance, and then leaned in very close and
gave me advice from her own life's struggles and heartbreak: "That
was wonderful, but don't think that any of these people are your
friends." With that, she kissed me and walked away.

In May of 1987 I was heartbroken, as was all of Europe, to hear
that she had committed suicide. It is possible that she never knew
how much she really was loved.

It may seem ironic that life repeatedly took me back to Paris, but there
turned out to be unexpectedly positive rewards in being forced to
spend so much time there. Professionally speaking, I was allowed to
do things I would never have dreamed of.

But a more surprising aspect was the timing as far as my interest
in the Cointreau family business was concerned. I had never
considered myself to be a businessman, but as it turned out, all of
my shares might have been imperiled if I had not been in France
to protect them.

THE FAMILY PACT

Even though they had created a successful family business, the Cointreaus were a contentious lot and had often been at one another's throats. First cousins and brothers would outwardly smile at one another, while secretly plotting power plays behind their backs.

As a young man, my father had accompanied his uncle Louis Cointreau throughout the world, creating a market for Cointreau liqueurs in more than a hundred countries, but he was never a major power in the family business. In his youth, his two uncles were in charge; later, his three much younger cousins held all the cards because they inherited vast fortunes at a very early age, whereas my father was in his seventies when his mother died. So the roll of the family dice had made his cousins (one of them an only child) the major players, the only ones who really knew what the shares were worth, and they doled out the dividends any way they pleased—no questions asked.

Many years before, a Cointreau family pact had been created, whereby no one was allowed to sell their shares to anyone outside the family. If a husband died, the widow could receive dividends but only relatives could own the shares.

In 1979, my father had divided his shares between my brother and me. At the time, he told us that his cousins had led him to believe that there would never be much of an income from his shares. However, this did not make sense to me, since there were only a handful of shareholders and the worldwide brand name alone had to be of considerable value.

Shortly after I arrived in Paris for my appearance at Maxim's (which the family had read about in all the newspapers), a faction of my family attempted to convince me to join them in abolishing the family pact. Later I suspected that that was also the main reason they had come to see me perform in the gospel show at L'Espace Cardin.

For most of my life I had felt that my family frowned upon me for being the "sensitive" child, and now I was the "artistic" one who had gone into the questionable world of show business. When I was a child I had overheard my uncle Denis say to the family seated around the living room at Château Brillant, "If I had a son like Jacques-Henri I would kill myself!" A rare flash of psychic intuition immediately told me that although he was a young man, he would never have any children of his own—and he never did.

Common sense told me that the family must have a hidden agenda in wanting to abolish the pact, so I sought legal counsel. My lawyer confirmed that everything I owned would be in peril if I signed the agreement—the two majority stockholders who wanted to abolish the pact could then make for themselves any deal that they wished with a conglomerate, and leave me out in the cold.

In an effort to get rid of me, they offered in a series of meetings to buy my shares for a pittance. I refused. As luck would have it, I had discovered during one of the meetings that I held exactly enough shares to be the deciding factor in the vote on the family pact.

As I sat in a taxi on my way to the final meeting in which we would vote, I was sure of my decision, but uncomfortable over the fury that would ensue when I defied the family hierarchy. Their decisions had never before been questioned. These were people who had lived a lifetime in a tiny world they had always controlled by the good fortune of inheritance. Now I was going to need all my strength to face them in what I will always refer to as my "Joan Crawford 'Don't fuck with me, fellas,' moment" (from the movie *Mommie Dearest*). I remembered my mother's letters to her family when she was escaping the Germans at the beginning of the Second World War, and how much like her I was. I knew that I could rise to the occasion and face the formidable forces of my Cointreau family.

While crossing one of the bridges of Paris, I prayed for comfort and reassurance that I was not alone. At that moment, an extraordinary feeling of warmth and love crept through my body. All I could do was say a silent, "Thank you." I knew I was on the right track.

My brother, Richard, the president of Cointreau in Brazil, had given me his power of attorney and then made a dash for South America, leaving me to face the music alone. I must admit, though, that we remained united and in total accord in our decision to veto the resolution. As it turned out, his presence would have been for moral support only, since either of us had enough power to veto the vote on our own.

I was treated with kid gloves as a handful of us sat around what seemed to be the largest conference table in the world. As soon as the usual boring business was dispensed with, the President announced that we would now vote for the resolution to abolish the family pact by a show of hands. As the hands shot up around the table, I took a deep breath and announced, "No."

The President patted my arm and, as though talking to a child, let me know that I didn't understand—we were now voting *for* the resolution. He reassured me that I would sooner or later get it right, and we voted again. Once more I looked at my family and said, "No."

It was probably impossible for this man to accept the fact that I might have an inkling as to what I was doing, so he patiently explained it all *again*, and for the third time I answered, "No," and added that my brother and I were in agreement to vote against abolishing the family pact. Now it finally dawned on the group that we were serious.

There was a moment of complete silence as they digested the

information. My godfather, his face purple, turned to me in a rage and screamed, "You've stabbed us in the back!" and stormed out.

At this point I had to give the President credit for perseverance. After my three negative votes, he called me into another room and informed me that if I didn't change my mind, they could not go ahead with a secret deal (which I considered questionable) that they had made to purchase my uncle Jean's shares for a pittance in exchange for his vote to abolish the pact. Again I declined and said that I would be happy, at a calmer time, to explain exactly why my brother and I had voted against it.

Although I had protected my interests in that round, I knew we were not through yet.

Upon arriving at my lawyer's office the next day, I sensed before we even shook hands that he had been seduced by promises of greater things than I could offer him if he changed my mind. He then suggested for the first time that I should go along with the plans of that faction of my family and sign the agreement. How stupid of him to think that a total change of opinion overnight, for no good reason, would not arouse my suspicions! I cut our meeting short, paid him, and went out to find the meanest shark of a lawyer in all of Paris to protect my interests. If this was how the game was played, I had no fear.

Ultimately, I found the most hateful, powerful lawyer I had ever met in my life. The only way I could interest such a man was by intimating that there would be a substantial financial reward in store for him if he were to maneuver a deal with a conglomerate to buy the whole company. Of course, he also had to secure the future of my brother and me within that structure.

It worked like a dream. Within a few months my brother and I were on the Cointreau Board of Directors and had a contract including us equally in any outside deals. *Now* we could abolish the family pact.

It was never easy dealing with this lawyer, but my family acknowledged that he was brilliant and asked our permission to consult him in other company business. I was not surprised when I read in the papers that his brother had been posthumously accused of collaborating with the Nazis during World War II.

Since the reality of today's world dictates that only conglomerates survive, we eventually merged the Cointreau company and all its products with the Remy Martin Cognac family's empire. It was not only a positive move for Cointreau, but my brother and I finally discovered our actual worth.

I find it ironic that the Remy Martin Cognac family should once again have entered my life, all those years after Mr. Renaud helped my mother when she was fleeing the Nazis during World War II. By the time of the merger, Mr. Renaud was long dead, and ours were possibly the only two major family-owned liquor businesses left that had not been absorbed by a conglomerate. As far as I'm concerned, it was a merger made in heaven.

But if I had not been in Paris for my own work in 1984, I might easily have signed the paper abolishing the family pact without giving it a second thought, and the merger might never have happened.

The Cointreau family members I knew as a child at Château Brillant, mostly my father's cousins and their wives, are almost all dead now. Life took its toll on them—no one gets away from this world Scot-free.

A few years ago I felt a need to reach out to them and tell them that I only remember the good times—mainly the large luncheon and dinner parties at Château Brillant and La Richardière, and that in my eyes they will always remain the vital and in some cases beautiful young people I knew then. It had been ten years since I had had any contact with any of them, and without exception my every phone call or letter was responded to with enthusiasm and joy.

My last call was to my uncle Denis, whom my brother and I had both loved like an older brother before the fight over my grandmother's inheritance damaged our relationship. He was living in Angers, in the advanced stages of Alzheimer's. I spoke to his wife, Marie-Geneviève, who was watching her husband become a shadow of the vibrant young man she had married more than fifty years ago.

I was touched during our conversation when Denis, in a moment of lucidity, understood that it was *me* on the phone; he managed to say how happy he was that I called, and ended with, *"Je t'embrasse"* ("I embrace you"). Years of conflict had melted away in a moment.

The old power plays and battles over money don't seem to matter much any more.

The Best of Friends

In late September, 1986, I came home from the recording studio in Paris and phoned my answering machine in New York. There was a message from my father's doctor saying not to worry, but my 85-year-old father had been bleeding from an ulcer in his stomach after having taken two aspirins for his arthritis. He was now in the intensive care unit of Lenox Hill Hospital—where both my mother and Tata had died.

At first I believed the doctor's reassurances and tried to keep to my schedule. I was at the ballet that evening when I thought, "How in the world can I be sitting in this theater while my father is alone in a hospital in New York?"

I went home and booked the next flight to the United States.

My father lived for another three weeks in the intensive care unit and I was with him every moment. As his condition worsened, I vowed that I would "get it right." This time I almost made it to the end.

On the last evening of my father's life, the doctor told me that most of my father's major organs had shut down and that his heart had begun to fail. The words barely penetrated the outer recesses of my brain. Once again it was not possible for me to acknowledge that I was losing someone I loved, and I fled the hospital. An hour later, my father died.

As soon as I got the call that he was dead, I began to struggle with the guilt of having deserted him in his last moments. But as I laid him to rest beside my mother, I looked back on the last fifteen years of his life—the years when I finally got to know this stranger I had called my father.

After Mother's death, my father, who had a reputation as a great chef, offered to cook lunch for me at his home in New York. Before going, I said to Jim, "What am I going to say to this man whom I hardly know?" To my surprise, the conversation flowed freely, and for the next fifteen years we were able to open up to each other and share our lives. Ultimately we became the best of friends.

In the summer, he would invite Jim and me to stay with him in his home in the Loire Valley in France, where he had bought several cases of an Anjou wine that we particularly loved. He kept this wine in the cellar and would let no one else touch it. Each time we came he let us know that he had saved every bottle of it for us.

A year before he died, he told me that I was the one person he trusted more than any other in the world. Could any son have asked for more?

By the time my father died, I had already realized many of my professional dreams. Now I began to think about fulfilling another dream that I had had for a long time, to give back to the world some of the fruits of my life experience.

And though I didn't know it yet, I would soon meet the little Albanian nun who had long intrigued me—and who would become my *third* "other mother."

PART II

The Last Mother

CALCUTTA

In 1979, Jim and I attended a dinner party in Beverly Hills at which someone asked, "Who in the world would you most like to meet?"

There was a chorus of famous and glamorous names in the arts and politics. And then I said, "Mother Teresa."

Everyone knew who she was, and that she had received the Nobel Peace Prize, but I was not prepared for their hoots of laughter and disbelief. Although I had only very recently heard of Mother Teresa, I had already been deeply inspired by her work with the "poorest of the poor" and her example of unconditional love. In later years, most of the people at the party would have felt honored to meet her, but back then it was probably naive of me to think that she had had as much of an impact on my friends as on me.

I had read that volunteers from around the world were welcome to join in her work. Indelibly imprinted on my brain was a magazine photograph of a volunteer in Mother Teresa's Home for the Dying in Calcutta, carrying a dying man in his arms. The photograph both frightened and inspired me.

I wondered if this could be the deeper meaning that I had been searching for in my life. I remained intrigued by Mother Teresa and in the back of my mind I retained the thought that she might one day bring me from my world of châteaux and show business to the world of "doing small things with great love."

തി മ

It wasn't until 1989, while I was still doing concerts and recording in Europe, that I felt emotionally ready to make the trip to Calcutta and meet Mother Teresa and her Missionaries of Charity, the religious order she had founded in 1950. This is the army of thousands of nuns who are sent all over the world to care for the sick, the dying, the hungry, and especially the unwanted and the unloved.

Religious fervor was certainly not what inspired me to go halfway around the world to volunteer my services. It was the people. I felt an empathy that I hoped would transcend cultural and social barriers. In spite of a lifelong fear of poverty and abandonment, I began to plan my trip to Calcutta, one of the poorest cities in the world, to work in Mother Teresa's Home for the Dying.

I was pleased when Jim agreed to go with me. Unlike me, he is a truly adventurous soul who loves to travel and will go anywhere in the world to see something new. Knowing me as well as he did, he probably suspected that I might need support amid the unrelenting poverty of Calcutta.

When we drove into Calcutta after our long flight from Paris, I could see that the city was in an appalling condition. Beautiful buildings that had once been very grand were now falling apart. There was an immediate assault on all our senses—smell, sight and sound. Legions of homeless were cooking on the sidewalks with dried cow dung, which added to the pollution of the city and infiltrated everything with a not-unpleasant sweet burning smell. It got in your hair, your clothes, and, we discovered later, even in the sheets at the hotel.

Emaciated cows wandered about as they pleased, and zillions of ancient cars careened in all directions. Car horns seemed to have little to do with the flow of traffic, and their cacophonous sounds simply added to the chaos of the city.

In the midst of this immense poverty, we drove to the Oberoi Grand Hotel, a marble palace situated at the end of a long driveway which the beggars and homeless could not enter. What stunned me was that even though there was no gate, they *knew* they could not enter. Inside the hotel, we found the epitome of old-world elegance, while outside, whole families camped out on the sidewalk, trying to survive.

It was early afternoon, so we quickly unpacked and went downstairs for some tea and chicken sandwiches. I said to Jim, "After ten years, my dream is becoming a reality."

At this point I felt quite ecstatic about flying first class halfway around the world, landing in a marble palace, and preparing to offer my services to the poorest of the poor dying in Nirmal Hriday— "Home of the Pure Heart." What's wrong with this picture? Maybe nothing. I certainly believe my motives were pure. Until then I had only known first class, marble palaces, and high tea, so it seemed perfectly natural to be staying in that environment, without realizing the irony of the situation.

After our refreshments, we decided to go to Mother Teresa's headquarters, known as the Motherhouse, and inquire about my volunteering in the Home for the Dying. I still had no idea what I was in for. But I was enthusiastic, if nothing else.

We drove a short distance from the hotel to Lower Circular Road, through the worst poverty I had ever seen in my life. The driver stopped the car, pointed down a narrow street and told us, "The Motherhouse is down there—the little door on the right." I peered out the window and looked down a dark alley lined with desperately poor and handicapped people waiting for someone to come by on their way to see Mother Teresa and give them something—anything.

I stared at the dismal scene and stammered, "I'm not—I can't go down that alley."

The driver seemed to understand my dilemma and said, "I'll go with you."

Not only did he go with us as we inched our way past the sea of human misery—outstretched hands and pleading eyes, deformed and mutilated bodies dressed in rags—but he also had to knock on the door and ring the bell. I couldn't even do *that*. I stood frozen in shock at the horror of what I had just seen in that short walk down the alley from the car to the front door.

It seemed like ages but was probably only a few moments until one of the Sisters opened the door and ushered us inside. I told her that I had come to Calcutta because I wanted to work as a volunteer in the Home for the Dying. She told me to come the next morning for six o'clock Mass—an unheard-of hour for me, since I was used to working in theaters and clubs until late at night—and talk to the Sister in charge of volunteers.

Before we knew it, we were back outside, once again facing the gauntlet of the alley. We had gone only a few steps when an agitated young man appeared directly behind me, breathing down my neck and yelling at me in a language I, of course, did not understand. When we got in the car, he wouldn't let us close the door until two Sisters who were leaving the Motherhouse heard the commotion and rushed over to calm him.

Since it was still early afternoon, we decided to visit the orphanage, Shishu Bhavan, a short distance away. This time there was no alley— the entrance was right on Lower Circular Road. A Sister opened the front door, led us through the courtyard, and invited us in.

The first room she took us through was filled with rows of empty cribs. We understood why they were empty when we entered a large, brightly painted and sunny room with toddlers crawling all over the spotlessly clean floor. They were happily playing with each other and taking turns being cuddled by the Sisters and volunteers.

Some of the children had been found on garbage heaps; others had been brought to the door by unwed mothers or by destitute parents. The parents knew that any time they were financially able to care for their children, they were welcome to take them home. Most of the children seemed healthy and well fed; but on one side of the room we noticed cribs holding young children who looked very ill.

One little girl, no more than two years old, with beautiful black hair and dark eyes, came up to us with her hand in front of her mouth. Sister picked her up and said, "We have a surgeon who's coming to operate on this child's harelip. Doctors come from many countries to volunteer their services for the children." She also told us that Mother Teresa's Missionaries of Charity arrange for many of the orphans to be adopted all over the world. Those who do not find a home are given an education and taught a trade. And when they marry, their spouses often consider the Sisters their "in-laws."

Sister walked with us back through the courtyard where other nuns, volunteers, and some of the older children were putting up colorful paper streamers and garlands of flowers. Mother Teresa had recently been ill, and they were going to entertain her with songs and dances to celebrate her recovery. We were awed by the enormous joy and reverence that went into this expression of love for their beloved Mother Teresa.

The stark image of the rows of cribs for abandoned children haunted me as we left Shishu Bhavan.

Still, we decided to go on to Nirmal Hriday, where I was particularly drawn to working. This was Mother Teresa's first Home for the Dying, which she opened in 1952 in an ancient Hindu temple in a section of Calcutta called Kalighat, and it is often referred to as her first love. It was here that Mother was first allowed to give the destitute and dying people from the streets a place to die, surrounded in peace and love.

As we approached Kalighat, the poverty was beyond anything we had yet encountered. The city seemed to disintegrate before our eyes, with a new level of noise, chaos and desperation.

Outside the front door of Nirmal Hriday, a woman sat on the ground, with her face mostly gone—simply eaten away. It was unnerving, but nothing could deter me at this point. We slid past her and at last I entered the place I had heard so much about.

Inside the entrance was a man who had just died and had been prepared for burial or cremation—whichever his religion dictated. He was neatly dressed, and a beautiful flower had been placed in his hands.

We walked past his body and through an open doorway into a long room with large windows high on the walls and about fifty cots for dying men; on the other side of the building were about fifty cots for women.

Every day Sisters and volunteers combed the city for the "poorest of the poor" lying in the streets and gutters, eaten up by disease and worms, and brought them to Nirmal Hriday to be cared for.

Although it was difficult for us to face so many human beings in such a diseased and skeletal condition, Jim and I both felt it was the most peaceful room we had ever entered in our lives. We stayed only a few minutes. No one spoke to us, but we watched in awe as a young volunteer slowly gave a dying man a drink of water—one drop at a time. This was what I had come so far to witness and, hopefully, be a part of.

Again, we were struck by how clean Nirmal Hriday was and by the effort Mother Teresa's Missionaries of Charity had made to decorate the walls with inspirational pictures and sayings.

When we left this extraordinary home, we were jolted back into the reality of the streets. Jim, ever the consummate shopper, spotted a bazaar nearby and said, "Come on, let's go see what they're selling."

I didn't think I would find my heart's desire in a bazaar in Kalighat, but reluctantly followed Jim around the stalls anyway. Then for the second time that afternoon a beggar came up behind me, screaming in a language I did not understand. When it became obvious that he was not going to go away, I turned to Jim and asked, "Jim, could we please go back to the car?"

At the same time, I glanced over to where we had left the car, and noticed a crowd swarming all over it, with our driver calmly standing by.

It was a mystery to me why our old car had become such an attraction and I had no idea how we were going to maneuver ourselves past this throng. We knew they all wanted money, but we had been advised by the Sisters not to give any out—it would only create more hysteria. The screaming man followed me closely while I fought my way through the crowd and collapsed into the safety of the back seat, praying for the driver to get us out of there as quickly as possible.

We had driven only a few yards from Nirmal Hriday when traffic was blocked by a funeral procession. We could not move. When the mourners reached us, we saw a beautiful young woman lying on a wooden stretcher, her face elaborately made up. She was dressed in a colorful sari and covered with flowers.

The driver explained that Kali is the Hindu goddess of destruction and the "ghat" in Kalighat is where the bodies are burnt. The woman was on her way to be cremated, and her ashes would be thrown into the Ganges. He added that, if we wished, he could arrange for us to witness the whole ceremony—the burning of the body and its disposal in the river.

By this time I felt that I had seen enough for one day and declined his offer, saying, "I really think we should be getting back to the hotel."

We returned to the Oberoi Grand Hotel without further incident and opted for an early dinner in the comforting luxury of its French restaurant. After dinner, it was still light outside and we decided to take a walk, as we would in any other great city in the world. But the moment we stepped onto the sidewalk, a woman approached me and, like the two men earlier in the day, started screaming at the top of her voice. She could have been any age, but she looked elderly. I could see she was out of her mind with hopelessness and pain.

Half a block later, she was still right behind us, so Jim and I decided we had no choice but to turn back. Strolling through the streets of Calcutta was not an option. I could have given her a few rupees, but I was afraid the other beggars would surround us and make it impossible for us to get back to the hotel.

We stepped off the sidewalk and onto the long driveway to the hotel, where the woman knew she could not follow us—she was not allowed to cross that line. All the way to the front door we could hear her shrieking, "No! *No! NO! NO!*" in a rising crescendo burning into our backs. That driveway was the longest walk I have ever taken in my life. I had never felt so completely helpless as I did then, facing the enormity of the suffering we had witnessed in just these few hours.

When we got back to the room, Jim and I, feeling physically and emotionally drained, decided to call it a night. It had been a very full twenty-four hours, first with the long plane rides from Paris and then the visits to the Motherhouse, Shishu Bhavan, and Nirmal Hriday— not to mention an "almost cremation" and the city of Calcutta itself.

I slept soundly until about 2:30 a.m., when I was suddenly awakened by a feeling of terror at what my good intentions had gotten me into. As the panic rose, I knew that I was in way over my head.

Out of India

I lay in my bed at the Oberoi Grand Hotel in Calcutta, transformed into a helpless child waking up from a nightmare and desperately trying to control the overwhelming emotions that threatened to tear me apart. I realized that it had begun at the orphanage, somehow regressing me to that young age when I had been so helpless in the face of a world where love was conditional and I had been at the mercy of Mr. Fuller.

My upbringing had been such that I was too ashamed to unveil my fears and vulnerability to another human being, but the day had been so traumatic that I could no longer keep it all in. I wandered around the room making noises and hoping that Jim would wake up. As soon as he opened one eye and asked, "What's happening?" I completely fell apart. I cried for the first time in my adult life. I was totally incoherent and finally sobbed, "I can't do it. I just can't do it."

All my fears came rushing out in a torrent. I tried to explain to Jim how frightened I was of dealing with the poverty and despair I had experienced that day in Calcutta. I knew I couldn't do it—not then, maybe never. And I felt so guilty.

It didn't take long for Jim to understand and he was wise enough to say all the things I most needed to hear. "It's okay, you don't have to feel guilty. You don't have to do this. You're not ready, so don't do it. Nobody's judging you." He kept telling me there was no shame in not being able to do it now, and that I was good enough the way I was.

Needless to say, we did not go to the Motherhouse at dawn; instead, we began a massive struggle to get out of India. With airline computers out of order and a long waiting list for all aircraft out of the city, we tried in vain to book seats on Air India to New Delhi and then an Air France flight to Paris.

I did not want to tell the travel agent the real reason we were leaving his country, so I explained that Jim's sister, Louise, was dying and we had to get home as quickly as possible. (We were aware that she had cancer but we did not know how serious her condition really was.) Our problem was presented to an airline official who, for forty dollars, told us he could arrange for a reservation to New Delhi in only four days. Four days! From that moment on, our only thought was of getting home.

We tried to do some sightseeing, but all I remember is mothers coming up to the car, with maimed or sick children in their arms. I had been told that it was common practice for a poor family to maim one of their children so they could beg more effectively, and that those few rupees might make the difference between life and death for the whole family. I'll never forget an old woman who came up to the window of the car with little tin cans hanging from two stumps where her wrists ended. Could she have been one of those tragic children?

I was ecstatic when the four days were up and we finally boarded a 7:00 a.m. flight out of Calcutta on a small plane. We were seated in the second row of seats on the left.

While we sat anxiously waiting for the plane to take off, I noticed an elderly Indian Holy Man with long white hair and a bare chest in the open doorway. On one side of him was a stewardess and on the other a young man with a painted face and long Rastafarian-style hair. They appeared to be holding him up, and since I could see only the top half of his body, I suddenly thought, "Oh my God, they're probably carrying him because he doesn't have any legs."

The stewardess was obviously looking for the best place to seat him, and pointed in the direction of the aisle next to me. They guided him to the front row of the center section, where I could see that he was wearing a loincloth and *did* have two legs. Once seated, he crossed his legs in a lotus position as though in a state of meditation. Occasionally he would bend slightly to his right and mutter something to his young helper.

We had relaxed in our seats and were looking forward to our first meal of the day when we became aware of a horrific smell going through the cabin. It was so awful that I thought the plane's sewage system had backed up. It was only when the stewardess put a tray in front of me that I realized that the smell was *breakfast.* I am not usually fussy about food, but this time I could not even eat the bread. (On the tray was a little card that I still keep in my wallet; on it was the name of the caterer, "Maureen of Calcutta." I will never forget her.)

The Holy Man, however, had no such problem and was being fed by his assistant. I particularly enjoyed watching the young man take the yoghurt on his fingers and slap it into the old man's mouth. It was neatly done and the Holy Man ate every mouthful.

At the end of the meal, the old man turned his head and whispered something in the young man's ear. The assistant reached into a bag at his feet and took out what looked like a milk bottle, and, to my astonishment, lifted the Holy Man's loincloth so he could relieve himself in the bottle.

Jim and I held our breath, wondering what the young man would do with the "urinal." He calmly bent down and put it—without a lid—under the seat. This seemed precarious at best, especially on an airplane with turbulence, so I made it my job to keep an eye out for any rivers flowing down the aisle. When the plane landed, the young man reached under the seat, pulled out the bottle and put it back in his bag. We couldn't believe it—the bottle was empty! The mystery of the Holy Man's urine will live with us forever.

Eighteen hours later we finally boarded our flight to Paris. My only uneasy moment occurred when the passport control in New Delhi insisted that I did not look like my picture. I wanted to tell him that I had aged twenty years in the short time I had spent in Calcutta, but I did not think this was the right time to make any enemies.

There was no room in business or first class, but I was glad to be assigned a comfortable seat in an exit row in coach, with lots of room for my long legs. The flight had originated in another country and was almost full when we boarded in New Delhi. I don't know where the other passengers came from but none of them wanted to sit in their seats. Instead they insisted on lying down in the aisles. In the bathroom, which was near my seat, I noticed that some of them had not bothered to use the toilet but had done their business wherever they pleased. The odor became a nostalgic reminder of "Maureen of Calcutta's" breakfast.

Once we arrived in Paris, we discovered that Jim's sister Louise had indeed taken a turn for the worse. We quickly gathered up some clothes without the smell of burning cow dung in them and took the next flight home to New York.

Jim adored Louise, and over the years she had become the sister I never had. She was one of the kindest women I have ever known, and cared more about others than about herself. Now she was in a hospital in Vermont, ravaged at the age of fifty-nine with a relentless cancer that was rapidly taking her away from us.

Jim and I arrived in Vermont in the evening and drove directly from the airport to the hospital, where we were able to spend forty-five minutes talking with Louise and telling her how much we loved her. By morning she was in a coma, and we were grateful to have arrived in time to share those few moments with her the night before.

Never in my adult life had I been able to fully acknowledge the loss of someone I loved. Perhaps that's why I had been so drawn to the Home for the Dying in Calcutta. But this time I was determined to be fully present and face the reality of Louise's death. For the next five days Jim and I stayed with her, holding her hand and talking to her, until she peacefully died on December 5, 1989.

I will never regret my first trip to Calcutta. The fact that my fears drove me away made it possible for me to face the death of someone I loved back home. However, I still did not see the need for professional help, and in fact didn't yet understand the connection between my childhood traumas and what had happened to me in Calcutta.

Even though it had not been possible for me to cope with the realities of Calcutta, Mother Teresa's saying that "Life is not worthwhile unless it is lived for others" remained in my mind. I knew that I could never be another Mother Teresa and that I did not have a religious calling. But I was drawn to Mother Teresa, the ultimate mother figure—the mother of the world—and felt compelled to heal the inner child still striving to be perfect, and to discover a deeper layer of myself by trying to follow her example.

Several years earlier, Mother Teresa had visited a prison in New York, and met inmates who were dying of AIDS. When the men asked her if she could open a home for them to die in, Mother Teresa promised that she would, and set about founding one of the first hospices for AIDS patients in New York City. She personally greeted these dying inmates as they entered "Gift of Love," the home she opened for them on Christmas Eve, 1985, "as a birthday gift to Jesus."

At that time, AIDS was a death sentence, with no cure in sight; doctors did not even know how it was transmitted. Not only was there a universal fear of AIDS, but also a stigma associated with having it, because in America it mainly affected the gay population and intravenous drug users.

In April 1990, a few months after my return to New York from Calcutta, I remembered Mother Teresa's words: "If we look around us we will surely find someone in need. We needn't go halfway around the world to be of service. There are people everywhere starving for our love."

When I reached for the phone book to volunteer my services at Gift of Love, I didn't know what I would be asked to do, what I would see, or how I would react. But I knew I wanted to do it.

I never could have suspected that I was embarking on one of the greatest journeys of my life.

GIFT OF LOVE

On Wednesday, April 4th, 1990, I put on a green shirt with a bright yellow sweater over it—as though the colorful outfit would give me courage—left my apartment on Park Avenue, got into a cab, and headed for Greenwich Village. We drove through Central Park and made our way down Ninth Avenue, made a right turn onto 14th Street and entered the meatpacking district. I had opened my window, but closed it when the first smell of bloody carcasses assaulted my nostrils. Looking through the dirty glass, I kept my eyes peeled for evidence of the other world that I knew would emerge after dark—a world of transvestite prostitutes and sex clubs.

There was not much traffic in this part of town. Within moments we pulled up in front of an old four-story stone and brick townhouse on Washington Street, a block away from the Hudson River.

I knew I was in the right place when I saw a sign next to the front door that said, "Missionaries of Charity, Gift of Love"—Mother Teresa's home for destitute men dying of AIDS.

While I waited in the entrance for Sister Maria Lucy, the Superior with whom I had an appointment for an interview, it looked as if there were dozens of nuns scurrying around, but it turned out to be only four very busy Sisters. Although the sparse furnishings were of the simplest kind, this was one of the cleanest houses I had ever seen. I could tell that every inch of it had recently been thoroughly scrubbed and disinfected.

Directly in front of me was a large picture of Mother Teresa, with the quote, "Life is not worth living unless it is lived for others."

Soon a tiny and very beautiful Indian woman with wide-set deep brown eyes appeared before me. I was astonished that she looked so young. Like the nuns I had met in Calcutta, she had a big smile and wore the simple habit designed by Mother Teresa for her Missionaries of Charity—a white cotton sari trimmed with blue. She introduced herself as Sister Maria Lucy, and began the interview by asking me, "What kind of work do you do?"

I told her that I wasn't too qualified for anything, but that I was working on a record album, putting the music together, and had some free time to do something else.

She said, "It doesn't take much training to mop floors and change diapers and clean up and talk to the men, just in general do whatever has to be done." Finally she asked, "Do you know that these are AIDS patients? Are you afraid of being around people with this disease?"

"I'm a lot more frightened of walking down certain streets in New York." I didn't tell her that my own doctor had advised me, "Don't go there." He thought exposure to AIDS was too dangerous. I told him, "If we don't do this for each other as human beings, there is no hope."

Sister Maria Lucy asked, "How much time can you give us?"

I was still dividing my time between New York and my work in France, so I said, "How about two days a week when I am in town? Tuesdays and Fridays?" Little did I know that the Sisters will take anything you offer them with a smile, and never let you know what you've just gotten yourself into.

When she asked if I would like to go upstairs and meet some of the patients in the lounge, my moment of truth had arrived. Once again, as in Calcutta, I began to feel apprehensive. I was not afraid of the kind of reception I would get from dying men whose backgrounds were so different from mine. Rather, my greatest concern was that I had always found it difficult to cope with any medical emergency involving even one drop of blood or a needle—and I had no idea what kind of physical condition these AIDS patients might be in.

I took a deep breath and followed the little nun, who was much too tiny to catch this six-foot two-inch giant if he should suddenly come crashing to the ground.

The first thing I noticed on the men's faces was the pain—physical pain, emotional pain, just pain. There was a whole gamut of conditions, from those who were still in good shape, to some who were already visibly destroyed by AIDS.

Five young men, dressed in bathrobes or jogging suits, sat in comfortable leather armchairs lined up around the room; a large black man, blind and partially paralyzed, lay on the couch. One tall, emaciated man named Wendell, who did most of the talking, had the purple blotches of Kaposi's sarcoma (a type of cancer often associated with AIDS) all over his face, even on the tip of his nose.

I leaned against the doorway to control the shaking in my legs while the men looked me over. I hoped I looked relaxed.

Everyone seemed friendly and curious about this new face entering into their world. Within a few minutes I felt that we were relating to each other normally in what was actually for me a very abnormal situation. The men even managed to make me feel that I would be a welcome addition to the house.

Then Sister Maria Lucy gave me a tour of the building, which, before it became Mother Teresa's Gift of Love, had been the rectory for St. Veronica's Church. A skylight directly over the staircase filtered light throughout the house, and kept it from being dark and gloomy. Everything in the house was practical, designed to be easy to clean and maintain. All told, there was room for about fourteen men.

When I asked where the Sisters lived, Sister Maria Lucy replied, "In the basement, which is private, where we have our own little chapel."

As we walked back downstairs, I asked, "What about the men's families?"

She said, "*We* are their families," and explained that because of the widespread fear and ignorance of AIDS, most of the patients had been abandoned by their friends and loved ones.

On the ground floor, Sister Maria Lucy opened a door to what had once been the parlor and asked, "Would you like to see the main chapel?"

In the semi-darkness of the evening I saw an altar, and a large crucifix with the words "I Thirst" on the wall behind it. Sister told me, "The chairs on the right side are for the men and volunteers. The Sisters sit and kneel on the floor."

At the front door I turned and asked if I could start work on Friday, and she answered, "We have Mass at seven a.m."

I took a deep breath and said, "Well, Sister, what time is Mass over?"

"Eight o'clock."

"In my show business life, that's the middle of the night, but I'd be happy to come at eight o'clock. I could try for seven, but no guarantees."

We both laughed and waved goodbye.

I left the hospice and went home to ponder what I had gotten myself into this time. At Gift of Love, I would be faced with everything I had spent my life fearing, such as poverty and abandonment. Beauty and pretty wrappings had always been the things that had held me together when all else failed. I sensed that this time it would be different—and there would be no running away.

TONY THE VOLUNTEER

I had butterflies in my stomach when I walked in the front door of Gift of Love that Friday morning, April 6, 1990, wondering what my first day of volunteering would bring. I was nervous, I have to admit—I didn't know what to expect. I didn't know what I was going to do, what I was going to see, how I was going to react. But I knew I wanted to do it. I knew it was important for me to meet this challenge, and to open my life to something more.

Singing in arenas for thousands of people or before millions on television was never a problem for me, but now I feared that I would not be good enough at the tasks required of me at Gift of Love. My insecurities were such that I expected the Sisters to greet me politely at the front door and say that they didn't require my services after all.

But Sister Maria Lucy, with a twinkle in her eye, opened the door and only said, "You missed Mass."

There were so many things to learn on my first day, and little time for the Sisters to explain it all to me. So I carefully watched how things were done.

On that first day, I was asked to help cook and serve the meals, and then help with the other daily chores—to mop the floors and wash three flights of stairs on my hands and knees, using detergent and bleach (the only thing known to kill the AIDS virus). Every table and every chair also had to be cleaned and disinfected.

My very first task was to hand the men their medicine. I discovered that I had mixed up the medicine for two of the men, and was terrified that I had just killed two patients. When I confessed to Sister Maria Lucy what I had done, she told me, "Don't worry, they are on the same medication." I was careful never to make that mistake again.

After breakfast, Sister Maria Lucy taught me how to wash the dishes, in a tiny windowless room next to the dining room. In it were three sinks. The first was for washing with detergent and bleach, the second for rinsing, and the third for disinfecting with boiling water. I sweated from the heat and my eyes burned from the bleach, but it was comforting to know that this routine, like the others, would never vary.

One thing I learned that day was that as the men became more debilitated, they were unable to get to the bathroom and had to wear diapers. The one task I really dreaded was that sooner or later I would be asked to change a diaper on a grown man.

By two o'clock when the Sisters went into the Chapel for Holy Hour—during which they pray, sing, and meditate in front of the Blessed Sacrament on the altar—I was exhausted. I had been running up and down the three flights of stairs all day to answer the door, answer the phone, see to the men's needs, and in general do whatever had to be done.

Just when I was ready to sit down in the Chapel, Wendell, the young man whose face was covered with Kaposi's sarcoma, came to me and asked for a new colostomy bag.

I vaguely knew what a colostomy bag was, and was relieved that he knew how to care for it himself. I was having a hard enough time coming to terms with so much suffering on the face of a kid, without facing the raw physical evidence too intimately. I could see that Wendell's body was also covered with Kaposi's sarcoma, and I assumed that he had had the colostomy because the cancer had spread to his internal organs.

Sister Maria Lucy had told me that my most important job would be to communicate with the men. So I waited in the lounge while

Wendell connected the bag to his abdomen. When it was in place, he came in and sat down next to me. He told me that he had run away from an intolerable family situation in Tennessee when he was thirteen, and made his way to New York, where he supported himself as a transvestite prostitute. He was now twenty-six years old.

He had also been an entertainer in gay clubs, dressing up as Barbra Streisand or Ann-Margret and lip-syncing their records. I could see past the lesions on his face to a time when he must have been quite pretty, and remarked, "I would think you were probably too pretty to do Barbra Streisand," which made him smile. He said that he had been very, very good at his impersonations.

I could tell he really meant it, so I replied, "Anyone in this world who can honestly say, 'I was very, very good' at something can be quite proud."

By four o'clock I knew I had had enough for my first day. There had been a lot of new stuff thrown at me, a lot of procedure, a lot of things to examine and see how I felt about them. While I felt good about having made it through the day, part of me was left with a feeling of helplessness at all the suffering I had witnessed. You just feel at a loss—"What can I do?" To do even the menial jobs for these patients, you have to know how; you have to be comfortable with doing these things. It's all new. You're not going to just waltz in and *pfoom!*, there you are, Mr. Wonderful.

I left the hospice and walked down Christopher Street, breathed in the evening air of the outside world, and gave thanks for my health, my beautiful home, and the life I had been blessed with.

When I staggered into bed that night, I wondered if I would have the physical stamina to continue with the work at Gift of Love. After all, I was forty-nine years old—not a kid anymore.

Finally, as I drifted off to sleep, I decided that whether I was good or bad at mopping a floor or washing three flights of stairs, I had to go back. The men had touched me in a way that I couldn't explain. I felt as though my whole life had been leading up to this point.

It wasn't long before the two days a week that I had expected to work at Gift of Love had expanded to four days or more. With fourteen men in the house and several of them reaching the final stages of AIDS, I worked whenever I was needed.

The Sisters would often tell me as I was leaving in the evening, "We have no other volunteer tomorrow. Can you come in?"

How could I say "No"?

Some days were so long—ten to twelve hours—that it would take me two days of rest, whenever possible, to recover from that one day of work. Every part of me felt exhausted and much of the time I was running on nervous energy. My hip hurt and my calves twitched from constantly going up and down those three flights of stairs. I once put a pedometer on my ankle and found I had walked 10.6 miles in the house that day—most of it up and down the stairs.

Ironically, one of my favorite tasks was washing those same stairs on my hands and knees; the humility of what I was doing felt like a meditation or a prayer. It was also a time when the men seemed most comfortable coming to me with their problems; they could see that I was serious about my work at Gift of Love and that I was there for them.

Before long, these men were no longer nameless, faceless people I might have passed silently on the street—they became real human beings with a face and a story I could understand. They were mostly young people who had been brought up in an environment of crime and drugs, young men who never had much of a chance in life to begin with. When they came to Mother Teresa's hospice, for the first time in their lives they entered a world of unconditional love.

The more they trusted me and depended on me, the more I could see what Sister Maria Lucy had meant about our being their family.

I also came to understand what one of the other Sisters had told me, "There is something beautiful in each of the men."

Most of the men at Gift of Love were young, young enough to be my children. They were just kids—playing, joking, being sad, or needing someone to talk to or give them a hug at a time when most people were afraid to touch AIDS patients. It wasn't long before I was thinking of them as "my kids."

At first I was able to block out the fact that there was no cure for AIDS and they were all going to die. It was only while I was looking through the scrapbook of photos the Sisters had kept of the men who had been at Gift of Love one year earlier, in 1989, that I realized that not one of them had survived.

In taking care of "my kids" during my first months at Gift of Love, I learned that AIDS was often accompanied by dementia, especially in those days, when there was no effective treatment for AIDS.

I learned that in a few weeks a robust young man could waste away to skin and bones.

I also learned how to do the thing I had dreaded the most—changing diapers. The amazing thing was that during my first diaper change it was as though a scrim had been put in front of my face to block the smell. From that moment on, no matter what body fluids I was asked to deal with, there was never any odor.

Another devastating side effect of AIDS was blindness. Many men would spend eight hours a day hooked up to an IV in an often futile effort to save their sight.

One of the men summed up the disease by saying, "With AIDS, it's always something."

What I would never have believed my first week at Gift of Love was that within five months, all the young men I thought of as "my kids" would be dead.

It seemed that every hour we were faced with another crisis, and death was a constant presence. The only way I could deal with this was to follow the Sisters' example. Not only was my life enriched by helping the men in their final days, but also through my growing relationship with the nuns.

I had first been inspired to be of service because of Mother Teresa's example of compassion, but now I learned that one did not have to go to Calcutta to discover the secret of unconditional love and joy. It could be found in each of the Sisters I worked with.

These women who had taken a serious vow of poverty and service to the "poorest of the poor" were filled with laughter and good humor.

One sunny spring afternoon I heard laughter from the Sisters' cement courtyard below. I peeked out the back window and saw five nuns sitting in a circle on metal chairs, sharing what looked like a single mango, and having a wonderful, joyous time. I couldn't yet understand where that wellspring of joy came from, or how they plugged into it to that extent.

These women were constantly confronted with the sordid side of life. They went into crack houses. They took care of the homeless, the drug addicts, the sick, the elderly and the dying. And all they had in their hearts was joy, which they gladly shared with everyone, including me.

One of the greatest differences between Mother Teresa's Missionaries of Charity and other religious orders is their vow to *live* as the "poorest of the poor." Mother Teresa did not feel that she and her Sisters could really understand the poor that they had vowed to serve if they were not able to say, "I too know what it is to be hungry; to be thirsty; to be too hot or to be cold." However, Mother Teresa was wise enough to make the distinction that she and her nuns would have the luxury of *choosing* to live that way.

Each Sister owns only two saris. Every morning one sari is worn while the other is washed in a bucket of water and hung outside to dry. The same bucket is filled with cold water so they can wash themselves every day at dawn. The Sisters and their saris, just like their homes, are always spotlessly clean.

The day a young woman becomes a Missionary of Charity she is given her two saris and a crucifix, which is pinned near her heart. These few items and her rosary become her only possessions.

I laughed the day I overheard a volunteer ask a Sister who was being transferred to another part of the world if she was already packed. She smiled sweetly and answered, "But I don't own anything."

The reality of the Missionaries of Charity's way of life was brought home to me even more the day they asked me to help them make some mattresses for the Sisters to sleep on—another task that was way outside my realm of experience. First we put on masks and opened bags filled with cotton batting. Then we took two pieces of fabric which felt like potato sacks, sewed three sides together, tore the cotton into small pieces, put the pieces inside the "mattress" and sewed (by hand, of course) the fourth side. They were not very thick nor did they look comfortable but they cost practically nothing to make.

Also, the Sisters never accept any food or drink in public. They wait until they are back in the convent. Mother Teresa was worried that if the poor felt obliged to show their hospitality they might not have enough to feed their families that day. She knew that if the rule applied to *everyone* they visited then no one would feel offended. Even when she won the Nobel Peace Prize she asked that instead of a banquet, the organizers give the food to the poor.

Following this way of life never appeared to be a hardship for the Sisters and only increased their sense of appreciation for the little blessings in their lives—blessings as small as a single mango for the five of them.

It's no wonder that so many young men at Gift of Love wanted to spend their last moments in this atmosphere of unconditional love. The Sisters made it seem like a house of life and joy, rather than a house of death.

Not only was Gift of Love a source of peace for the men, but it was equally gratifying for a volunteer like me to be working in such a unique environment. I felt as though I had a dozen new mothers to learn from and it always made me happy to be around them.

There was another benefit for me at Gift of Love that I had not expected. For the first time in my life, no one knew anything about my last name or background. It was a great feeling to be judged on nothing but my willingness to be of service. There may have been others who could mop a floor in less time or with more skill than I, but at Gift of Love the Sisters liked me just the way I was. And when I added to that all the new friends I found among the patients, it was a wonderful feeling to be accepted as Tony, the volunteer. Period.

"My Kids"

Throughout my life I had never been able to fully acknowledge the deaths of those I loved, but had always gone on as though nothing had happened—the way Mother and Tata had trained me to do when I was growing up. But as the summer wore on and "my kids" started to die, death was all around me and was impossible to ignore. Seven of my eight kids died in little more than four months, and my armor began to crack. The last one left alive was Wilfredo.

Although Wilfredo was twenty-six years old and knew his disease was a death sentence, he often put his suffering aside and acted like the kid he had never been allowed to be. His favorite pastime, which I never discouraged, was playing practical jokes on me.

One morning I went up to his room, where I found him lying in bed in obvious discomfort. He looked up at me with tears of exhaustion on his face and complained that he had stayed awake vomiting all night. When I felt something unusual around my feet I looked down and saw that, in spite of his very real suffering, he had surreptitiously dropped one hand to the floor while we were talking and had untied my shoelaces.

That was pure Wilfredo.

On his last trip to the hospital the doctors decided that there was nothing more they could do for Wilfredo. He told them, "Whatever time I have left, I want to spend at Gift of Love."

The idea seemed absurd to the medical community, who insisted that he would probably not even survive the trip. The Sisters, however, immediately made arrangements for an ambulance to bring him home.

When the ambulance attendants carried Wilfredo through the front door of Gift of Love that Tuesday afternoon I tried to hide my shock at his deterioration. The first time I had met him, only four-and-a-half short months before, he had been fairly robust from a life of physical labor, but now he could not have weighed more than sixty pounds, and was in obvious pain.

There were three ambulance workers—one woman and two men. They used a sheet to lift Wilfredo from the stretcher into a wheelchair with a minimum of pain; then I helped them carry him upstairs in the chair. In his room, they again lifted him with the sheet and gently lowered him onto his bed.

The team was so moved by Wilfredo's suffering that before they left, each one in turn stood by his bed and spoke a few words to him. The last one touched his hand and said, "God bless you, brother."

I accompanied the ambulance attendants back downstairs and had just closed the front door behind them when Sister Maria Lucy appeared beside me. She looked closely into my face and said, "You look tired."

I nodded, "Yeah."

She looked again and said softly, "It's hard to see him this way, isn't it?"

I couldn't speak but simply nodded my head and turned away so she could not see the tears welling up in my eyes.

I slowly climbed up the stairs to Wilfredo's room. Now my job was to make him as comfortable as possible.

It was difficult to understand his speech in his weakened condition, but he seemed happy to be home, and wanted us to know about a beautiful woman he had seen. The Sisters were convinced it was the Blessed Mother.

I cared for him until seven o'clock, when the night volunteer arrived. Then, for the first time since I started work at Gift of Love, I walked down to the end of the pier so only the Hudson River would see my tears.

Two days later, on Thursday, Wilfredo had his first visitor—his favorite brother, Edouardo. Edouardo told me that most of the family had not been told that Wilfredo had AIDS.

Edouardo stood in the doorway for a long time, not daring to venture into the room. I continued to quietly care for Wilfredo, while Edouardo watched from a safe distance. My intention was to show him by my actions that, unless we were dealing with certain body fluids, we could touch Wilfredo the same way we would anyone else.

Finally I turned and said, "You know, Edouardo, we're not stupid. We know it's not that easy to catch this disease. Many people who are afraid to come into this house and hold someone's hand or give them a hug are going to leave here and do something that will really put their lives in danger and give them AIDS. Many people are afraid because they don't know any better, but maybe you could go out in the world and enlighten them."

Slowly, Edouardo approached Wilfredo's bed. By now he was not as frightened of the illness as he was of his own emotions while watching his brother's suffering. As he came closer, I said, "Tell him what's in your heart, Edouardo, just speak from the heart."

He called softly, "Willie, Willie. It's Edouardo, Willie," and started to sob.

I saw Edouardo touch his brother's head under the pretext of checking his fever, and quietly left them alone in the room. From the hallway, I heard him repeat, "Willie, Willie, *mira, mira.*" They were both laughing and crying at the same time.

The next day, Friday, Wilfredo was still fully conscious and able to let me know when he needed something. His mouth and throat were raw from an infection and it was difficult for him to swallow, so I took a big Q-Tip with lemon and glycerine to wet his lips and mouth. Then I dipped it in water and let him suck on it. There were so few things that I could do to give him any physical comfort that I didn't mind doing them as often as necessary.

During the afternoon, Wilfredo's breathing became very labored, and I decided that since it was only the two of us, I would quietly sing as I went about my duties. The song I chose was "Take My Hand, Precious Lord."

I had been singing softly for about fifteen minutes, when I noticed that he was no longer gasping for air. His whole being seemed to relax and I could move him with a minimum of pain.

I would never again question the healing power of music.

Wilfredo died Saturday afternoon. I was not with him that day but Sister Maria Lucy left a message on my answering machine within minutes of his passing. I was touched because it showed that it mattered to the Sisters that I was there, and that they appreciated and honored the love that I gave.

The most beautiful part of Wilfredo's death was that he knew how much he was loved. He remained conscious and at peace until the very end, when Father Tom said, "God bless you, Wilfredo," and he replied, "God bless you, Father."

Wilfredo was the last of my kids to die during my first summer at Gift of Love. After that, unfortunately, there were always others to take their places—others with whom I would also develop a bond. But there was something about that first group that set them apart from the rest. They were rather like my firstborn.

The hardest part of losing any of them was the emptiness in the house when they died. I saw them around every corner and felt their presence in every room. I didn't give myself time to grieve, and instead tried to pretend that it was "business as usual" in spite of the huge void.

స్తా స్తా

When Wilfredo died, I was scheduled to go to Paris. During my first few months at Gift of Love, periodically I had to go back to Europe for a few weeks at a time to do concerts or to work on a new CD. After my work was over, I would rush back to New York to be with my kids.

On the morning of Wilfredo's funeral, Jim and I arrived at St. Veronica's church at 9:30 with our luggage in the car so we could make the one o'clock Concorde flight to Paris.

Sister Maria Lucy asked them to reopen the casket so we could see Wilfredo beautifully dressed in a suit and tie, wearing a little guardian angel pin and a miraculous medal that Mother Teresa had blessed. For me the most comforting part was seeing his face filled with peace.

Sitting in the front row were several members of Wilfredo's family with a guitar, singing hymns in Spanish. The pews were filled with Sisters, friends, patients, and volunteers. At the altar were Father Tom and Father Anthony, two priests who had known Wilfredo well during his days at Gift of Love.

Father Anthony was the first to speak. Apparently he had recently had a serious illness and a crisis of faith. As soon as he was physically well, he came back to visit the men at Gift of Love. Wilfredo had greeted him at the door with open arms and said, "Father, I have received the Sacraments and I'm happy. Now I can go in peace." It was then that Father Anthony's faith had been miraculously restored. As he told us how Wilfredo had given him back his faith, he broke down and unabashedly wept in front of the congregation.

Father Tom, whose life had also been deeply touched by Wilfredo, and who had been with him when he died, spoke next. I was fortunate to receive a copy of his eulogy and I believe that it says as much about all the men as it does about Wilfredo.

Here it is in part:

*Today we come together to bury a good friend and
a loving teacher, one who tried his best to follow Jesus*

and bore in his own body hard suffering not unlike that of his Master.

For many of us here at Gift of Love, but for myself in particular, Wilfredo was a leader, the one who showed me the face of God in the way he cared for others. The way he was willing to give of himself so often, and certainly in the way he suffered and died, slowly enduring an incredible pain that often brought him to tears—never complaining and always worrying that he might be too much of a burden.

This Wilfredo was not well educated or successful in the eyes of the world, but he was very wise. Wilfredo was materially poor, but rich in the most important of ways. He was of a shy nature but had many friends. Wilfredo was not outwardly pious, but had a great faith and devotion.

Wilfredo suffered terribly in his dying but perhaps even more so in his living. No doubt he carried in his heart many scars which he received from wounds inflicted by others in his youth. For me, Wilfredo was an instrument of God. He let God heal him. He let God change what could have been bitterness into simple and beautiful acts of mercy.

There was a certain innocence about Wilfredo and I can almost see him as one of the sheep in the Gospel story today, standing before the king and asking him, "But when, Lord, did I see you hungry and feed you, or thirsty and give you drink? When did I see you a stranger and welcome you, naked and clothe you, ill or in prison and visit you?"

And so his beloved Jesus will look at Wilfredo with love and say, "Wilfredo, whatever you did for these least brothers of mine—whatever you did for the other men at Gift of Love, whatever you did for the Sisters, the volunteers, the priests or Father Tom, that you did for Me. Come enter the kingdom prepared for you from the beginning."

After the service, Jim, who had never been to Gift of Love before, or to a funeral for one of our men, observed that even though Wilfredo was in what looked like a plain wood coffin, no head of state or "important person" in this world could have a service filled with so much love.

Then we all gathered in the street to sing with the Sisters and to throw holy water on the casket. As soon as the hearse drove away, we went back to Gift of Love to have coffee and cake and celebrate Wilfredo's life and the love with which he touched us all.

Before I knew it, it was time for me to leave the world of Gift of Love, and go to the totally different world that once again awaited me in Paris.

THE MAN IN BLACK

By the time Jim and I landed in Paris, I was totally overcome by the suffering and death I had witnessed at Gift of Love. All I wanted to do was close the bedroom drapes, crawl under the covers, and withdraw from the world while I came to terms with the loss of "my kids."

However, I was scheduled to start the master recordings of a CD the day after my arrival in Paris. But in my present state of mind, I didn't know how I could possibly stop grieving, get out of bed, and function in a recording studio. In desperation, I called the producer, Marc François. He and the creative director, Eric Duval, were sympathetic, but explained that the studio had already been booked and the best musicians hired for several weeks of work.

Then Marc offered, "How about taking this weekend off? All I want is the work—it doesn't matter what hours you choose to record. If you feel like starting at eight o'clock in the evening and working through the night, it's okay with us."

I suspect they were smart enough to know that my being on the emotional edge might bring another dimension to my work.

It was not possible, however, for me to travel three thousand miles and just forget Gift of Love. The Sisters, the other volunteers and the men were never far from my thoughts. I called the house regularly for updates and wrote to the men I had left behind so they would not feel that I had cavalierly run off to another continent and forgotten about them.

Singing to the men had been a part of my daily routine at Gift of Love. One morning I woke up and thought, "Why couldn't I go into the studio, sit at the piano, and make a tape for the Sisters, the men, and Mother Teresa?" I could talk to everyone and sing some of the inspirational songs I had so often sung at the house. This way I would really be able to let my friends know that I was thinking about them.

I got permission from Marc and went into the studio that very afternoon with a vague sketch in my head of about twenty minutes of song and chatter. I wanted to make the entire tape in one long take—no stopping. Only four other people were present, and they were all in the control room: Jim; Eric Duval; the sound engineer; and his assistant. I was separated from them by an enormous window through which they could see me—and the entire studio—clearly at all times.

The room I would be recording in was huge, with a soundproof door that was eighteen inches thick and filled with sand. Outside the room were red lights and signs saying, "Do Not Enter. Recording In Progress!"

I sat down at the grand piano facing the door and waited for the signal to begin. I was well into the second song, "Take My Hand, Precious Lord," which I had sung constantly to Wilfredo during his last days, when I was startled to hear a noise at the door. My surprise turned to anger when the door creaked open and a man walked in.

I was wearing glasses that allowed me to see the piano, but everything else in the room, including the man, was slightly out of focus. Frantically pointing to the microphone, I continued to sing and play the piano. The man standing before me was all in black—black suit, black hair, black briefcase. I couldn't see well enough to make out his features, but all that black seemed to shine. Then, ignoring my agitated gestures, the man started speaking to me. When he was through, he calmly turned around, walked out, and shut the door behind him.

By this time I could barely control my anger. But I didn't want to spoil the taping or discuss what had just happened, so I stopped singing and told the engineer, "We don't have to start at the beginning, but we can pick it up at the top of the song."

The moment I finished recording, I burst into the control room screaming, "Who was that idiot who walked in on me and even spoke while I was recording? How could anyone be so dumb?!"

Jim, Eric, and the two engineers in the control room looked at me in shock. They had no idea what I was talking about. They had seen and heard no one. There were no other sounds on the tape. And there was no way anyone could have gotten into the building that day, let alone into the studio, without buzzing the control room. Actually, they had all been puzzled as to why I wanted to start the song over.

I have often thought about this incident, and I know I saw and heard someone come into that room and talk to me. The identity of the man in black will always remain a mystery. Could it have been my friend Wilfredo, playing another one of his pranks? If so, I wish I had listened to what he had to say.

In retrospect, having to divide my time between working in Paris and volunteering at Gift of Love in New York turned out to be a blessing. The work with the dying men might have burned me out if I had not had my professional life to go to—no matter how difficult it may have been for me to live in Paris. And the contrast of being just Tony, the volunteer, created a balance between life at Gift of Love in New York City and the rather unreal way that the world revolved around me when I was performing in show business.

Eventually I realized that experiences I would have killed for when I was younger no longer carried the same weight and meaning. After all I had lived through at Gift of Love, my values were beginning to change.

While I took care of so many men in their last hours, I came to realize how little worldly success or power really matters in those final moments of life. At Gift of Love, what really mattered was that the dying were surrounded with peace and love. As Mother Teresa—whom I would soon meet for the first time when I returned to New York—said, "We are all created to love and be loved." In the end, the rest doesn't really matter very much.

Not My Fault

One morning not long after that trip to Paris, I was standing in the shower, and realized that silent tears were coming down my face.

But the tears were not for "my kids" who had just died; they were for me. Lately, as I had allowed death to penetrate my emotional armor, fleeting memories of Mr. Fuller had begun to assault my consciousness. Since I was eight years old—more than forty years earlier—I had never so much as mentioned his name to anyone, not even Jim, and during much of that time I had tried to block out his abuse completely.

My parents, not knowing what had happened, had ignored all the emotional consequences and neurotic behavior that had so drastically affected my life—from an excessive need for cleanliness and perfection to agoraphobia and panic attacks.

I knew it was finally time for me to seek professional help.

It was in Los Angeles, where I was doing some re-mixing on one of my recordings, that I found a therapist, a compassionate, middle-aged woman with grown children. After several sessions I still couldn't say it. I was asking questions and going around in circles, trying to find a way to approach the subject, but unable to get the words out.

She finally understood what I was trying to tell her and said it for me. She explained to me that it was not my fault, and I was not to blame. *I* had done nothing wrong. She told me that a child molester like Mr. Fuller has an instinct for picking victims like me, who are so vulnerable and in such need of attention that they will not tell. He knew full well that he could easily manipulate my innocence and my needs in order to fulfill his perverted desires. Then I cried—not because I was ashamed, but for the innocent child who had been forced to live with so much pain.

Jim was waiting for me in the car when I left the therapist's office. He was the first person I was able to verbalize the abuse to. His response was as wise and supportive this time as it had been in Calcutta.

Shortly afterward, my brother visited me at my country home in Vermont.

Although we had taken different paths in life, as adults we left our childhood battles behind us and began to communicate. My brother once told me, "We both had the same childhood, we just reacted to it in a totally different way."

I decided to share the story of my early sexual molestation with him. He was devastated. "It might never have happened if I had been nicer to you," Richard said.

"You were only a child yourself," I told him, "and you were doing the best you could with what you had."

His genuine concern and regret became an important part of my healing.

When I returned to New York, I invited Lucy, my old nurse, over for lunch. Afterwards we sat alone together and I said, "Lucy, there is something that I want to tell you. When I was a little boy, I was sexually molested."

She looked at me with a big smile on her face and replied, "Oh, you mean Mr. Fuller. He was such a lovely man."

I was so shocked that all I could say was, "Mother questioned me about him, but I never told her."

Then Lucy said, "I *knew* you'd never tell your mother!"

I couldn't believe what I was hearing. Did she mean that she *knew* I was being molested? When I confronted her later on the phone about her bizarre reply, she dismissed me by saying, "I have to wash my hair," and refused to discuss it again.

I'll never know if she was avoiding the subject out of guilt at not having protected me, or if she was still jealous because Mr. Fuller preferred me, an eight-year-old child in her care, to her. If that were the case, she had never given any thought at all to the physical and emotional price that I had had to pay over the years.

Toward the end of Lucy's life, during one of my visits to her, my mother was mentioned, and Lucy said rather indignantly, "*I* was your mother."

And I thought, "Not a chance in hell."

I was never able to hate Mr. Fuller for what he did to me, but I had a hard time coming to grips with the feeling of having been betrayed by the nurse I had always thought was supposed to have been there to protect me.

MEETING MOTHER TERESA:
MY THIRD "OTHER MOTHER"

Sister Maria Lucy had exciting news for me when I returned from Los Angeles in the fall of 1990. She could hardly wait to tell me that Mother Teresa was on her way to New York, and I was not only invited to join her and the Sisters for Mass on her first morning, but also to meet with her privately afterwards.

I had waited eleven years, ever since I had first read about her, for this day to arrive.

When I started work at Gift of Love, I had no idea that Mother Teresa would ever be coming to New York. As far as I knew, she spent most of her time in Calcutta. So I was surprised when Sister Maria Lucy told me that Mother Teresa often visited her convent in the South Bronx, called Queen of Peace, which was one of several convents around the world where young women received their training to become Missionaries of Charity.

The convent was in a dangerous part of town that I would not be going to if it were not for Mother Teresa—an area filled with poverty, gangs, prostitution, and drugs. I had been told that one could sometimes hear gunfire outside the chapel during Mass.

I had decided the only way I could feel safe was to hire a car and chauffeur and hope that the Sisters would not notice that I had not taken public transportation. After all, Mother Teresa and her

Missionaries of Charity were not known for riding in luxury and I did not want to stand out.

Mass at Queen of Peace was scheduled for 6:00 a.m.—still not my favorite time of day. At that hour on a cold autumn morning, the streets of the South Bronx were deserted except for groups of homeless men and women huddled around fires set in large steel drums.

It was easy to recognize the convent, which had a statue of the Virgin Mary out front and was surrounded by a fence topped with barbed wire. I tried to get out of my car unnoticed, but one of the nuns saw me and opened the gates to their private garden so we would not have to park on the dangerous street. So much for my being discreet!

I was a few minutes early, so I went into what was back in those days a tiny chapel and watched the Sisters slowly file in. I waited in anticipation until finally, a few moments before Mass, a bent-over elderly lady in a mended blue-and-white sari and gnarled, bare feet came in and knelt on the floor behind me. Mother Teresa had arrived.

From the moment Mother Teresa entered the chapel that morning, she was clearly in charge. First she made sure that there was enough room for the Cardinal of New York, John O'Connor, who traditionally celebrated Mass in her honor on her first morning in New York, to make his way through the crowded room filled with nuns. During Mass, she kept getting up to turn lights off as daylight began to filter through the windows.

For me, the most moving thing about the Mass was that it was Mother Teresa's voice behind me leading the prayers.

After Mass, I waited until Mother Teresa was ready to meet me. She was even shorter than I had expected, and she laughed when I got down on one knee and explained, "Mother, this isn't totally out of reverence, it's just that I'm too tall for you."

I marveled that in spite of a trip halfway around the world and having a serious heart condition, she showed no signs of fatigue. She gave me her full attention and made me feel as though I was the only person in the world. It made no difference to her if I was a beggar on the streets of Calcutta, Tony the volunteer, or the Pope—I was all that mattered at that moment.

The Sisters had told her that I was a singer, so she asked me about my work. For the first time in my life I was tongue-tied. *My* work seemed so unimportant compared to the difference that she had made in the world. And when I told her how much Gift of Love had changed my life, she asked me if I would come share in the work in Calcutta.

Not wanting to divulge the trauma I had experienced in Calcutta the year before, I laughingly asked, "Mother, if I come to Calcutta, will you work me as hard as you do at Gift of Love?"

Her answer was to take my hand in hers, and repeat Jesus's words, "Whatever you do to the least of my brothers and sisters, YOU DID IT TO ME." And for the first of many times over the next seven years, she pointed to a different finger on my hand for each of the last five words.

All I could see was her smile as she put her hands on my head and blessed me.

When it was time for me to leave, I reluctantly said goodbye to the Sisters and went out to the garden, where my car was parked. There I discovered that the exit was blocked by the Cardinal's car, a dark blue sedan identical to mine. I jokingly complained to a volunteer that I couldn't leave because the Cardinal's car was in the way, and before I could stop her, she had run into the convent to tell him.

I was thoroughly embarrassed when the Cardinal came running out a few moments later, apologized profusely for holding me up, got into his car, and drove off.

As my driver backed the car in front of the convent, I saw Mother Teresa standing on the sidewalk in front of a group of nuns, all singing and bowing in my direction. It dawned on me that this display was not for me but for the Cardinal, who, unbeknownst to the Sisters, had already left. Since I looked nothing like the Cardinal, I hunched down in my seat and whispered to the driver to get us out of there before they noticed.

Unfortunately, my chauffeur took one look out the window, saw Mother Teresa next to the car, and froze at the wheel. Slowly the Sisters started to realize their error, and, one by one, began to laugh. When we finally drove off, I tried to imagine what Mother and the Sisters were going to think of their volunteer in a chauffeur-driven car, impersonating the Cardinal of New York.

In fact, I knew that neither Mother Teresa nor the Sisters would ever condemn me for my luxurious lifestyle, so different from theirs, and would only find it amusing—their sense of humor being one of their strongest attributes. By the time I reached Gift of Love that afternoon, word had already spread, and for quite some time afterward I was jokingly referred to as "the Cardinal."

On November 10, 1990, not long after our first meeting, Mother Teresa wrote me a letter saying how happy she was that I had found so much joy working at Gift of Love. She wrote, *"… even the rich are hungry for love, for being cared for, for being wanted, for having someone to call their own … "* At the end of the letter she added,

> *Be kind, show kindness in your eyes,*
> *kindness in your smile.…*
> *To all who suffer and are lonely,*
> *Give always a happy smile.*
> *God bless you,*
> *Mother Teresa, M.C.*

After that, whenever Mother Teresa came to New York, the Superior at Gift of Love always arranged for Mother and me to spend time alone with each other.

My conversations with Mother Teresa were usually very simple. Mostly she spoke of her gratitude to God for having given her the privilege of serving Him for so many years. Her joy came from the humble tasks that God had asked of her and she was very emphatic about the fact that she had "never said 'No' to God." Mother always asked me about my music and if I continued to sing for the men at Gift of Love. It was always a thrill for me, each time we met, when she put her hands on my head and blessed me.

When Pat Kennedy Lawford told me that she said the rosary every day for world peace, I asked for permission to bring Pat to the convent to meet Mother Teresa. I felt that a daily rosary for world peace deserved something!

At the time, Mother desperately wanted to get permission from the Chinese government to open a home in China. Never one to miss an opportunity, Mother asked Pat if she knew of any way she could accomplish this goal before her death. Mother Teresa felt that once the Missionaries of Charity opened a home for the poor in China, she would then be free to go home to God. I left the convent that day selfishly hoping that Mother would not find a way to accomplish this task for some time if it meant that she might die. In spite of her age and failing health, I didn't feel that the rest of the world and I were ready to give her up quite yet.

When you think about meeting someone who is considered a living saint, you almost expect thunder and lightning and miracles going on around them. But there was nothing about Mother Teresa that *seemed* extraordinary at first glance. She was a saint who acted like an ordinary woman, and who loved to laugh. Her only philosophy was the simple words of Jesus, but when I left her, I knew I had been in the presence of an extraordinary ordinary woman.

Mother Teresa, without ever seeking fame, had become one of the most famous women in the world—a symbol of unconditional love and peace. The way she dealt with what she considered the burden of public and media attention was characteristically simple. She said, "My deal with Jesus: for each photo, one soul out of purgatory."

Years later I told Dominick Dunne, the writer who openly admitted to a lifelong love affair with anything related to fame, that after knowing Mother Teresa, I could never again be seduced by mere celebrity.

CHOICES

After I had been working at Mother Teresa's home for the dying for six years, I began to understand how misguided I had been in blaming myself for having repeatedly denied the reality of the deaths in my family. But what else could one expect of someone who was raised not to acknowledge emotion?

In spite of my upbringing, though, on some level I always suspected that death was an important phase of life that should not be ignored. I finally realized that death was something I needed to come to terms with and accept in order to become a whole person.

Perhaps this is why I was drawn to working with the dying. Singing my songs at Gift of Love, touching the men, and talking with them about death in a way that I was never able to do with my family allowed me to break through the emotional boundaries that had been set for me as a child.

I opened up in other ways as well. Because the physical and emotional demands of being a caregiver were so great, I found that I too needed a support system. As surely as the men at Gift of Love shouldn't die alone and afraid, I as the caregiver couldn't go it alone either. My strength came from sharing my experiences with Jim and slowly learning how to open up to my close friends and to other caregivers who were always available at the right time to hear about *my* pain and *my* loss. Allowing myself not only to grieve but also to meet the needs of the dying became a part of my own healing in that it gave me the opportunity to release emotions that had been closed off for so long.

Oscar, one of the patients who always encouraged me to keep going when I felt overwhelmed, said, "Tony, the real work you do at Gift of Love is not cleaning or mopping, but talking to me, touching a patient's shoulder as he walks by—the little things that show us you care."

One of the most important lessons I learned during my years at Gift of Love is that there is no formula for dying. Death is a totally individual experience that, whenever possible, should be filled with options. It is a time when each person needs the freedom to find their own way.

Although all the men at Gift of Love knew they were going to die, it was comforting for these patients to feel that they still had choices. A choice could be as profound as deciding when to refuse life support, or as seemingly frivolous as a concern about some aspect of their physical appearance. They could die in the hospital or with us. They could choose to continue their medications or not. They could accept all the spiritual guidance and support that they felt they needed. It was even okay for a patient to ask me for a salami sandwich that he was ultimately not able to eat.

Nothing was too small or unimportant. It was a question of their still feeling some control over whatever was left of their lives. Most of all, the men were given choices because they were loved, and because they were loved, they felt free to express their own love.

I remembered that when Ethel Merman was in the last stages of brain cancer she rarely bothered to wear the wig that hid the loss of her hair, but she derived pleasure from seeing that her nails were always perfectly manicured with bright red polish. Ethel's mother, Agnes, had also had lovely hands, and during the eight months that Agnes was in a coma before she died, Ethel saw to it that her mother's hands were always beautifully manicured. It might not have mattered to someone else, but it did to Ethel. And when Ethel herself was dying, I never failed to tell her how pretty her hands were, even when it was doubtful that she could hear me.

Another thing I learned at Gift of Love was that there were as many ways to die as there were people, and each death was touching and unique.

A young man named Michael, who had been quite uncertain about the transition from this world to the next, asked the priest, Father Tom, to stay with him till the end. Every so often, drifting in and out of consciousness, he would open his eyes wide and ask, "Am I dead yet, Father? Am I dead yet?" Father Tom remained at his side until Michael peacefully passed on.

Another young patient, Miguel, weighed no more than sixty-five pounds as he neared his final moments. Early one morning, as Mass was about to begin, the night volunteer felt inspired to ask the boy, "Do you want to see Jesus? Do you want to go see Jesus?"

The young man enthusiastically nodded, "Yes, yes."

The volunteer scooped Miguel's frail body up in his arms, carried him down the stairs to the chapel, and knelt in front of the altar. The chapel was totally silent while Miguel looked up in rapture at the sight of Christ on the cross. After a few moments, his head fell back and his body became totally limp. Although he had not yet died, the Savior in whom he had put all his trust was possibly the last thing he saw with his earthly eyes.

None of the men at Gift of Love died alone if we could help it. When a patient was not able to come home in time to die, the Sisters would make sure that one of us was always with him in the hospital.

One exception, however, was my friend Wendell, the young man who was covered with Kaposi's sarcoma, even on the tip of his nose. When he was almost too weak to walk, he chose to go out with some old friends. Sister Maria Lucy was frantic, because not only was he too ill, but once before, these "friends" had used Wendell's money to get strung out on drugs and then had left him unconscious in the street. In spite of Sister's pleading, Wendell remained adamant. He wanted to go into the world one more time. Finally he became irate and said, "I'm not staying where I'm not trusted."

It broke Sister Maria Lucy's heart to watch him gather a few belongings, take his money and leave. I was not there that day, and will always wonder if I could possibly have changed his mind.

Two days later, a hospital on Staten Island called, saying that the police had picked Wendell up in the Staten Island ferry terminal and had taken him to the Emergency Room. He was in terrible pain and had no more money or belongings. Someone had even stripped him of a beautiful watch that he cherished.

The Sisters flew out of the house, but all the elements conspired against them. First there was a traffic jam. Then they had difficulty finding the hospital. Finally, they got off the elevator on Wendell's floor and went the wrong way. When they found him, it was 1:45 in the afternoon. Wendell had died ten minutes earlier.

I found some comfort in the fact that one of the nurses recognized him from an earlier stay. He could no longer speak, but smiled when she asked if he remembered her.

In any case, he chose to leave us and died alone, when he could have been surrounded by so many people who loved him.

When we visited our men in the hospital, it was painful to see people who had no place like Gift of Love to go home to, and we did what we could to assist them while we were there. A volunteer called Michael was visiting a patient at Bellevue Hospital when he spotted what looked like an empty bed. As he came closer with a yellow rose in his hand, he saw a man who could not have weighed more than sixty pounds open his eyes and reach for the flower with his face. Michael let the man breathe in the scent and asked him if he wanted to pray.

He couldn't understand the reply, but when he started reciting the "Our Father," he saw the young man's lips begin to move. A nurse later told Michael that the man had been in a coma for a month. The next time Michael came to visit, he had passed away. How beautiful that he woke up long enough to smell the rose and pray.

I found that the many relationships that I treasured at Gift of Love were relationships that I am convinced continue beyond the moment of death and will remain with me for the rest of my life.

When I sing songs such as "His Eye Is on the Sparrow" that I first associated with my friend James back in 1990, or "Take My Hand, Precious Lord," which I sang hundreds of times to the men in their last days, hours, and moments of life, I swear I can feel them smiling and singing along beside me.

As I have said before, they gave me so much more than I could ever have given them.

"A Light That Leads Home"

During my years abroad, I discovered that just as the men had choices in their dying, I had choices in my living.

Back in 1994, I was in Paris in the middle of a new recording, when I decided that it was time to return to America on a more permanent basis. Paris had given me the opportunity to accomplish many of the things that I had wanted to do professionally, but after my years at Gift of Love it no longer held the same meaning in my life. When I told my producer that I was leaving, his reply was, "We'll talk about it."

But within two weeks, I had made a reservation to go back to New York and had given away all the furniture in my apartment and all my clothes.

My last recording was a song called "*Un Rayon de Lumière*" (A Ray of Light). The music was written for me by Patrick Fiori, and the lyrics by Bernard Di Domenico. The lyrics for the English version, called "A Light That Leads Home," were written by my friend Glynnis Snow. I always say that this song does not mention Mother Teresa's name, but it was inspired by all the Mother Teresas in the world, everyone who gives of themselves in service.

Before leaving Paris, I was asked to sing at a benefit gala for the Variety Club International at the legendary Folies-Bergère in the heart of Paris. I felt that a charity for handicapped children seemed an appropriate way to launch this particular song. At rehearsal, the normally blasé technicians couldn't restrain their enthusiasm. That night, the audience reacted in the same way. And as I held the last note, I stretched my arms out and could feel every one of my friends from Gift of Love beside me on that stage.

On my last morning in Paris, I *knew* I had made the right decision.

My friend Geneviève, one of the closest friends I made on my return to Paris in 1984, recently told me, "When I first met you, I hoped to live long enough to see you grow from the person you were then, the person who had a certain definition of success—worldly goods and public acclaim—to the person I knew you could become. You had to learn that the most important thing in life is the love that you give."

Back to Calcutta

In 1997, after seven years of volunteering at Gift of Love, I felt that the time had finally come for me to go back to Calcutta to visit Mother Teresa, whom by now I had come to consider my third "other mother."

Peggy Dolan, a volunteer I had gotten to know during my early days at Gift of Love, had called me in January to say that her greatest wish was to visit Calcutta, but she would only go if I went with her. For years I had resisted going back to India, despite Mother Teresa's frequent invitations, and I told Peggy I would have to think about it. But in my heart I knew I was ready.

I ran the idea past Jim and asked him if he would be interested in going. It was, of course, a silly question, since I already knew he would go anywhere in the world at a moment's notice.

While we planned the trip to Calcutta, we went to Nashville, Tennessee, to work on both the French and English versions of a music video of my last recording in Paris, "A Light That Leads Home"—a song that was so meaningful to my life.

When I told the production team about our trip to Calcutta, they asked if we could film in some of Mother Teresa's homes. Not knowing how Mother would react to my request, I decided to wait until we were in Calcutta to ask for her permission. In the meantime, Jim bought a discreet digital video camera that fit in the palm of his hand.

Our only problem now was when to go to Calcutta.

Because of the severity of Mother Teresa's heart condition, she was preparing to step down as Superior General of the Missionaries of Charity. It was now painfully obvious that at eighty-six she would probably not survive to serve another six-year term. Her successor would be elected by a group of about a hundred Missionaries of Charity delegates from around the world, and there was even speculation as to whether she would live long enough to see her successor named.

Believing that the Council would have finished its work by Easter, we decided to go the week before. As it turned out, the meetings ended the day before we arrived, and Sister Nirmala, who had been the head of the Contemplative Missionaries of Charity nuns, had been elected to replace Mother Teresa. (Unlike the active nuns I had worked with, the Contemplatives spend most of the day praying in their own convents and go out each day for short periods of time to help the poor in their neighborhood.)

On the plane, Jim and I saw Peggy reading a book about India, and laughed at the thought that it would give her the slightest inkling of the cultural shock she was in for. When she assured us that she was well prepared for Calcutta, Jim and I looked knowingly at each other and thought, "You have no idea!"

The first thing we saw as we descended from the plane was a huge banner leading to the interior of the airport saying, "WELCOME TO CALCUTTA". Underneath it were the decaying remains of an enormous dog. I saw Peggy turn pale as she carefully stepped around the carcass. As for the wild taxi ride from the airport to the Oberoi Grand Hotel, Peggy laughingly described it as "a near death experience."

Although she was proving herself to be a good sport, Peggy was clearly overwhelmed by the number of beggars we witnessed on the way to the hotel. Later, in the comfort of our suite, when I asked what she thought so far, she answered, "We came from Heaven and landed in Hell."

Even though the city had vastly improved since 1989, it was still evident that no guidebook could adequately prepare a Westerner for the poverty of Calcutta.

It was already evening by the time we arrived at the hotel on Monday night, so I immediately called Sister Priscilla, Mother Teresa's right hand, who was expecting us. She told us that Mother would be happy to receive us the next morning.

Tuesday morning, after rising at our leisure, we met our driver for the week, a young man called Jamal. As we drove through the streets in broad daylight, Peggy had to hide her eyes from the endless stream of mothers with babies in their arms coming up to the car at stoplights, begging for a few rupees. This time, as we neared the alley to the Motherhouse that had so terrified me on my first trip, my only concern was for Peggy, who found it increasingly difficult to say "No" to the small children with their arms stretched out to us.

An elderly nun quickly let us in the front door and took us up the stairs to the inner balcony overlooking the courtyard. The sparsely furnished house was filled not only with the noise of traffic from the main road outside, but also with the Sisters' laughter as they cleaned the Motherhouse in preparation for the religious ceremonies of Easter week.

Sister Priscilla greeted us on the terrace outside the office, from which we could hear old-fashioned typewriters clicking away, and told us that Mother was looking forward to our visit.

As soon as she said that, the curtains parted and a radiant Mother Teresa walked out onto the balcony, with her arms outstretched and a big smile on her face. Not only was this not the dying lady we had expected, she looked to be in the best of health.

Mother immediately took me away from the others to a little bench on her terrace and looked at me with eyes that saw right through to my soul. The two of us sat alone and talked about my spiritual journey and how much the seven years at Gift of Love had meant to me. I also wanted to tell her just once before she died what an inspiration she had been in my life.

We were basking in the sunlight when I felt a sudden need to open up my heart to Mother Teresa as I had rarely done to anyone. I told her about the emotional problems that had so often gotten in the way of my life, and how my work with her Sisters had become a great source of comfort.

Mother sat quietly for a moment. Then she put her hands on my head and prayed softly. As she prayed, I felt a wave of peace wash through my body, and when I looked up, I saw a gentle, understanding smile on her face.

At the time, what happened to me felt like a miracle. This woman I had come to think of as "another mother" had in a few timeless moments helped ease the pain of a lifetime.

Another fascinating thing about this encounter is that in a photo that was taken of us during our conversation, although we were both sitting in bright sunlight, everything is in shadow, including me—only parts of Mother Teresa are illuminated. One can see a very strong light behind her, lending a brilliant aura, like a halo, to the back of her head and on her left hand.

When I saw the photograph I knew that I had been in the presence of something extraordinary—something one might call a miracle.

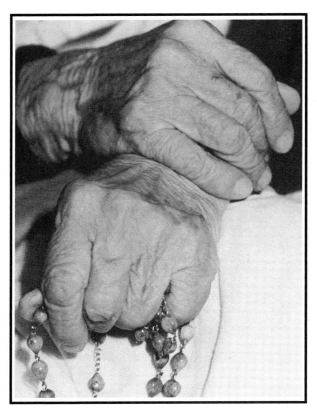

Mother Teresa's hands.

The front entrance to Mother
Teresa's Gift of Love, New York City.

Ready for a day's work
at Gift of Love.

I'm celebrating the Confirmation of patient Wendell (seated)
with another volunteer and patient Gilbert.

Jim and I arrive in Calcutta, 1997.

Even on one knee, I was still taller
than Mother Teresa.

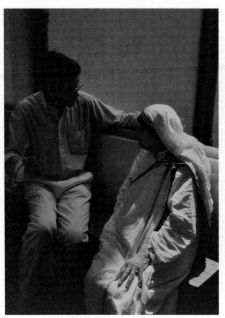

The "miracle" photo.

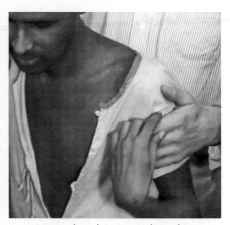

Man clutching my hand in
Mother Teresa's Home for
the Dying in Calcutta.

Mother Teresa, Jim, and me on her terrace in Calcutta.

With the children at Mother Teresa's orphanage in Calcutta.

One of the lepers showing me how the looms work.

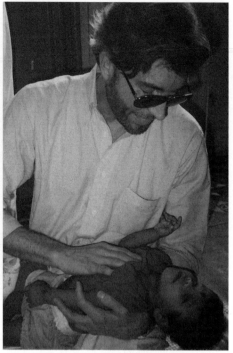

Mother Teresa's Home for
the Dying in Calcutta.

Comforting a blind baby
in Mother Teresa's orphanage
in Calcutta.

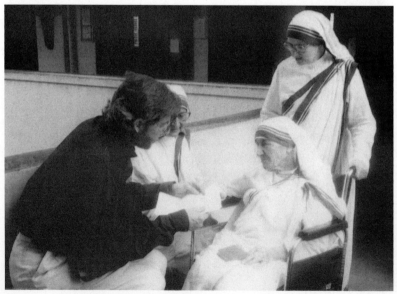

I read the lyrics of "A Light That Leads Home" to
Mother Teresa on her balcony in Calcutta.

Mother Teresa took one look at herself and joked, "Look at that *old* face!"

The Boys' Towns of Italy presents me with the first "Chance in Life Award," 2004. (Left to right) Robert Osborne, me, Laurence Auriana, Brother D'Adamo.

One of the last photos taken of Lee, me and Jim together.

On November 1, 2008, after 42 years together, Jim and I were married at the Peninsula Hotel in Beverly Hills, California. It was about time!

MOTHER TERESA'S LAST EASTER

Easter week, 1997, Jim and I visited with Mother Teresa every day.

When we approached Mother with the subject of the music video, I told her that it was not the purpose of our visit but wondered if we could have her permission to film in some of her homes for the poor.

Although this was a woman who may never have been in a movie theater in her life, and who said, "My tabernacle is my television," she understood what we were asking, and said, "Oh, you mean a short film where you sing in front of images!"

I answered, "Yes, Mother, that's exactly it."

"Well, Tony, you'll need written permission for that but if you come back this evening we'll have the letter ready for you."

Mother Teresa told me again about the more than five hundred homes she had opened for the poor in over a hundred countries of the world. I looked at her in awe and said, "And to think, you started it all in the slums of Calcutta with only a few rupees in your pocket."

Mother Teresa smiled at me and answered, "Yes, isn't it wonderful how God can take someone so completely useless and do so much?"

Later that afternoon we were given the priceless document that Mother had signed, giving us permission to film in Nirmal Hriday (the Home for the Dying), Shishu Bhavan (the orphanage), Prem Dan (a home for the mentally ill and the handicapped), and Gandiji Prem Nivas (a leprosy center in Titagargh). We were also granted permission to film Mother Teresa alone on her terrace. We realized that these were privileges rarely given.

The next morning our plan was to visit the Home for the Dying in Kalighat. I was delighted to learn that the Superior of the Home for the Dying was my old friend Sister Dolores, whom I had known in the Bronx when she was the Superior of the East Coast.

I walked into the familiar doorway in Kalighat, and asked the first nun I saw if I could speak to Sister Dolores. She started to laugh and said, "Tony! Don't you know me?"

"Sister Dolores?"

"Of course! How come you didn't recognize me?"

I looked closer and indeed, she was no longer the rather stout woman I remembered. Sister Dolores had slimmed down considerably in the heat of Calcutta.

She seemed in such good humor that I said, "I'm sorry, Sister, but there's a lot less of you now than there was in New York."

When I presented her the letter signed by Mother Teresa, Sister Dolores was very cooperative. She suggested that we come back and film on Good Friday.

Since our next stop was the Motherhouse, and Sister Dolores needed to go there too, she asked if we could give her a ride.

On the way to the Motherhouse, I asked Sister Dolores, "Why did God give some people the grace of knowing the joy of giving, and others not?"

"God didn't choose that. He gave it to everyone. *We* choose which path we want to take. It's not God, it's us. He gave everyone free will, and the choice to love. It's like when the rain comes down and someone says, 'I need some water.' They put a glass outside, take a little water, and bring it in. Someone else, however, will take the biggest bucket they can find, put *that* out, and fill it with water. And that's their choice.

"We have to trust in God, because He knows the past, present, and future. We must allow Him to do what He will with our lives. He knows. Often, we have to fail in order to learn—and sometimes fall. It's like the little baby. The mother has to allow her child to fall when it walks, and then it learns. We have to allow ourselves the same thing, but never be discouraged because God has the perfect plan for each of us.

"Jesus picked only very ordinary people as disciples. Thomas doubted him, Judas betrayed him, and Simon was afraid. They were only human beings. When Jesus arrived at the foot of Mount Calvary, he was too weak to go any further, so they forced Simon, who wanted no part of it, to help Him carry His cross to the top. And that is where Simon found his faith."

When we arrived at the Motherhouse, Mother Teresa was tired and sitting in a wheelchair. I was concerned about her health, but she seemed happy to see us and insisted on going ahead with our filmed interview.

For about twenty-five minutes, we sat together and talked while Jim recorded it all on video. My eyes were drawn to her worn hands, which told their own story of much hard work combined with a loving and gentle touch, for a disfigured leper or a dying child. These were the same hands that held mine at least half a dozen times during our interview while she quoted the words of Christ, "Whatever you do to the least of my brothers and sisters, *you did it to me*," in an effort to impress upon me that every act of charity is an act of love for God. More often than not, though, without saying a word, she would simply take one of my hands in hers and point to a different one of my fingers for each of the last five words, "You—did—it—to—me."

She had been doing this since the first time I met her, and it had taken me years to fully comprehend and to attempt to live those five words. But each time I felt too weary to climb the steps at Gift of Love one more time at the end of a long day in answer to a patient's cry, or I hesitated to stop and help some poor soul on the street during the course of what I considered to be my busy day, or I simply needed a little more patience to comfort an elderly person, Mother's words would come back to me and make me give just a little bit more of myself, of my time, or of my patience. Those words that Mother engraved on the five fingers of my hand told me that God resides in each of those people, and therefore I was truly doing it to Him. I can't say that I always succeeded, but I believe that the warmth that always spread through me and gave me strength during those times was God smiling from the depths of that person's soul into mine.

Mother Teresa, who started out as a schoolteacher, never stopped teaching us how to live, how to love, and how human one must really be in order to become a saint.

Mother Teresa told me that if she had not taken that first dying person off the streets of Calcutta, she would never have rescued the many thousands of others after that. To me, this meant that she was so involved in the moment that there was no room for doubt to creep in and prevent her from accomplishing that task. And that task, multiplied thousands of times, created a miracle around the world.

We sat together on her tiny balcony and talked about the increasing poverty in the world—the lack of food and material goods, and, worst of all, the absence of love in so many people's lives. The need for each human being to be loved and cared for was always uppermost in her mind. She also worried about the increase in AIDS cases around the world, and constantly asked me why, for which I had no answer except "Ignorance and drugs."

Mother Teresa joyously told me once again how wonderful God had been to her Missionaries of Charity, making it possible for them, in a period of almost fifty years, to open five hundred homes for the poor in more than one hundred countries, while drawing approximately five thousand young men and women to this order— which requires them not only to serve the poorest of the poor, but also to *live* as the poorest of the poor. Again she told me, "The poor are very great people."

Mother Teresa seemed particularly proud of the self-supporting "city" in Titagargh that the Missionaries of Charity had created for the leprosy patients, and she insisted that I go see it.

She never tired of telling me, "God has been very good to us," and that she was merely a "pencil in God's hands. He does the writing— everything," but I could never ignore the enormous sacrifice that it took every moment of every day to fully submit to His will—a sobering thought for a very ordinary human being such as myself, riddled with fears and uncertainty.

It was only her great humility and simplicity that made it possible for me to sit there, look into her loving face, and talk about the poor as though I could begin to understand one iota of the wisdom that she had acquired through a lifetime of service. The best way I knew how to express what was in my heart was to ask her if I could sing a song of praise, "I Bowed On My Knees," just for her. This is a song about a man dreaming of visiting the glories of Heaven. Mother Teresa smiled and nodded deeply in agreement when I sang the words, *"But I said, I want to see Jesus, 'cause he's the one who died for me."*

I had sung for her many times, and although there were moments during my song when she seemed to be looking far into the distance, I knew she was always fully present and listening to every word.

At the end of the song, she responded with one of her favorite words, "Beautiful," and asked me if I would sing at the Home for the Dying on Easter Sunday.

Then she blessed us once again and went back inside.

That afternoon, we set out with our chauffeur for Prem Dan, a home primarily for mentally and physically handicapped men and women whom the Sisters had rescued from the streets.

When we approached Prem Dan, our driver had to dodge children and dogs in narrow alleys filled with sewage. The living conditions were a nightmare compared to anything we had seen before—houses that were mostly open huts, with families sharing tiny spaces that barely shielded them from the heat and rain. As always, Mother Teresa had built a home for the poor in one of the poorest areas of the city, where it was needed most.

If someone hadn't opened the gates of Prem Dan, I don't know if I could have stepped out of the car. As it was, the smell from the street nearly overwhelmed us.

Jim's word to describe Prem Dan was "gloom." At Nirmal Hriday, the Home for the Dying, there were beautiful pictures of Mother Teresa and inspirational sayings on the walls that made it homelike, but here we saw nothing. It went beyond the walls to a feeling of hopelessness that we never felt in the other homes. And yet we could see how grateful these people were, when a man silently came up to Sister and kissed the ground in front of her sandals.

Although I had explained to the Superior that we had been given permission to film in the home, Jim and I instantly felt that we could not intrude upon this kind of misery with a camera.

We decided to visit the orphanage, Shishu Bhavan, on Thursday morning because that was when Sister Maria Lucy worked there. It would be an extra treat for us to see her again.

In a large room, we saw many toddlers scurrying around on the floor playing with lots of toys including a tiny slide, while others were content taking turns being held by the novices.

Jim was busy filming the children at play when I instinctively reached out to a child lying face down on the floor. It was only when I picked him up that I realized he was blind. At first he was very agitated, so I sat down on the floor, placed him on his back in my lap and sang to him while gently rubbing his chest. After a few moments, his little body relaxed completely and he lay there with a smile of pure contentment on his face.

Upstairs, the Sisters led us to a separate area for severely handicapped children. It also had colorful cribs and a large playing area. The children who were not able to sit up had special chairs built like highchairs with desks in front that enabled them to participate in the activities to the best of their abilities. Some, who could at least crawl on the mats, were thrilled to be lifted in the air by a six-foot-two-inch giant such as me, and squealed in glee as I held them up in a standing position and sang.

I was later told that many of the children were blind because of the primitive techniques that had been used in an effort to abort them. For many years Mother Teresa had asked everyone not to abort their unborn children but to give them to her. She promised to see that they were either adopted or raised and educated by her and her Sisters. And throughout a lifetime of work in many countries of the world, she always had room for one more child.

After Shishu Bhavan, we returned to the Motherhouse to spend more time with Mother Teresa before our next stop. As always, she greeted us with a big smile and a blessing. She was especially happy that our destination that afternoon would finally be the leprosy center that she had built in Titagargh.

The Center, which was called "Abode of Love," was built along several acres of railroad tracks and we were amazed to see that it was a completely self-supporting little "city. " It had a hospital, dormitories for single patients, and homes for families. The patients raised their own food and livestock, and earned a living making sandals and colorful materials for saris. These handicapped men and women— many without fingers or toes—worked the old-fashioned looms and created, among other fabrics, the white and blue saris worn by the Missionaries of Charity Sisters all over the world.

It was at the very least a revolutionary idea for lepers in India to be treated with respect as useful members of society, and only Mother Teresa's vision and tenacity was able to make it a reality.

Even though drugs have been discovered that can cure the disease in its early stages, ignorance and poverty still cause millions of victims in third-world countries to seek help only after disfigurement and deformity have set in. Many still don't know that leprosy is not an irreversible curse created by "karma," but is a progressive infectious disease caused by a bacterium that attacks the skin, flesh, and nerves. The Missionaries of Charity have opened many centers, some of them nothing more than a van, from which they medicate and educate the huge population of lepers throughout the world.

Since it was known that children are not born with leprosy, the babies at Titagargh were separated from their mothers at birth. Parents could see them, but had to wait to hold or feed them. Meanwhile, Mother Teresa saw to it that the children were assured of an education and a trade in order to someday be self-supporting.

Again we didn't feel comfortable filming in Titagargh, but the lepers were proud to show us the fruits of their labor, and smiled as we took still photographs of them at work.

That evening we returned to the Motherhouse for Mass. It was Holy Thursday, which meant that the priests would wash the feet of twelve men who represented the Apostles.

At the last moment, Mother Teresa entered in her wheelchair and took her usual place in the back. When several Sisters rose to take different offerings to the altar, Mother left her wheelchair and followed them, with the communion chalice in her hands.

We were deeply moved, watching the love with which this holy woman carried the symbolic Body of her Spouse to the priest.

Good Friday
At 8:00 a.m. we made our way through the wild traffic of Calcutta to visit my "new friend," Sister Dolores, at the Home for the Dying.

In the car, Peggy said there was no way she could handle doing any work, while Jim told me, "You care for the patients and I'll hold the camera!" Although it seemed that they were both getting cold feet, this time I felt no apprehension at what the day might bring. After all, how different could it be from Gift of Love?

The moment Sister Dolores saw us walk in, she told Peggy and me to put on aprons and get to work.

One of my charges was a young man whom I carried in my arms into the bath. He was only skin and bones and was racked with spasms, especially when he attempted to help me wash him. He did his best, but the harder he tried the less he could control his movements. After I had washed him and dressed him in fresh pajamas, another volunteer told me to put a lotion all over his body. When I asked what it was for, he informed me that my young patient was covered with scabies. I wasn't quite sure what scabies was but I knew it was something I didn't want to catch, and quickly put on the rubber gloves I had so far resisted wearing.

It now amazes me when I think of the ease with which I talked to these men, whose language was probably Hindu or Bengali, and never felt a lack of communication. In fact, the language barrier never even occurred to me. I instinctively knew when my spastic friend needed a way to raise his head, or when to give him water, drop by drop, as I had seen a volunteer do so many years ago on my first trip to the Home for the Dying in Calcutta.

During this time I lost track of Peggy, whose resolve to sit and watch only lasted long enough for her to walk in the front door. As for Jim, he followed Sister Dolores around, getting it all on film. It was only when Sister showed him a patient being carried into the tiny morgue that the camera began to visibly shake. She didn't realize that, unlike me, Jim had not dealt with death on such intimate terms before.

In spite of that, Jim courageously filmed both sides of the little room where the dead lay while waiting for whatever their religion dictated. On one side a sign said, "I'M ON MY WAY TO HEAVEN", and on the other side a sign said, "THANK YOU FOR TAKING ME TO HEAVEN".

Sister also showed us a private area where the patients were first brought in from the streets and gutters. Here they were washed and, when necessary, the worms carefully taken out of their bodies. Overhead Mother Teresa had put a sign that said, "THE BODY OF CHRIST". Never for a moment did she want us to forget that we must treat the poor with as much tenderness and love as we would Christ Himself.

The last thing I noted before we left the Home for the Dying was that in 45 years 68,055 patients had been admitted to Nirmal Hriday and 29,269 had died—two of them that day.

The next day, Saturday, I was sitting on the balcony of the Motherhouse, reading the English translation of the lyrics of *Un Rayon de Lumière* to Mother Teresa. She listened carefully, and seemed deeply moved. Then, with a big smile on her face, she asked me for a copy.

When I told Mother that on Good Friday I had washed the body of Christ, clothed the body of Christ, and fed the body of Christ, in the Home for the Dying, she smiled broadly and said "Good! Do it again!"

Late that afternoon we once again returned to the Motherhouse. We stood a discreet distance away while Mother Teresa stood in the midst of several people who were taking pictures and asking for a blessing. One of them was on her knees, weeping at Mother's feet.

Before we knew it, Mother had left the crowd and sauntered over to us with her usual smile, ready for what had become our daily chat. She was embarrassed at public displays of adulation and seemed to enjoy the fact that we treated her like a normal person. With us she was also free to laugh and to indulge in a sense of humor that few people were aware of.

While she was talking, we asked her to sign some large photographs the Sisters had given us. One picture was particularly interesting: a candle with a large flame in Mother's hand illuminated her face, accentuating every wrinkle. Mother took one look at herself and joked, "Look at that *old* face!"

When I told Mother that she was the only person in the world I would get up at dawn for, and pointed out how grey my hair had become during the seven years at Gift of Love, she wasn't particularly impressed. She touched my hair and said, "There's still a lot of black in there."

As the afternoon wore on, I realized that Mother was enjoying our conversation and seemed in no hurry to go back to any pressing duties. The impressive part for us was the fact that she appeared to be just "hanging out," as they say, with no pressure to be on display. We considered that a great compliment.

Mother Teresa repeated how great the poor are—"Even when the Sisters take them off the streets and remove the worms from their bodies, they never complain. And they all die such a beautiful death." Then, as so many times before, she took my hand and repeated Christ's words, touching each finger, "You—did—it—to—me."

Her final words, as she blessed us and told us again of her many Homes around the world, were, "Yes, God has been very good to us."

Before we left the Motherhouse, we discovered that some of the Sisters were becoming curious about our lengthy discussions with Mother and wondered what fascinating information we had that kept her chatting away every day. It was Sister Nirmala who finally came up to us once after Mother had gone inside, hesitated, and asked, "The Sisters and I are dying to know, what on earth do you all talk about every day?"

I said, "Everything and nothing."

It had been that way with Ethel Merman, too. We had laughed and talked every day, about anything. It is hard enough to deal with the public when you are a great star, with people grabbing at you and everybody wanting a piece of you; I can only imagine how difficult it must be when the world considers you to be a living saint, weeping and touching you and expecting you to get them to heaven somehow. Even Mother Teresa's nuns didn't understand the demands that were made on her. Ethel Merman and Mother Teresa were both comfortable with Jim and me, because we treated both of them like ordinary extraordinary human beings. We laughed, talked, and cried together about everything and anything.

Easter Sunday

Our last day in Calcutta began with the worldly question of what clean clothes I had left to wear for Mass on Easter Sunday at the Home for the Dying. Jim only laughed when all I could find was a Versace shirt that he considered inappropriate for the occasion. Finally I unearthed a plain button-down shirt and khaki pants from the Army/Navy store that looked presentable enough for me to sing in.

At ten o'clock Easter morning, the Home for the Dying was beautifully decorated and an altar set up near the entrance on the men's side. All the women patients were dressed in colorful yellow dresses, and those who were able to do so came over for the Mass. The priest went through the home blessing everyone with an olive branch and holy water; no one was ignored.

When it came time for me to sing, I looked out at volunteers holding on to emaciated hands in their final hours of life. It was overwhelming to think that this might be the last music some of these men and women would hear on this earth.

Afterwards, I told Jim and Peggy that there is no award in the world that could have meant more to me than the honor of sharing my music in Kalighat on Easter Sunday, 1997.

Later in the day, we went to the Motherhouse to say goodbye to Mother Teresa. I thanked her and told her how much it had meant to me to sing at the Home for the Dying that Easter morning. She then blessed me one more time, held my hand, and said, "What a blessing for Easter!"

I doubted that Jim and Peggy and I would ever be quite the same again.

Agnes Bojaxhiu

On September 5, 1997, at 8:15 in the evening, the Sisters noticed that Mother Teresa was in obvious distress. Her immense heart, which had touched so many people around the world, had failed her in the end. Somehow Mother found the strength to kiss a crown of thorns hanging on the wall beside her bed and say, "Jesus, I love you. Jesus, I trust in you. Jesus…"

Those were her last words before she went home to the God whom she had faithfully served for eighty-seven years.

How grateful I was to have spent so much time with her over the last seven years, and especially during her last Easter Week on earth, just five months before.

I couldn't help but think back upon the awesome effect this holy woman had on me the first few times we met in New York City. I would feel a sense of timelessness come over me, while my mind ceased to function as a part of this world, and words became just meaningless sounds—in essence, being with Mother Teresa had been like being in the presence of a living prayer.

While looking back upon Mother Teresa's lifetime of sacrifice and unfaltering selfless giving, I wished I had known Agnes Bojaxhiu, the girl who would grow up to be Mother Teresa.

I remembered meeting Dimitri, the *maitre d'* of a Russian restaurant in Los Angeles, whose mother had been a childhood friend of Mother Teresa's family, living only two doors away from them in Skopje, Albania. Dimitri's "Mum," who was three years younger than Agnes, would often go to the Bojaxhiu home for embroidery lessons, and Agnes would always make a point of accompanying her safely home.

After young Agnes left home at eighteen to become a nun, sixty years passed before the government would allow Mother Teresa to return to Skopje. By that time, both her mother and sister, who had remained in Albania, had died. But Mother Teresa went anyway, in 1991, using the opportunity to open homes for the poor and to visit her old friend, Dimitri's Mum.

Dimitri explained to me that in their culture, a woman's major purpose in life was to bear children. So when these two old friends were finally reunited, Dimitri's Mum asked Mother Teresa if she regretted never having had any children of her own. Mother's immediate reply was, "Yes, very much, but I had no choice."

In 1994, Dimitri, who had never met Mother Teresa, went to Calcutta to visit her. Mother happily greeted him and told him of his family, whom she had known well, and that he was the image of his granddaddy. They spent several hours together, speaking in Serbian, while she wept and touched his head and his hands as the memories flooded back.

Dimitri's story made me even more aware of the great sacrifice Mother never showed the world when she left home at such an early age and gave her life to the "poorest of the poor."

I was invited to attend the ceremony for the beatification of Mother Teresa in Rome on October 19, 2003. It is one of the steps on her way to becoming a saint. As far as I am concerned, she doesn't need confirmation from the Vatican—she was a saint long before her death.

Between Two Worlds

One Christmas Eve the Sisters invited Jim and me to go out into the streets of the South Bronx after Midnight Mass to give blankets, clothes, food, and hot chocolate to the homeless. They knew just where to go—under bridges, on the streets and into abandoned buildings. These were areas that the police had told us to avoid, but with the Missionaries of Charity, all things are possible. I had no fear.

We drove around in a van on a freezing, rainy night. Prostitutes, drug addicts, and just plain folks down on their luck came out to greet us. All these human beings whom most people would have avoided if they passed them in their neighborhood turned out to be among the most polite and gentle people we had ever met—and so grateful. Many asked for things to take back to their friends who were too sick to come outside themselves, and all of them patiently waited their turn in the cold.

At four o'clock Christmas morning, we stood on the street, holding hands in a large circle and singing "Silent Night." During the moment of silence that followed the song, I asked if anyone wanted to say a prayer. In spite of the rain and cold, these homeless men and women took off their hats out of respect. One of them simply said, "I give thanks for everything." Another man looked around the circle and said, "I can't believe somebody cared about us tonight."

Although Mother Teresa devoted her life to serving the "poorest of the poor" and was considered by many to be a "living saint," I believe she considered *these* people to be the real saints.

☙ ❧

Jim and I finally returned home at five o'clock in the morning knowing that we had a few hours in which to rest before going to our second Christmas celebration of the day. This time it would be at our friend Lee Lehman's luxurious home on Fifth Avenue.

When I was thirteen years old, Lee had become my first "other mother," and over the years remained one of my best friends. Even though she still lived with the effects of damage to the motor portion of her brain after her suicide attempt at the age of forty-nine, holidays were always a time for us to celebrate together. She had slowly become a recluse, but her spirit was such that even after all these years she still had her make-up man and hairdresser come to the house every day. On this Christmas Day, I knew she would once again greet me looking her most beautiful. I was not disappointed.

Before dinner, we drank champagne in her massive living room, surrounded by priceless paintings, eighteenth-century furniture, and porcelain de Sèvres while we laughed and talked about old times. Almost a half-century after our first meeting, she was as fascinating as ever. Nothing seemed to have changed. We were still an important part of each other's lives.

I knew how difficult it would be for her to help herself to the buffet, so I fixed her a plate of turkey with all the trimmings. She was radiant in the candlelight, and, as I took my place next to her at the table, I realized how much love I had found serving people in two very different worlds that day.

GOODBYE, MY BEAUTIFUL FRIEND

It was hard for me to believe that Lee Lehman was eighty-seven years old in 2006. She was still beautiful to look at but no longer left her bedroom. Over the years her speech had become even more difficult to understand and it was apparent that her right hand lay immobile in her lap. Fortunately, there were aides around the clock to care for her.

The first thing Jim and I would see when we made the long walk down the hallway to her bedroom was the wheelchair outside the door. Beyond that was a hunched-over figure sitting motionless in front of a television set.

But the moment Lee saw us she became the woman Jim and I had always adored. The smile was radiant, the make-up and hair were perfect, and the laughter was still there. We talked about the trips we took together years ago and remembered the good times we shared.

At the height of Lee's beauty, when I first met her, she told me that all of her lovers said they wanted to be there when she was old, to push her wheelchair. Lee looked at me with a wry smile and a knowing look on her face, and said, "They won't be there."

I thought to myself, "I'll be there." And I was.

On a sunny afternoon, June 10, 2006, I received a call from Lee's daughter Pam in California informing me that her mother had been admitted to Lenox Hill Hospital's Emergency Room. She asked me if I would please run over and see what was happening. I went into my safe and took out Lee's Living Will, which she had entrusted to me.

When I arrived at the hospital, I told the nurse at the desk that I was Mrs. Lehman's son (a white lie that I hoped might save me some bureaucratic problems). A sympathetic doctor immediately approached me and told me that Mrs. Lehman had a massive infection in her body.

"What are her chances of surviving this episode?" I asked.

Without a moment's hesitation, the doctor answered, "None!"

I appreciated his candor and told him that I had brought her Living Will, of which I was the executor.

"Thank God," he said. "Now we can give her life a compassionate ending."

The first thing I saw as I entered the tiny cubicle were tubes—lots and lots of tubes coming out of every part of her body. But in spite of the swelling in her face, it was not hard to recognize my still-beautiful friend.

I watched as the doctor removed the now-useless life support system and gave her morphine to ease her discomfort. Before leaving the little cubicle he said that he could not predict how long it might be before she took her last breath, but not to be surprised if she survived for no more than twenty minutes. I was prepared.

I sat alone with her for the next two hours during which I held her hand, caressed her forehead and spoke comforting words to her. I told her how much she was loved, and that a brilliant white light surrounded her. She had done her work well while she was here, and could now rest peacefully.

I then called Jim, who came over and sat with me in the comfortable room they mercifully moved her to. She was now surrounded by two people who loved her unconditionally.

At midnight, Lee's breathing became progressively slower. She could not hang on much longer. Finally at 2:40 a.m. my first "other mother" peacefully died. It was over. I had sat next to her for twelve hours and Jim had been there for eight.

☙ ❧

A few moments after Lee took her last breath, Jim and I were both aware that the body of the woman we had known and loved was now an empty shell. As I leaned over the bed to kiss her goodbye, I felt the room filling up with her vibrant spirit. I could almost touch it.

Jim stood by her bed with me and said, "She's young and beautiful again."

On my way home through the empty streets of New York, I thought back to the last time I had visited my old friend in her lonely bedroom.

Before leaving her, I had said, "One of the most amazing things about you, Lee, is that in fifty-two years I have never heard you say an unkind word about anyone."

"Why would I?" she replied. "I was given so much."

$$—\!\!\!-\!\!\blacklozenge\!\!-\!\!\!—$$

"That Was Your First Mistake"

Pam outlived Lee by a year, and I was grateful that Lee did not have to suffer the tragedy of losing her daughter.

When Pam was diagnosed with stage four ovarian cancer, she called me and said, "Will you be there to help me to die?"

And I said, "Of course, Pam." And I was, just as I had been for Lee.

Pam's son Chris, whom I had loved unconditionally all his life, called us on Friday before Thanksgiving, sobbing, "Please come to California—I need you." We flew to California the next day.

I remembered the first time I ever saw Chris, shortly after he was born. Pam and her husband were staying with the Lehmans in the Park Avenue apartment, and Lee took me into the room where Chris was being cared for by a very stiff old-fashioned Irish nurse. Lee walked with me over to the crib, leaned over it, and said, "Chris, I want you to meet your *real* daddy!"

The nurse, not having much of a sense of humor, started crossing herself and praying for the heathens in the house, with "Hail Mary's" flying around the room.

Lee wasn't far wrong, because, to me, Chris has always been like a son. I could not love him more if I were his biological father.

Chris did not tell Pam that we were coming. When we walked into her room on Sunday morning, she looked at Chris and smiled, and said, "Does this mean I'm dying?"

I said, "Pam, it means we love you."

She laughed and pointed her finger at me and said, "That was your first mistake."

We spent half an hour talking, just talking, just like with Mother Teresa. It wasn't about death or dying, it wasn't about anything but life. After half an hour I could see she was growing tired. I said, "Pam, we're going to go downstairs. We'll come back upstairs later, and you rest."

It was the last lucid half-hour that she had. She died on Thanksgiving morning, and I held her in my arms after she died.

Chris was distraught and ran out of the house. I cleaned Pam up and put her in a comfortable position on the bed, and suddenly there was a beautiful smile on her face.

I said to Jim, "Please call Chris back, I want him to see her the way she is now, not the way she was when she passed. I want him to remember her this way."

Then we sent him away again, because I didn't want him to be there when they came to take her out of the house.

We buried Pam's ashes with her husband's ashes. I dropped into the grave, on top of the urn, a "miraculous medal" that had been blessed and kissed by Mother Teresa.

Our Wedding

I don't know how much I could have accomplished in my life without Jim's unfailing support. Therefore I would find it hard to finish telling my story without acknowledging his role in bringing endless joy into my life and for never letting a day go by without making me laugh.

Over the years Jim has been my manager, my best friend, my emotional support, and, most of all, the person I have lived and shared my life with in every way for more than four decades. In the era we grew up in, our relationship would never have been accepted. Fortunately we have bridged the gap of time and it has always been, as far as I know, a non-issue for our families, for my "other mothers," in my professional career, and ultimately in my work with the sick and the dying.

On November 1, 2008, at six o'clock in the evening, Jim Russo and I were married at the Peninsula Hotel in Beverly Hills, California. It was four days before Proposition 8 was passed and all 18,000 gay couples who had already been joined in matrimony in that state remained married, including us.

Our ceremony took place in a large patio, where bowls of gardenias and huge vases of white calla lilies surrounded a flowing fountain whose splashing waters sparkled and danced in the candlelight that outlined it. Forty-six friends from around the world came to share this momentous event with us. Who would have thought when we were growing up in the 1950s that such a miraculous and wonderful blessing would be possible in our lifetime?

Each of the forty-six guests represented a beautiful thread in the tapestry of our lives.

Among our friends who were present that night was Ronda Copeland, with her flaming red hair, wearing a black lace dress on her still-perfect figure. She had been Jim's date the night we first met at a Halloween party, and she had become like a sister to me. As witnesses and ring bearers, we were honored to have Lee Lehman's grandson, Christopher, who is like a son to me, and his fiancée, Ruth.

A couple of days before the great day, I had asked Ethel Merman's son, Bob Levitt, whom I had known since 1959 when I first met his sister Little Ethel at a summer acting class for teenagers, if he would be kind enough to say a few words before the ceremony. He did not hesitate for a moment before saying a resounding, "Yes!"

I knew that Bob usually shied away from publicly bringing his mother's celebrity into his world. But this evening he stunned us all with a meaningful and touching speech that brought us all to tears—especially with the amazing gift he gave us all at the end.

Here it is in part:

—

In my mother's twilight year of life, she was bedridden with a brain tumor. All her friends gathered to take care of her in New York City, and I, the family member on the scene, began to socialize with my mother's friends in a way that I never had in my lifetime. I moved in very different circles than my mom did and so I got the first intense look at the way my mother's circle were behaving around her—the love that they were sharing with her. And right in the heartbeat of that love were Tony and Jimmy, because their dearest friend, Ethel, was suffering the reduction from the great and magnificent ETHEL MERMAN to the simple and quietly, barely surviving Ethel. And I watched Tony and Jimmy redefine for me what heart's love was about in friends.

I grew up all my life celebrating the union of gay people. My "aunties and uncles," most of them that Mom cherished friendships with, were gay. I grew up loving gay people and being loved by gay people. And at a certain point it all blended in for me to "people."

I think that the forty-two years that Jimmy and Tony have spent in their union, which we will now celebrate with a kind of exclamation point in this formal ceremony, is one of the most precious, loving, tender, openhearted and elegantly graceful relationships that I have ever seen. And I admire them and love them deeply and it's my honor and my every heartbeat's privilege to know them as my brothers.

I'd like to end by playing something for them and for all of us that I thought would be appropriate in this moment, which is something that I would like to give to their hearts.

We had thought that we were going to surprise Bob when we came down the aisle to a slow piano and cello rendition of Ethel's first big hit song, "I Got Rhythm," the song that first put her on the map in Gershwin's *Girl Crazy* in 1930. To our surprise, Bob trumped us when he put the microphone on a tape recorder which filled the whole outdoors with his mother singing George Gershwin's "Someone To Watch Over Me."

There was not a dry eye in the house.

When it was over, all forty-six guests stood up as a weeping Jimmy and I walked down that aisle.

Now that we are in our forty-seventh year together, in 2013, Jimmy always says, "It was the perfect song. It told us that Ethel was watching over us and we were watching over each other."

EPILOGUE

All aspects of my existence continue to be enriched as a result of my years of experience with Mother Teresa and the Missionaries of Charity.

After twelve years, I was forced to stop my work at Gift of Love because of what my neurologist, after many tests, finally diagnosed as peripheral neuropathy. Although many things can cause neuropathy, in my case, the doctor concluded that it was congenital, inherited from my mother.

Since this is a disease that attacks and destroys the nerves in the arms and legs, eventually the work and the three flights of stairs at Gift of Love became too much for me to handle. Although neuropathy has made my daily life increasingly difficult as I lose more of the use of my legs, I take comfort in the fact that I was well enough to be in the front lines of the battle against AIDS for twelve years, when I was needed most.

Now I know what Ethel Merman meant when she would come home from a day's work volunteering at Roosevelt Hospital— which she did every Wednesday for ten years, whenever she was in Manhattan—and she would call me and tell me about her day: "It was a long day, but it just makes me feel so good." Although I was not consciously thinking about Ethel when I volunteered at Gift of Love, she had already set the example for me.

When I first started volunteering with Mother Teresa and the Missionaries of Charity, I found myself flailing around in panic and insecurity. But no matter how incompetent I may have felt then, ultimately I came away with the knowledge that if *I* could do it, then *anyone* could do it. *I* had no special gifts or talents to bring to the house. In the end, all that really mattered was my willingness to share a small part of myself with others. I no longer had to be "perfect."

A Tribute to "My Kids"

I volunteered at Gift of Love for twelve years. During that time I helped almost a hundred men who were dying of AIDS.

In the early years, when there was no effective treatment for AIDS, and hospitals and prisons didn't know how to deal with this unpredictable and always terminal disease, I often worked ten- to twelve-hour days several times a week.

Ultimately, the men's courage, humor, and generosity helped me with *my* growth. This was, for me, the real story of Gift of Love— transforming it into a place of life, not of death. Here are a few of their stories:

Joseph
Joseph was a white, college-educated, middle-class youth of Irish descent. He was also a slight, effeminate, twenty-six-year-old gay man who offered no apologies to anyone for the way God had made him.

The first time I saw Joseph at Gift of Love he was helping the Sisters carry platters of food up to the dining room for breakfast. When I asked Sister Maria Lucy if we had a new volunteer in the house she answered, "No, Tony, that's Joseph, one of our new patients."

After the meal Joseph and I stood at the foot of the stairs and discussed the fact that unlike him, many of the men in the house had been infected with AIDS through intravenous drug use.

Joseph told me that his father had accepted his being gay, but his mother could not. She apparently would have preferred it if he had contracted AIDS from drugs.

I'll never forget his final words that morning as he swept grandly up the staircase, looked down at me with a big grin and announced, "But I told her that I got it the *normal* way!"

Until he died a few months later, I remained in awe of the way Joseph used humor to deal with a disease that eventually would destroy his body but never his spirit.

Wendell

Although the men were generous in caring for each other, it was hard for some of them to acknowledge when one of their friends had been moved into the "dying room" (a single room set apart, where the dying man could be cared for peacefully around the clock without disturbing the other patients). The door was always left open so that the sounds of life were still present and others would feel welcome to come in and visit if they wished. Of course the question on everyone's mind was, "Am I next?"

One morning while I was taking care of Wilfredo, Wendell, who was only twenty-six years old himself, shuffled into the dying room dressed in his slippers and robe, approached Wilfredo's bed and said, "Wilfredo, I'm going to die soon—just like you. Last night, while you were sleeping, you didn't know it, but I came and sat by your bed and said a rosary for you."

I could only wonder where this kind of courage came from.

Oscar

Oscar was one of those rare patients who was always there for me if *I* needed someone to talk to; he understood the complexities of the house and the other patients that I had to deal with. He was also a talented artist who was losing his sight.

One day he showed me a beautiful wooden box that he had made for Peggy, one of the volunteers, with her name written in gold on the top. He then hinted that he was working on another project for me. I found it tragic that he was rushing to finish these gifts while he could still see.

Oscar kept his sight long enough to make another wooden box, with my name on the outside. Inside, he had written in gold letters, "To Tony for being so kind, nice and generous. We love you: Thanks. God bless you. The guys of Gift of Love."

He told me, "I am doing my best to begin to see you all with my heart and not with my eyes."

Oscar and Herbert

But not all the patients were as easy to get along with as Oscar.

When Herbert, who had always been a demanding patient, was moved into the dying room, he became increasingly disagreeable toward the Sisters and volunteers. Sometimes it seemed as if he saved up his energy to figure out how to provoke us the most. A particularly trying incident prompted one of the Sisters to say, "Tony, I know we're supposed to love everyone, but, Lord, Herbert makes it so difficult!"

One day, after giving Herbert a diaper change and enduring a litany of abuse, I went into Oscar's room next door and said through gritted teeth, "Oscar, I'm not a saint. I can't deal with this man any more."

After blowing off some steam, I went back to Herbert's room with a smile on my face and noticed that he had slipped down towards the foot of the bed. When I put my arms around him and started to lift, I saw a flash of light before my eyes. My first thought was, "What's happening to me? Maybe I'm having the Big One."

Then I turned around and saw Oscar taking pictures of me helping Herbert.

Oscar, knowing how upset I was, told me, "Now if you need tangible proof of what you do, that you are a valuable person, and a valuable volunteer, I'm going to give it to you."

I tell you, every day was a miracle.

Bruce

Bruce was raised by a poor Pentecostal family down South, and as a child had loved Jesus so much that he wanted to be just like him in every way.

At the age of twelve, after years of physical abuse, he made the mistake of wearing his father's tie for his first day of school in the seventh grade—without permission. When his father came home, he went into a rage and kicked Bruce so hard he broke his lower spine.

As he grew up, Bruce prayed to God to rescue him from the pain of his home life, and when that didn't work, he prayed to the devil; but there was no help there either. Eventually he withdrew into his own world where no one could hurt him.

When Bruce was eighteen, he escaped from his family by joining the army, and was sent to Vietnam. He wouldn't elaborate on his life after returning from the war, but told me that he cared for no one and did many things of which he was now ashamed. Years later, when he became ill, a V.A. doctor bluntly told him that he had the AIDS virus.

It was at Gift of Love that Bruce started to make his peace with God and with his past. The Sisters assured him that AIDS was not a punishment from God, but that God loved him unconditionally and wanted him to use the situation in which he had been placed to open his heart to others. Soon he began to accept that he was loved, and even started to help me take care of other patients in the house.

When his health improved enough for him to leave us—which rarely happened in those days—I asked him what his plans were. He said that he wasn't quite ready to go yet since one of the friends he had made at Gift of Love was dying. He added, "I'll go back to North Carolina after Charles is gone. I don't want to abandon him now."

Then he told me that his birthday was next week.

"How wonderful—we can have a celebration!"

"You know, Tony, I'm forty-eight years old, and I have never, ever in my life had a birthday party."

I thought it was time we celebrated.

James

James was a 200-pound gentle giant of a man who had lost the use of his arms and legs. He could move them but he couldn't make them do what he wanted. He had also lost the ability to speak. Again, he could make sounds but could not articulate words. On top of all that, he had lost his sight.

On one of my many trips up and down the three flights of stairs I looked at the photograph of Mother Teresa next to the chapel door—and silently begged her for guidance: What could I do for this man who was imprisoned in his body and could no longer communicate?

The next time I passed by the lounge where James lay on the couch, I was inspired to pull up a stool next to him and say, "James, why don't we sing?"

Seeing a flicker of interest on his face, I took his hand and started to sing an old spiritual called "His Eye Is On The Sparrow." Before I finished the first line his face lit up with the most extraordinary smile. He grabbed my hand with all his strength and started to sing along. Of course, he was only making sounds, but I could tell that he knew the song perfectly and was singing every word with me.

That morning I learned that I could make a difference by calling upon the same talents I had used for years in the world of show business.

I also learned that joy can still be found no matter what the human condition.

Carlos

Some days, when I was particularly tired, it was easy to lose sight of the real reason I had volunteered my services at Gift of Love and I would grumble to myself as I washed another bathroom floor or cleaned the front steps.

One beautiful spring day, the men were upstairs resting, and I was alone in the kitchen, peeling endless potatoes, and thinking, "This is so boring. What am I doing here with these potatoes? I'm of no use at all."

The Sisters were downstairs in the convent so I went into the chapel for a change of scenery. When I heard footsteps coming down the stairs I walked out of the chapel and saw a young man who had just arrived at Gift of Love that morning. As I sat down quietly nearby, he looked me right in the eye and spoke loudly and haltingly—the only way he was able to speak—"I... WANT... TO DIE. ..."

I then listened while he told me of his life in the ghetto, his involvement with drugs, and how when he was eighteen years old a neighborhood gang had beaten him with baseball bats and clubs, causing serious damage to the motor portion of his brain. For the last eight years he had lived with partial paralysis and had difficulty speaking.

After about an hour I asked him, "There's something I don't understand. How can a human being take a club or a baseball bat and bash another human being's head in? How can he do that?"

Again he looked me right in the eye, shrugged his shoulders, and answered in his painful way, "WELL, ... ONCE... THERE WAS... A... MAN... WHO WAS... CRUCIFIED... BECAUSE... HE LOVED."

Finally, as he got up to go back to his room, he turned to me, a virtual stranger, and with a beautiful smile, thanked me for listening. Then he said, "NOW... I KNOW... I... HAVE A FRIEND."

It was then that I discovered my real purpose for staying and peeling endless potatoes at Gift of Love that day.

José

The first time I met José, I was talking to Sister Dominga in the hallway when he walked by and said, "Good morning." At the same time he made it perfectly clear that it was anything but a good morning by making a gesture as though to hang himself.

Sister didn't let it go by, and after telling him that he didn't have to walk alone because Jesus was with him, she asked me to go and talk to him.

José and I went into the dining room, where he told me, "Everyone tells me about heaven. I know it's wonderful, but I'm thirty-one years old and I think *this* life is beautiful too. I want to enjoy my life here also."

He explained that his major problem stemmed from a severe case of Kaposi's sarcoma that covered the lower half of his body. Then he asked me, "Tony, you haven't seen the lower half of my body, have you?"

"No, I haven't."

He stood up and said, "You'd better hold on to the table."

I repeatedly forgot that over the years I had not seen everything, even when I thought I had. This was one of those moments when I sat there, complacently believing I knew what Kaposi's sarcoma looked like at its worst. But when José lowered his pants, it was one of the most terrifying sights I had ever seen. All I could think of was that if a Hollywood makeup artist had attempted to create a half-man, half-alien monster he would have been hard put to come up with something this frightening. The only way I could begin to describe it would be to imagine thick, black alligator skin with deep cracks through which you could see raw flesh and seeping blood.

It was particularly difficult coming to terms with the sight of José's beautiful face and torso on top of these monstrous legs.

José looked me right in the eye and asked, "What do you think?"

I couldn't lie or insult his intelligence, so I answered, "That's quite something."

"When I get up in the morning, my own body disgusts me. I wake up to a nightmare. And I don't want people telling me different. I know how terrible it is. The first thing I do when I get up in the morning is look in the mirror and check my face."

Later in the day, at lunchtime, I asked José what he would like to eat. After he gave me his order, I asked, "Anything else?"

"Yeah, a magic wand."

"José, if I had one, you'd be the first one I'd use it on."

These were only a few of the many inspiring moments the dying men at Gift of Love shared with me on our journey together.

I had gone to Gift of Love on my first day with no training in nursing or in caring for the dying. All I had was my willingness to learn and care and love. It was sometimes overwhelming to have to assimilate so much information and learn so many lessons that struck the very core of my heart and soul.

As time went on, I knew that I was no longer the same person who had walked into Gift of Love in 1990. I had grown stronger while facing the daily traumas at Gift of Love, and had learned to cope with increasing confidence as each new crisis arose. I had also learned what Mother Teresa meant when she said that "we can do no great things, only small things with great love."

As I told my friend Wendell shortly before his death, "When it is my turn to pass over, I know that my friends from Gift of Love will be there to greet me with a big smile and open arms."

Till then, I will remember them all with gratitude and love.